Raising Cain

RAISING CAIN

Blackface Performance from Jim Crow to Hip Hop

W. T. LHAMON JR.

Harvard University Press
Cambridge, Massachusetts
London, England
1998

Library of Congress Cataloging-in-Publication Data
Lhamon, W. T.
    Raising Cain : blackface performance from Jim Crow to Hip Hop /
W.T. Lhamon, Jr.
      p.   cm.
    Includes bibliographical references and index.
    ISBN 0-674-74711-9 (alk. paper)
    1. Minstrel shows—United States—History.
    2. Blackface entertainers—United States—Biography.
    3. United States—Race relations.
    4. Minstrel music.   I. Title.
    PN1969.M5L53   1998
    791'.12'0973—dc21   97-28735

For F.

Contents

Figures

Raising Cain

1

Dancing for Eels
at Catherine Market

After the Jersey negroes had disposed of their masters' produce at
the "Bear Market," which sometimes was early done, and then the
advantage of a late tide, they would "shin it" for the Catherine
Market to enter the lists with the Long Islanders, and in the end,
an equal division of the proceeds took place. The success which
attended them brought our city negroes down there, who, after a
time, even exceeded them both, and if money was not to be had
"they would dance for a bunch of eels or fish."

— Thomas F. De Voe, *The Market Book*

We want to dance, too. Let's shin it for the Catherine Market ourselves.
Let's enter the lists with the Long Islanders. Shucking our constraints, let's
admit their old, low, and large ambition is also ours. Success attended them,
De Voe says, and it has since attended others. Fascination adheres in these
gestures, their contest, and their coining. To coin those gestures was to
produce currency for exchange. As this currency accumulated interest, it
was codified and it persisted. The gestures gathered momentum. When we
can see their momentum, we can see their economy: the conditions of their
cultural transmission. It is pretty to think that we might all share "in the
end, an equal division of the proceeds." We all want those eels.[1]

Catherine Market was a short sail in breezy weather, or a moderate row
on still days, across the East River from the truck farms of Long Island.
The skiffs from Long Island came from towns just on the other side, from

1

Williamsburgh and Brooklyn, and tied up at Catherine Slip. At its edge was Catherine Market, which joined the Slip to Catherine Street, and thence to the rest of the city via the Five Points, which was six blocks up to Chatham Square and two over. From Chatham Square and the Five Points, the Bowery went uptown, Pearl Street downtown, Worth and Canal Streets across town one way and Division the other. Maps today still give us "Catherine Slip" at the wide spot where the market was.

Today, Catherine Slip seems to bisect the territory between the Brooklyn and Manhattan bridges that have put it in parentheses. The more recent subway tunnels further bracket the market a little way along in each direction, north toward Corlears Hook, south toward the Battery. In its day Catherine Slip handled most of the traffic that all those conduits came to replace. The bridges and tunnels made massive arteries to replace the delicately negotiating capillary action of Catherine Market, the Five Points, and its tributary veins.

Catherine Market was the spot where the goods of Long Island slipped in and out of the isle of Manhattan when the river was both a boundary and a conveyance. Catherine Market, like all traditional markets, paradoxically smudged that borderline and also reinforced it. The market's presence as the membrane of the city emphasized its border, but managed its permeability, too. The culture in and of the market did the same, as we shall see: the culture of Catherine Market drew boundaries and managed their crossings.

At Catherine Slip the pedestrian and the riparian overlapped, like a skiff pulled across a shoreline, and those men who flourished in both realms had a special cachet. That's an initial reason why the slaves who planted and grubbed the potatoes, then rowed them across the water, then called their sales in the market were paid to dance there. Jersey, Williamsburgh, Brooklyn, and "our own" Negroes, said Thomas De Voe, danced out their regional affiliation and their identity. This overlap is first among several that are important in these early commercial performances of an independent Atlantic popular culture.

From its earliest instances, probably in the eighteenth century, this dancing for eels at Catherine Market addressed the issue of overlap. It appealed to several audiences who were finding different values in the dance at the same time. It was a yoking across perceived differences at least as much as it was a closing out or a separation. When they tied their hair in tea-lead, combed it out to imitate and mock the long wigs then in fashion, or wound their foreheads in eelskins, the dancers played out charismatic singularities that were to be made available to others. After all, appeal and exchange was what display in a market was about. And from the outset this dancing was supported, applauded, and desired by others.

Fascinated whites and blacks congregated to pay for that style and copy it. These marks of grace and difference they appreciated and wanted to absorb. They wanted to overlay this black cachet on their own identities— even *as* their own identities. And they did. Anyone today can see that the cultures of the Atlantic world are in good measure joinings and mergers that follow from such fascinations as occurred at Catherine Market. The dancing for eels was a performance of eclecticism that modeled later performance in the Atlantic world.

This early support of blacks dancing for eels is a sure instance of a public becoming patron to a specific style. In doing so it risks slippage from *patron* to *patronize*, nurture to condescension. So much depends on the slippery difference between the two. The crudest mistake we can make, however, is to assume that the connection between public and performance is un-alloyed—either simple patrons or simple patronization. In blackface performance, both attitudes converge at once, kinetic in each other.

The overlays of rural and riparian, seafaring and metropolitan cultures indicated a willingness to merge and make combinatory that is associated with markets and bazaars. Roger Abrahams has studied market performance up and down the Americas. He describes market places as edgy areas, contact zones between cultures on the outskirts of towns or up against their walls. In markets, people wink at various civic constraints so that exchange may take place. In order to sell goods, creole language develops and extravagant gestures thrive. "For trade to occur," he has written, "frontiers have to be established that can be crossed, or zones created in which different peoples may come together with impunity. These sanctuaries are fire free zones, places in which difference itself, especially stylistic difference, is transvalued. In such environs, what other peoples make and perform becomes positively attractive."[2]

I begin my study of the Atlantic blackface lore cycle in Catherine Market because I want to insist, with Abrahams, on the mingled behavior that "fire free zones" encouraged in the traditional market. At Catherine Market and other early spots for the performances of American culture there was an eagerness to combine, share, join, draw from opposites, play on opposition. An enthusiasm for the underlying possibilities in difference continually reappears in this popular-folk culture of the Atlantic diaspora. People in the market at Catherine Slip articulated these possibilities early. The market at Catherine Slip was a relay in the conduction of that culture, a relay that stamped what it passed on.

These overlaps of difference so attractive in the market will later be pointed at formally by the blackface mask. The mask is itself an excellent signifier of overlap as a principle. We wear the mask, said blackface performers, a good century before Paul Lawrence Dunbar enlisted the phrase for his poem.

We wear the mask, said Bob Rowley. Belonging to the Long Island farmer William Bennett, Bob Rowley was one of the favorites among the men dancing for eels at Catherine Market. When Rowley performed he overlaid his slave name with a performance name: "Bobolink Bob." The name was catchy in its alliteration but, more significantly, it pointed at his overlapping identity. The Bobolink (*Dolichonyx oryzivorus*) is a field bird, a new world passerine, rarely vagrant in Europe, whose male's brown underparts and face change to black while it breeds in spring. Joining himself to these attributes, Bobolink Bob crossed close rural observations with the requirements of market performance. He was a proto-blackface performer for a new North Atlantic culture. One wants very much to have heard Bobolink Bob's whistle. I will show that this whistle is one of the most talismanic aspects of blackface performance, retained and referenced even as late as Al Jolson's performance in *The Jazz Singer* (1927).[3]

Today Catherine Slip and the spot of its former market are surrounded by some of New York's earliest public housing: Knickerbocker Village to the east and the Governor Smith Houses to the west. China Town supplants the European and African ethnic mixture that in the late eighteenth and early nineteenth centuries populated the Five Points and Chatham Square. During the waves of Atlantic immigration that rolled up the East River throughout the nineteenth century, this area gradually became the "Jew-town" that would bring forth Irving Berlin and a large portion of Tin Pan Alley.[4] But the culture that came out of it had Catherine Market and the gestures of the Slip working through it no matter what the overlay.

The East River Drive hugging the shoreline stops pedestrian movement. Out on the river, Circle Liners, tugs, and barges press against the current. One hears the dull traffic on the bridges and highways, the white noise of the city's churning. But at Catherine Slip, now, the human touches of enterprise and exchange sound distant. The structures of the present baffle what went on here. Standing in the midst of these physical overlays it is hard to imagine how the capillary connections of Catherine Slip were commercially significant in its formative moment, around 1820. More important to imagine is how at Catherine Market cultural work was performed that proved important well beyond the city.

Gestures gathered into dance contests. Habits of response clustered observers into publics providing patronage. Conventions of praise and blame arched around the performances in the lists of Catherine Market. All these stimuli and responses arranged themselves in patterns like iron filings around a magnet. Their apparently mutable and delicate tracings—so easy to turn away from or scatter on the surface—conform to enduring force fields deeper than we have realized. Beneath these surface clues, patterns organize relations among citizens not only in the United States but also throughout the Atlantic world. This persisting template held for Catherine Market, as for its nearly neighboring theatres—the Bowery and the Chatham. It survived transatlantic crossing and held sway both south and north of the Thames. It held for the traveling minstrel show in metropolitan and frontier venues. It survived, even showed the way for, silent and talking films. It was popular on TV in the fifties and even now organizes much of MTV.[5]

We will have to push back the fortress façades of Knickerbocker Village, forget the autos, erase the limited-access highways, bring down the bridges, and fill up the subways if we wish to recall Catherine Market as it was and enter the lists with the Long Islanders. There is also a further structure muffling the actuality of Catherine Market that we must sidestep.

We must work against inherited abstractions that have distorted or erased those who danced for eels at Catherine Market. People have tried to tell stories that made sense, and did damage, according to their needs. The first chroniclers of blackface performance accepted its declared premises. These first historians said blackface was about happy Negroes. Minstrelsy told of black people's genius for contentment, they said; it told of their supposedly simple southern ways. Theirs was organic harmony on the Plantation; the hands were in the fields; Ol' Massa and Missus were deservedly well-loved in the big house. From Fanny Kemble's fancied discovery in 1838 of "Jim Crow—the veritable James" to Charles Dickens's *American Notes* in 1842 and Robert Nevin writing in the *Atlantic Monthly* in 1867 right up through Brander Matthews in *Scribner's Magazine* in 1915 and even Constance Rourke's path-breaking *American Humor* in 1931, historians of several sorts repeatedly validated the southern authenticity of blackface performance.[6]

Then Hans Nathan's study of Dan Emmett in 1962 and particularly Robert Toll's history of minstrelsy in 1974 reversed many of the earlier understandings of the form. The racism in minstrelsy appalled Toll and the form's subsequent critics. The newly conventional embarrassment at white racism popularized in the fifties and sixties had so determined public responses that simply underlining the stereotypes in minstrelsy served as a satisfactory analytic maneuver for this new wave of scholarship. Current historians have extended Toll's noticing that the minstrel show was neither about authentic black life nor about an authentic South. Alexander Saxton, David Roediger, and Eric Lott have more recently argued that blackface performance was a fantasy of northern white performers, largely from middle-class homes, who knew little or nothing of black life.[7]

Although I have lived in the same culture that shaped the attitudes of this more recent group of critics, the story I will tell is rather different. One does not approve the abhorrent racism in most minstrelsy by emphasizing its presence, then moving on to discuss the form's other—even its counter—aspects. I analyze the multiple aspects in blackface performance because it was not a fixed thing, but slippery in its uses and effects. Indeed, this late in the cycle, it seems most important to notice how blackface performance can work also and simultaneously *against* racial stereotyping. The way minstrelsy saps racism from within has almost never been mentioned. Its anti-racist dimensions—occasionally abolitionist but usually supplemental to both abolitionist and anti-abolitionist doctrine—are remaining secrets among the phenomena of blackface performance.

Raising Cain is about this resistance to racism, for sure, but also about a wider recalcitrance. I want to bring out the broad interracial refusal of middle-class channeling that working men and women of all hues mounted using the corrupt tools bequeathed them by the marketplaces and other locations where they could make spectacles of themselves. Their refusal was not set in amber. It pulsed and warped over time. It was human—vibrant, confused, always mixed. Many of the workers in minstrelsy, most often early but also late, took the racism that was the given of their days and raised it against its original wielders. People work with what they have. What they have is mixed and messy. To think otherwise is the real fantasy in this business.

Much might be said regarding the shifting accounts of minstrelsy that obscure its complex cultural work. Historians have covered over what performers were doing as much as the altered physical structure of Catherine Market has obscured the early activities danced out on its ground. Commentators' shifting analyses say as much or more about the needs of successive eras as about minstrelsy. Nevertheless, the vernacular tradition—right up through Michael Jackson (who emblemizes the conflicted nature of blackface performance)—keeps alive insouciant practices whose party I, for one, am little loath to join. The patterns in these disdained actions persist down all the years of their exclusion from respect.

I, too, am doubtless misusing, therefore abusing, the legacy of blackface performance. What might I say in my defense? Only what is compelling in the stories I tell. What distinguishes my approach from those who have told their stories before me? I am not surprised to find culture corrupt and its measures mixed. Minstrelsy is often racist, growing more complex and more codified as time went on. So much is true of human action by all peoples. Minstrelsy usually misrepresents women, as have most men and women throughout history. In its development, minstrelsy bellied up to power; show me a movement that has not. When I speak about the achievements of blackface performance, I hardly condone its denigration of blacks or its misogyny. I condemn them. What I want most to account for, however, is the way blackface actions have often contradicted what was expected of them. Like the teeming, recoiling eels which early figured it, the conundrums of blackface performance have certainly flopped out of, and knocked over, all the buckets into which people poured them.

> The negroes who visited here were principally slaves from Long Island, who had leave of their masters for certain holidays, among which "Pinkster" was the principal one; when, for "pocket-money," they would gather up everything that would bring a few pence or shillings, such as roots, berries, herbs, yellow or other birds, fish, clams, oysters, &c., and bring them with them in their skiffs to this market; then, as they had usually three days holiday, they were ever ready, by their "negro sayings or doings," to make a few shillings more.
>
> —Thomas F. De Voe, *The Market Book*

There was long an informal market at the square abutting Catherine Slip. To regulate this activity, a formal license was proposed in 1786 and an enlarged building completed in 1800. New Yorkers seeking fish and vegetables during the first two decades of the nineteenth century went to Catherine Market. It was noisy with stalls, docks, a clustering of rope and sail makers, ship chandleries, and the like. By 1820 Longworth's City Directory locates Micah Hawkins's all-purpose tavern, store, and hotel at number 8. It had its piano under the staircase, some say, or behind the bar, and that's where Hawkins composed the first American opera: *The Saw Mill; or A Yankee Trick* (1824). It's also where he probably worked up one of the earliest American blackface songs, "Champlain and Plattsburgh" (also known as "The Siege of Plattsburgh" and "Backside Albany") in 1815.[8]

These strands of Atlantic music, Euro- and Afro-derived operas, which tradition has increasingly defined as opposite, did not seem opposite to Hawkins. He was responding to the ragged, mixed inspiration directly between his door and the Slip, on the wide, worn ground of the market. Present there were all the customary incantations—"roots, berries, herbs, yellow or other birds . . . 'negro sayings or doings.' " Sailors and roustabouts swapped curses, verses, and winks with servants and slaves. History has not recorded the grog shops and oyster houses that lubricated these passing exchanges, but we can be sure they were there, as always at such threshold spots.

Directly across from Hawkins's tavern, for example, was the sort of place that has come down to us in a skimpy couple of citations: Burnel Brown's Ship Chandlery. I focus on it because on the northeastern edge of the densely peopled part of Manhattan island in the first decade of the nineteenth century, the cobbles to the front of Brown's shop were marked off as at once a liminal area and a center for small crowds come from within the city and beyond. This spot was a precipitate. It was to the market what the market was to the city. Citizens and slaves mingled here to gather, perform, and learn the stylistic gestures that sorted out their problems. It was an urban edge and a nexus, a determinative cultural valve sorting nutrients and waste. They all passed through Catherine Slip, turning for inspection, payment, and learning in Catherine Market—right here on the shingle in front of Brown's Chandlery. The turning began to inscribe—drill in—the gestures as practices. They were becoming texts, of sorts. We read them still.

> So they would be hired by some joking butcher or individual to engage in a jig or break-down, as that was one of their pastimes at home on the barn-floor, or in a frolic, and those that could and would dance soon raised a collection; but some of them did more in "turning around and shying off" from the designated spot than keeping to the regular "shake-down," which caused them all to be confined to a "board," (or shingle, as they called it,) and not allowed off it.
>
> —Thomas F. De Voe, *The Market Book*

This "turning around and shying off" beckons to us. Already in these early North American instances of black performance coming into commerce there is this turning away. (The shying off at Catherine Market may remind us of Miles Davis's controversial turning his back on audiences, or walking off stage, during quartet and quintet performances in the 1950s.) The shying at the Market may mean that the dancer was taking his act away from the individual "joking butcher" who hired his breakdown; he was spinning off to other patrons. It may mean the dancer was turning inward and private, reserving gestures for which the patron thought he paid. Many of the song sheets of purported black songs, from about 1840, are of faux plantation frolics. One of their most repeated tropes is this shingle, as in Figures 1.1 and 1.2. The shingle is one real connection among these northern, urban, breakdowns in the early years of the century, the cornshucking dances that Abrahams authenticates on southern plantations, and the minstrel stage. The word, *shingle,* as well as the dancing on the board, may well be African retentions. If so, then the shingle and its practice are further connections in the Atlantic world.[9]

Abrahams describes the dancing of the slaves on the shingle as their preference rather than their confinement. Their feet dance the board the way hands play a drum. It is part of what Abrahams calls *apart-playing.* The board sets the dancer apart from his colleagues, but unites him with them, too, because they keep his time by patting juba for him; they hold the board down; and they jive with him as he performs. (Team jump-roping as it is still acted out in urban squares with rhymes and competitive steps is probably related to this dancing. So is tap dancing.) There is an apparent conflict, then, between the supposed confinement to the shingle and the dancers' preference for it. De Voe's description seemed to me at first to contradict this preference: he thought the shying slaves had to be confined to the shingle.

But perhaps the performer's turning away was a solicitation, a way of

JIM ALONG JOSY,

As sung by
MR. JOHN M. SMITH,
Arranged by
AN EMINENT PROFESSOR.

NEW YORK.
Published by WILLIAM HALL & SON 239 Broadway cor of Park Place.

1.1   Song sheet cover for "Jim Along Josy" (1840) as sung by Mr. John M. Smith

1.2 Song sheet cover showing J. W. Sweeney performing "Jenny Get Your Hoe Cake Done" pulling the butcher into the give-and-take of that apart-playing customary in the barn of the down-home frolic, or even in African festivity. You! Butcher, attend me more closely, Hey, push and pull with me. Thus, if the shingle was indeed an African retention, then the butchers who thought they were protecting their commodity were enticed instead into reinforcing African-American customary practice. This was Brer Rabbit and his briar patch carried on by other means. This shingle was a briar patch brought into the market not by the confining butchers but by the performers finding their identities on it. This shingle scene shows black performers early toying with the way patrons think they control black gestures. The shingle dancers are modulating or tendering—certainly playing within if not controlling—their presentation even as the joking butchers think *they* are patronizing the performers.

The shingle seems to be a rudimentary stage ready for enclosure in a theatre. But this rudimentary readiness also pulls in different directions. On the one hand, it seems to suggest capture of a separable part of black gesture, and its successful removal into the dominantly white space of a theatre. One solitary dancer of the 1840 examples is Joe Sweeney (see Figure 1.2). On the other hand, this separated part, once inside, will re-generate its customary context. Sweeney will by 1843 have called into being his colleagues in the Virginia Minstrels—Dan Emmett's famous troupe—to complete his act, pat juba with him, and, all the while, carry on the jive.[10] When the colleagues rejoin their parted player, the shingle separation will be annulled. Everything is not happy, however, because the struggle for control continues. And what has come inside is blackness, for the most part, not black people.

Other tropes in the dance passage underscore the ritual, even magic, aspect of this behavior. The dancers were herb men. They worked roots. They dealt in oysters and shellfish; they purveyed caged birds. These are the goods of magicians and vernacular medicine. Their history associates minstrel dances, therefore, even in this simple way with magic men and carnival life. Minstrel comes from *minister,* as in *minister to,* but these shingle dances at Catherine Market supplement this curative genealogy. The danc-ers dress in costume from beyond the pale, tying their hair in tea-lead and eel skins: "Many New Jersey negroes, mostly from Tappan, were after a time found among them, contending for the prize . . . they were known by their suppleness and plaited forelocks tied up with tea-lead. The Long Islanders usually tied up theirs in a cue, with dried eel-skin; but sometimes they combed it about their heads and shoulders, in the form of a wig, then all the fashion."[11] The dancers bring their skills from the country. They are outsiders, indeed, from across the water's real boundary—from Brooklyn and Williamsburgh on Long Island, from Tappan in New Jersey—and they contest the gestural style of Manhattan. The outsiders come to teach the insiders. The insiders master the gestures themselves; in time, they claim to do them better than the outsiders.

This was a contest, a cutting contest for money or eels, but also a representation of contested culture, of which even the white dance-novitiate could be aware. It was both a contest and self-aware, a pattern of a contest. It played with dance and with the frame, the use, of the dance. It was about the value of the dance and about its surplus value. All the participants knew that, even this early in the process of its marketing. And all the participants tempered that marketing. No one participant wholly owned or controlled it, even when as a joking butcher one bought it. Perhaps the joke was *on* the thought that anyone could buy a gesture, a person, a culture. This pattern of push and pull, of control and taking control back, of nested codes that generate and regenerate—all were part of the cultural valve that was Catherine Market. (See this push coming to shove at the nearby public space of Five Points in 1827 in Figure 1.3.)

If you go looking for that valve these days you cannot find it. Its physical structures are gone, overwritten. Other markets, at Fulton and Franklin Streets, diluted the dominance of Catherine Market by the middle of the nineteenth century. When the bridges were built, they obviated most of the need for a commercial slip. Eventually public housing obliterated the teeming community that had thrived there to negotiate the crossing of the water. And the cultural patterns that Catherine Market spawned and wrote into American bodily gesture were sent packing. To go looking for Catherine Slip, then, is to seek dispersal and its traces.

Reimagining the early American lists, today one walks toward Catherine Slip through the China Town now occupying the streets above it. If you go in summer, after feasting on Dim Sum, it will be appropriate to linger on a bench at Columbus Park, which supplants Five Points. You will not hear come-ons from hustlers in the doors of oyster houses calling, Get Your Oysters, We Got Mussels! Instead, you may peek at youths working their own enormous muscles, sweating out dips and pullups on the exercise bars where there used to be stews and brothels. Immaculate children in pinafores, calling in Chinese, chase one another across the jungle gyms. Farther

1.3 Five Points, 1827

down, under Roosevelt Drive and across South Street, where men and women once bartered chickens and eels, where bushels spilled beets with Williamsburgh loam still crusted on them, desultory fishermen now in airsole training shoes cast bait into the turgid river with polylaminate rods. What do they hope to catch? Whatever bites, they'll say. But little does.

Certainly, two hundred years ago, when Catherine Market was a functioning cultural valve, its hopes were specific. The waters were relatively clean, the nibbles plentiful. Hopes spilled like beets. Fears churned like eels. People of all sorts and all degrees of freedom mingled here, as did their competing ideologies. Not just dancers, but also attitudes, contended in the lists of Catherine Market. Neither the actors nor their audiences were homogeneous. One public cheered what alarmed another. They instigated each other, back and forth. Their mutual dependence set spinning one of the longest-lasting and most determinative cultural cycles of the Atlantic diaspora. These young black slaves and freemen come across the waters from Jersey and Long Island, as well as down from the farms along the northern cliffs of Manhattan itself, were dancing out their identity, and a lot more. Increasingly, they danced out the identities of their publics, who paid them for their gestures.

"Their" gestures. Who owned what? The way these men cocked a knee and raised the opposite hand came to stand for other people, too, and this is the heart of the matter here. Why choose *these* gestures? When a gesture comes to stand for someone other than its apparent originator, what is the meaning? How does it happen? Why? Once paid for, wasn't a gesture owned, then, by the buyer? Maybe a gesture could be sold and retained, too. Maybe marketing of gestures exhibited this complexity of cultural property: that it was saleable but never exclusive property. You could buy it and you could sell it, but you could not own it. Maybe the step took over the stepper, an inversion analogous to the tail wagging the dog. Certainly the gesture, itself, was precious: it has remained distinctive from the first drawings of it through the latest steps in downtown clubs. But was this step transmitted in an unbroken chain beneath all the bastardizations of it? Probably not, for that would entail a conscious chain.

Perhaps it remained an arbiter of getting things right to which black youths returned repeatedly at irregular moments in the transmission of black street culture. Their turn to the wheeling gesture seems to operate in the blackface lore cycle as a gestural touchstone that corrects any emulations which mutate too aberrantly. The wheel-about gesture lurks. It waits.

Then it announces: No, come back, *this* is how it goes. It is a fetishized mark of genuineness—a hub for street culture. It is one big wink.

These performers did not dance in a vacuum. They danced in a specific market, for profit: "if money was not to be had 'they would dance for a bunch of eels or fish.' " Until 1827 they danced in a slave state. Until 1863 they danced in a slave nation. New York City was until the end of the eighteenth century a slave city, and there were lots of slaves. In Brooklyn fully a third of the population were slaves in 1790. By 1820 the black population had dropped to 1,761 of 11,187 (almost 16 percent), and many of these came through Catherine Market, which was their entrance and exit from the city.[12] But the most important fact about the beginning of black charisma to whites at Catherine Market was that in the last year of the eighteenth century the *children* of slaves were thereafter freed in New York. Although New York was a legal slave state until 4 July 1827, the state's Gradual Manumission Act of 1799 had freed all Negroes born after 4 July 1799. Thus although parts of every age cohort in the New York Negro population were free, the youngest cohorts were—legally—entirely free.

The contrasts in degrees of freedom were intense. They were doubtless as intensely modulated at Catherine Market as anywhere in the country, perhaps anywhere in the world. Young blacks in the teen years of the nineteenth century had a good bit to dance about at Catherine Market. They were dancing a free identity in a place that valued it, against a backdrop of enslavement. Thus began the pungent metaphor that is still playing virtually two centuries later: runaway freedom within confinement.

Shane White has done careful work on slave demographics in the city. His work is important because it punctures the conventional thesis that northern minstrel pioneers could know nothing of black life since there was no significant black culture in the North for them to copy. Although there were probably never more than a hundred free black people in New York City during English rule, writes White, "in the years after the Revolution the free black population expanded rapidly, and by 1810 there were 7,140 blacks in this category, making up 8.1 percent of New York's population . . . The 1790s and early 1800s saw the genesis, therefore, of the most important urban black center in nineteenth- and twentieth-century America."[13]

Significantly, White establishes that the increase of the black population was *not* due to the decline of slavery in the Northeast or in the areas surrounding New York City. In these areas there were many slaves and their owners held on to them. Indeed, during the 1790s slaves increased in number in the city by more than a fifth and slaveholders by a third. These increases were due to the growth in relative importance of New York City in North America. New York overtook both Boston and Philadelphia after the Revolution and nearly doubled its numbers between 1790 and 1800: both in raw population and in the black share. On Staten Island and in rural parts of Kings County, more than half the households had slaves in 1790. When by 1810 the manumission statutes were beginning to have an effect, these rural blacks did not stay at home after they took or negotiated their freedom. Rather, like many other Americans and immigrants, they shinned it to the city. There was also a massive spillover before the 1804 Haitian revolution: "By 1793 about ten thousand people had fled the great slave rebellion in the French West Indian colony and had settled in America." These were free blacks and whites with black slaves.[14]

In 1800 New York City had 5,865 blacks in its population, second only to Charleston. In Charleston, however, blacks constituted a majority, while in New York the percentage was only around 10 percent of the city's population—to white New Yorkers, surely a much less threatening proportion, but nonetheless a critical mass. It was large enough to accumulate a distinctive style and send forth its representative stylists, like Bobolink Bob, to the world. By 1810 the black population of the city reached 8,918, of which 1,443 (16.2 percent) were still enslaved. There were more free blacks in New York City than anywhere else in the Americas.[15]

Further facts and conventions differentiated Catherine Market in the Seventh Ward of New York City from the rest of the country and indeed from the rest of the city. Catherine Market was specifically not New York's slave market; Fly Market served that purpose, and subsequent plays—like T. D. Rice's *Otello*—maintained the distinction well along in the century.[16] As might be expected of a district of wharves, immigration, and markets, the Seventh Ward was the most mixed area of the city. Catherine Street ran along the ward's western border between the Slip and the bottom of the Bowery. There the Seventh joined the corners of the Fourth, Sixth, and Tenth Wards. Each of these other wards had its own relative exclusivities of class and ethnic makeup. The Sixth Ward is often cited as the home of the city's black population in the early century, for instance. But in the Seventh Ward mingling was the fact, and it was a mingling of disdained equals, as we shall see.

This mingling was a difference that stood out as the Ward's specific identity. Therefore, in its functions of cultural display, Catherine Market served purposes increasingly opposed to the phony racial separations necessary to slavery as Europeans and their descendants practiced it in the Americas. In Catherine Market an attraction across difference was daily played out. At least some of the whites of Catherine Market watched those dancers as their champions, as people marking out differences for all of them.

> . . . what is much more amazing, to plot, conspire, consult, abet and encourage these black seed of Cain, to burn this city, and to kill and destroy us all. Good God!
>
> —Judge sentencing John Hughson to hang at Catherine Slip, 1741

In 1820 the specific area of Catherine Market was plagued with a fever so severe that dispute broke out in the papers and among the authorities about its treatment. One report had it that the plague was the dreaded yellow fever. Doctors from the New York Board of Health then issued a counter-report defending their diagnosis of typhoid fever. This report included house-by-house descriptions of the occupants, their color, and, in some cases of the female afflicted, generalizations about their trades. Its numerical details are exceptionally exact, covering August through November of 1820 and all residents in the area between Catherine Street and Pike Street (two blocks to the east) and along Bancker and Lombardy Streets—now Madison and Monroe. The ratio of whites to blacks in these blocks was three to one, or precisely 1,732 to 562.[17] These details confirm the thorough mixture of whites and blacks in one dense microdistrict which subsequent blackface performers have routinely connected to the origins of their acts. These blocks make up one incubator for the blackface lore cycle.

This area was also one of the poorest in the city, and in it blacks lived the lowest of the low, literally underground. For instance: "Out of 48 blacks, living in 10 cellars, (viz. Nos 138, 98, 96, 89, 79, 84, and 78 Bancker-street, at No. 53 Lombardy-street, and No 36 Pike-street,) 33 were sick, of whom 14 died; while out of 120 *whites*, living *immediately over their heads*, in *the apartments of the same houses, not one* even had the fever!" Frequently the writers specify that the whites who had the fever were living with or married to blacks:

At No. 85 Lombardy-street, in the third story, were 5 white females, and a black man, husband to one of them, and all of whom were sick of the fever . . . At No. 89 Bancker-street, in the front cellar, where a white woman and her black husband lived as boarders in a black family consisting of 6 persons, all of whom had the fever, and 4 of the blacks died . . . At No. 102 Bancker-street, where 4 white women kept a brothel in the *cellar,* and had constant intercourse with negro men. Two of these women had the fever, and one died. At No 124 Bancker-street, where a white woman and her black husband lived together in the front cellar, and the black man died of the fever.[18]

This report shows that at least at Catherine Market twenty-one years after New York State's Gradual Manumission Act, blacks and whites were clearly contracting intimate knowledge of one another. Although authorities were classifying them as separate categories, biological progeny that mixed and nixed the official classifications were proliferating. The marking of race was more observed by the authorities than practiced, at least in this neighborhood. Then as now, the ordinary people of these streets were attracted to one another well across "race," despite the fictions to which their doctors subscribed. Or, perhaps, part of their mutual attraction was *to* spite those authorities. Indeed, bedrooms in these streets from cellar to eave were serving as petri dishes for the production of crossed categories.

My supposition is that this mixed biological production excited the mixed cultural production of Catherine Market. The neighbors in this doctors' report trafficked and danced there, after all, in sickness as in health. My further supposition is that the relative integration of these streets was not usual. Strong creole communities had certainly developed in other Atlantic ports, Boston round to New Orleans. Even the Caribbean ports, however, did not have the specifics of Catherine Market. Other cities in the Atlantic did not have New York's synergy: maturing Manumission Acts interacting with such rapid expansion. Whether or not the scene at Catherine Market was as extraordinary as I believe, the alarm in the documents indicates that the local officials thought it was.

This specific context, with its distinctions from other markets, was surely relevant to the burgeoning charisma of black dance among the street sparrows, as the newspapers had started referring to the ruffians of the markets. These lads of the ward, not yet a class, were growing conscious of their differences, and I want to draw out a further dimension of how they might have come to understand their distinctiveness. The ground which became Catherine Market had half a century earlier been the spot where authorities chose to make a capital spectacle of John Hughson, tavernkeeper and white ringleader of an interracial revolutionary plot. Hughson had called meetings at his house over a period of many months, some reputedly including as many as forty Negroes. He riled them to swear "to burn and kill." Each was to set fire to his master's house, "kill master and mistress, and then fire the Fort" (Fort George).[19]

This "Great Negro Plot" was set for 17 March 1741, St. Patrick's Night. With its organization of laboring Irish, Spanish, English, and African mutualities it was hardly a "Negro" revolt. It was rather a poor persons' plot, a mixed-race conspiracy. But its participants, like the poor people still living in the area of the market in 1820, were not subscribing to the racial categories that their richer, more powerful fellow citizens thought were real. The 1741 plot "designed to destroy the city by fire, and massacre the inhabitants." And it is this cross-racial revolutionary intention that the authorities actually punished, even while their naming of it seemed to pin the blame on slaves. If slaves had been the problem the authorities feared, the punishment would have been meted out at Fly Market, where slaves were bought and sold. But the site of punishment for the plot's henchmen was Augustus Street between Pearl and Duane, near where City Hall stands today. There 14 Negroes, of the 154 imprisoned in this plot, were burned at the stake.

Authorities punished the plot's designated leaders on the ground at Catherine Slip that would later become licensed as Catherine Market. Hughson would be made a chained spectacle there, not hanging in the market where whites bought and sold blacks. At Fly Market his spectacle would have been redundant because there the border between "races," as between marketability and ownership, was absolute. Rather, he was hanged at Catherine Slip because that was the place in the city where those absolute demarcations between races were breaking, broken, tempered: transgressed. At Catherine Market white butchers paid young blacks in eels for dancing out differences that might become their mutualities. These mutualities were what was threatening, had to be misnamed the Negro Plot, and had to be hanged on their own ground. Authorities would make Hughson a terrifying spectacle precisely where that border between buying and owning race was being broken down by the charisma of performing blackness. That was the logic of Hughson's sentence.

Hanging Hughson was really the disciplining of the publics of Catherine Market, too. Here is what the sentencing Judge read aloud to John Hughson, his wife, his daughter, and his tenant "Irish Peggy" Sorubiero (aka Kerry, who was thought to be a prostitute consorting with blacks in Hughson's rooms). To the authorities, these whites were the most inexplicably terrifying members of the plot. Listen to the judge:

> for people who have been brought up and always lived in a christian country, and also called themselves christians, to be guilty not only of making negro slaves their equals, but even their superiors, by waiting upon, keeping with, and entertaining them with meat, drink and lodging, and what is much more amazing, to plot, conspire, consult, abet and encourage these black seed of Cain, to burn this city, and to kill and destroy us all. Good God! . . . All are satisfied that you justly merit a more severe death than is intended for you, having, in my opinion, been much worse than the negroes.[20]

Hanging Hughson at Catherine Slip was a disciplining of that practice which sought a common ground or a common symbolism in markers of difference.

I draw out Hughson's presence, and that of his executioners, in order to emphasize how they played parts on the preterrain of blackface actions. They set the stage. Hughson hanging in chains in Catherine Market documents the class and racial skirmishing that backgrounds popular culture in the Americas. The metaphor of the gallows hangs over the history of popular theatre even when actors and opponents outside their audiences pretend that such life-and-death struggle is far distant. A century after Hughson was hanged at Catherine Slip, during the years in which the formulaic minstrel show consolidated its form and popularity, Henry Ward Beecher asked this rhetorical question in 1844 in his lecture "Popular Amusements": "May not men do as they please in a free country, without being hung up in a gibbet of public remark?"[21] Characteristically, Beecher went on to answer no. But his essay actively hammers together such a gibbet.

When it has avoided the scaffold itself, insurgent culture has always had to avoid the noose of public remark. The fear of censure, sometimes violent, caused the motley culture that arose at the crossroads of surplus youth and surplus popularity to cloak itself in jive banter and punning wit. The apparent lightness of minstrelsy has helped its detractors classify it as folderol.

While no one would deny the goofing, it is important to deny that minstrel goofing is nonsense. Its foolery is what licenses or permits the multivalent slashing that is going on in blackface beneath its apparently simple mask. The goofiness keeps at bay the violence all sides have strewn across the historical ground where blackface performance does its tender stepping.

Blackface action is usually slashing back at the pretensions and politesse of authority more than at blackness. Certainly in these earliest instances of white fascination with black performance there was little laughing at blacks, alone or even primarily. Instead, there was laughter in the face of the gallows and violence, the gibbet of public remark, and preaching censure. Particularly at Catherine Market, there was dancing among the memory of the chains. The spectacular discipline left its traces on workers who were both enslaved and pressed, whipped and waged. What is mistaken is the suggestion that poor whites had no significant contact with black culture in nineteenth-century New York City.

The same year as the plague that occurred in the surrounding streets, a stallholder at the market composed a remarkable folk drawing: "Dancing for Eels *1820* Catharine Market" (Figure 1.4). The subjects are pressed among several layers of surveillance. In the left middle of the space are the three black performers—a dancer, a drummer, a second dancer who is watching and clapping for his colleague. To their left and our right is a threesome of tightly engaged white watchers, leaning intently into the dance. In front of the dancers is the artist, for whom each group performs in its way; certainly all in the center of the drawing are aware of being watched. Behind the dancers and their appreciative white threesome are an integrated crowd of onlookers. Notice how our view peers out from inside a stall. This drawing shelters the point of view of its maker: the roof covers the peeking artist, not the dancers nor the crowd watching beyond, who are exposed in the plain air.

This drawing is a hieroglyph suggesting many stories. The two most basic are of the market dance and of the comfort the artist draws in watching it—and they may prove inseparable. The dancer is clearly the focus of the drawing, but I start my discussion of its meaning by noticing the roof that segments off the watcher's comfort. These rudimentary boards provide a top for the drawer's stall. They mark out his space in the crowded market just as boards underlie the space for the dancers. As the dancer performs on his boards, the stallholder cries his wares under his. Furthermore, the roof lines are part of the linearity ruling the space in this folk drawing. All

1.4   Folk Drawing of "Dancing for Eels *1820* Catharine Market"

the human elements counteract that wooden straightness of buildings and masts. These boards segment planes for performance. Pressing in on the players, the vertical boards indicate the divisions that will most change during the development of this scene over the next quarter-century, as the butcher's crew incorporates the dancer and his crowd. Their gestures will be staged together inside theatres and inserted into Atlantic consciousness. The roof protected the artist; it thus distinguished the roofed stallholders from the unprotected dancers. The roof above the privileged watcher also marked a rudimentary destination for the black dancer: a cover to come under.

The drawing shows activities *taking place* in an elaborately ruled-off Catherine Market. Fluid activity jigs across a boarded structure, composing a poignant contest of formal elements. Dancers and stallholders try with their uneven powers to own the space they cohabit. The dancer's turning solicitations to the attending public are one sort of drawing in. What does he need from them beyond their porgies and eels? He needs their legitimation. When viewers gather to watch his gestures they warrant his position. His dancing lays claim to the place and his public attests his hold. At the same virtual time, the butcher is drawing the space from under his cover. He acts out a similar taking of place. The butcher is partly competing, partly wanting to join. These two performances, dancing and drawing, occupy one plane, pressed between shingle and roof. An incorporation of the participants into a shared event is going on here. Each is freely choosing to join the contest and draw in others. In the passage I quoted at the beginning of this chapter, De Voe called this eager joining a shinning "to enter the lists." In actions like this dancing for eels, and the drawing of that dance as responsive counterpoint, each participant tries to take the place with the differentiated others in it.

Further difficulties follow from these conflicts. These participants engage in mutual activities; but they are not wholly congenial; they occupy places that are unequal; and they use uneven power to do it. Some are sheltered, some shingled. Aggression, passivity, and types of power (ownership, charisma) are rapidly showing their hands—but nothing is swapping any faster than the paradoxes and pleasures of the cultural transmission which these overlays figure. Taking the other's place, willy-nilly, also means taking the other. Whether that is desired, as I think it usually is in blackface, or despised and feared, as others have emphasized, the incorporation means that blackness (or whiteness) comes along. It comes along like a burr beneath a saddle.

So far as curators know, this small (10¼ x 12 inches) folk drawing, this world of watching in colored India ink on draftsman's tracing cloth, has been exhibited just twice. The first time was in 1969, at the Downtown Gallery in New York, in an exhibit of American Folk Art. The second and last was for six days at Sotheby's, November 1973, when it sold as part of a large folk art collection. Its image was reproduced in a catalogue for the sale.[22] Thus this folk drawing has remained in recent times for all practical purposes out of view. It has certainly remained unenlisted in the study of blackface performance or black dance. Nevertheless, before it was closeted as a work of art, early in the nineteenth century this drawing did determinative cultural work as a robust market drawing. Once it was considered art, its work was inhibited. Nothing new about that. But I am reenlisting it. I try to read its signals again as its contemporaries did, in order to regain a sense of this first American popular culture from its own angle.

Among those on whom the 1820 drawing worked were Eliphalet Brown Jr. and his brother, James. The Brown brothers etched several lithographic portraits of New York street culture as theatre. Indeed, James and Eliphalet Brown were part of New Yorkers' general recognition that their streets were theatrical. In 1848 the brothers produced a lithograph, presumably at the behest of Frank Chanfrau, to advertise Chanfrau's hit play *New York as It Is* at the Chatham Theatre (Figures 1.5, 1.6). Various versions of this scene are signed by James and by both brothers.

Frank Chanfrau was from the neighborhood. He had been born near the Five Points, at the corner of Pell and Bowery, in 1821, son of a French immigrant who for a while hawked fruit on Catherine Street. At just the moment of the Browns' lithograph, young Chanfrau was finding himself suddenly thrust forward, the next leading man of the youth culture on the order of Daddy Rice. In fact Chanfrau had witnessed Rice's own phenomenal ascent. He had seen Rice go over the top to flounder in that thin air. Later he would generously attempt to prop up and rehabilitate his mentor.[23] Chanfrau had achieved sudden success at the end of February 1848, creating the role of Mose. A brawling lad who ran with the fire companies and spoke their propulsive argot, Mose preferred punching out thugs in a plug-muss to anything except saving babies from burning buildings. Mose was true to his Lize, who herself, being "one of 'em," never ran short on spunk. Were you to ask Mose, Is Lize "a gallus gal, anyhow," he would reply, "She ain't nothin' else." Another example: one thief tells another to "prig his wipe," meaning steal the victim's handkerchief. Another interchange, this time between Mose and one of the upstate lads he guides around the city:

GEORGE: What's foo foos?
MOSE: Foo foos is outsiders and outsiders is foo-foos.
GEORGE: I'm as wise now as ever.
MOSE: Well, as your a greenhorn, I'll enlighten you. A foo foo or outsiders is a chap as cant come de big figure.
GEORGE: What's the big figure?
MOSE: The big figure here is 3 cts. for a glass of grog and a night's lodging.[24]

The author of these lines, Benjamin A. Baker, was also from the neighborhood, born in the Bowery. He was the prompter at the Olympic Theatre

1.5 James Brown's lithograph advertising Frank Chanfrau's play at the Chatham Theatre

1.6   A variant of James Brown's image

when he wrote *A Glance at New York in 1848* for Chanfrau. Before this play opened Chanfrau was earning $11 a week. Just two weeks after the opening, Chanfrau was so confident that he bought the Chatham Theatre, announcing himself "sole proprietor and lessee" on "Friday March 3rd." In mid-April he opened a sequel for Mose, *New York as It Is*—and this is the play that reconnected to Catherine Market. If Chanfrau's initial success at the Olympic was as "lucky as it was unexpected," as his obituary in the *Clipper* put it, the move to the Chatham, and to Catherine Market, was cunning from the start.

In these plays about firemen, butcher b'hoys and the g'hals they preferred, Mose's apparent function was to guide greenhorns arriving from upstate or from New England. A chief part of his guidance was teaching them to protect their valuables in the tight spots of urban ethnicity. In varying proportions, these visitors were both afraid of and drawn to such spots as Catherine's Market, saloons, and Ladies' Bowling Gyms. These were the taboo terrains of the era, through which Mose would ease them. Barroom brawlers and market con men parted before the fists of Mose as waters had parted for the people of his Old Testament namesake. Mose delivered.

By the time Chanfrau's sequel opened two months after its predecessor, the actor had realized the meaning of his material. Audience responses had told him where the choke points, where the exhilarations were. By now he knew his presentations of this terrain were delivering local knowledge by displaying gestural vocabularies of the emerging popular culture to itself. These scenes also delivered this material to those beyond it who both feared and were drawn to it. That's one reason that for their Chatham sequel Chanfrau and Baker created the character of Porgy Joe "of Catharine Fish Market," acted by Jack Winans, whose big moment is when he "troubles the Fishermen for an Eel skin." Reason two for these market scenes is that, as I have been arguing, Catherine's Slip was one originating site of the gestures these plays were returning to their public. Chanfrau was consciously processing local history for a public growing larger and more congenial by the week.

By May 1848, reported the *Herald,* forty thousand customers had paid to see Porgy Joe and Mose at the Chatham—this in two weeks. By June 7 the dancing for eels at Catherine Market in scene six had become the distinctive episode of the sequel. There were other famous scenes: the "dumb belles" in the Ladies Gymnasium, the building in flames of the final tableau. But Chanfrau chose the dancing scene to make talismanic with the Browns' lithograph inserted at the top of the poster (Figure 1.5). Chanfrau judged that dancing for eels had more allure than visiting partially dressed women or burning buildings. *New York as It Is* became that spring, at the Chatham Theatre, the most popular play yet performed on an American stage. By summer's end Chanfrau was calling the theatre "Chanfrau's New National Theatre, formerly Chatham."[25]

The Chatham had gone from being a minor theatre whose managers scurried to find sufficient actors to mount an evening's bill in 1828, to proclaiming itself a National Theatre, whose plays were setting attendance records in 1848.[26] Partly to show the turbulent struggles that these changes rode out, equally to orient the discussion to come in later chapters, what I need here is a discussion of the way Catherine Street culture acted out its quarrel with the forces trying to police it at the Chatham. Here is a quick list of the events.

The Chatham's 1,300-seat amphitheater was the home for the first American opera, Micah Hawkins's *The Saw Mill* (1824). It was also the first theatre in the city to use gas lighting, as of 1825. This novelty was a tactical move at a time when the neighborhood had become scary to its middle-class clientele. But the novelty of gas lighting was an insufficient solution and by 1828, after two years of competing with the new Bowery and the old Park, the Chatham and the Lafayette had clearly "sunk to the level of 'minor' theatres."[27] Minor and major are of course relative terms, and from my angle of interest in the development of a distinctive motley consciousness, the deprecative "minor" is good news. Only when a theatre is removed from the prestige of the majors will it begin to expand its repertoire by building on excluded gestural practices.

At this point, in 1828, a neighborhood youth just twenty years old, Thomas Dartmouth Rice, was a backup actor at the Lafayette and the Chatham. He had apprenticed in smaller theatres that enter the historical record only parenthetically, being too small, too vernacular, perhaps too sodden and sordid even to classify as "minor."[28] At the top of the theatre bills for the Chatham this summer was George Washington Dixon, working out some of the earliest blackface material: "Coal Black Rose," for instance, and "Long-Tail'd Blue." Rice watched Dixon very closely. He had doubtless also watched market matters closely when he was a boy of twelve the year the folk drawing of dancing for eels was done.

By the autumn Dixon had embedded "Coal Black Rose" in an interlude he called "Love in a Cloud." He played it at the Lafayette Theatre. The next year he expanded this skit, bringing it and an expanded cast back to the Chatham, now calling it "The Duel or Coal Black Rose."[29] At the Chatham were born the first blackface plays building momentum toward minstrelsy. Why, when Rice returned from the provinces with his further enhancements of this mode in November 1832, did he not play them at the Chatham? Because in May 1832 the Chatham suffered a sea change.

Evangelist activists bought the Chatham Theatre and converted it to a chapel. They replaced the imitators of Bobolink Bob with Charles Grandison Finney, the evangelical preacher who had been working the Ohio frontier, as well as the "burned-over district" upstate. "The *sensation* that will be produced by converting the place with slight alterations into a church will be very great," Lewis Tappan wrote to Finney, "and curiosity will be excited." By May of 1832 Finney was creating converts in pews where clerks and *calicots* a few months before had congregated to watch actors in blackface sing songs of coded rebellion.[30]

> Question: What was going on at the Chatham that the tractarians would want to squelch?
> Answer: Only the beginnings of the American wing of the Atlantic youth culture becoming a self-conscious lumpenproletariat.

Because the Chatham had proved to be an important arena for the figuring out of their nascent culture, its customary public took neither lightly nor passively to the confiscation of its space. In May 1834, when its new abolitionist owners tried at the Chatham to interview a black carpenter just returned from Liberia, in order to show up the wretchedness of colonizationist affairs, the show was disrupted. That July Fourth, riots began at the Chatham when abolitionists scheduled a dry celebration of Abolition Day at the chapel. All blacks in New York had been finally freed on 4 July 1827, the end of the gradual manumission, and abolitionists were trying to substitute sober consideration of the end of slavery in the state for the customary carousing and costuming by which the general Independence Day was celebrated in Chatham Square and down Catherine to its market. The locals were having none of it. Then the dissatisfaction at the Chatham sparked another incident that week at the Bowery Theatre when its audience took offense at perceived anti-American remarks by the visiting English actor William Farren. A critical mass was reached on 9 July 1834 after the Bowery crowd tore up their theatre and spilled out to join the Chatham unrest. They burned homes and an integrated church. According to the diarist Philip Hone, the authorities were quite content to let the violence exhaust itself—until it seemed to be boiling beyond abolitionist targets.[31]

The Chatham Chapel was reclaimed as a secular theatre in September 1839.[32] It featured blackface acts through the forties, reaching a sort of culmination in early 1843. That's when Dan Emmett, Frank Brower, Dick Pelham, and Billy Whitlock joined together for their inaugural performance in New York City of the Virginia Minstrels on the stage of the Chatham. This performance is customarily described as the beginning of the classic minstrel show with its street stories in staccato rhythms, its rude interruptions and overlaps of market confrontation, and, perhaps above all, its flexibly short elements that encouraged improvisation and interaction with the audience. Did they like that song? Well, then, let's just draw it out, sing it again. Are these conundrums boring them? Cut 'em.

At the Chatham, too, during this period something else became prominent, again largely through the influence of the Virginia Minstrels. They and others at this juncture insisted that minstrelsy was delineation of plantation life. This was straight-up faux anthropology, done as theatre. It was the rage at home and became even more pronounced as troupes began doing England. The Virginia Minstrels announced their performance in a newspaper on 19 June 1843:

> In their delineations of the sports and pastimes of the Southern slave race of America they offer an exhibition that is both new and original, which they illustrate through the medium of songs, refrains, lectures and dances, accompanying themselves on instruments of a peculiar nature . . . Their melodies have all been produced at great toil and expense, from among the sable inhabitants of the Southern States in America, the subject of each ascribing the manner in which the slaves celebrate their holidays, which commence at the gathering-in of the sugar and cotton crops.[33]

Abstracted performance of crop festivities mingled with a robust olio of foreshortened Shakespeare and nationalist farces had been playing the Chatham for five years when Chanfrau bought it in 1848. Like the market nearby, this theatre had been a contested space. The Chatham was a wrangling ground for the control of the youth culture from the outside, and it was a switching yard from within. As switching yard, the Chatham had in its last five years switched the emphasis of blackface from interludes and dramas over to the new form of the classic minstrel show, with its hopped repartee and comic confrontations interspersed with songs, locomotive imitations, and crop-festival dances. These confrontations were now being represented in terms of southern blacks in slippery struggles with authority, figured as Ol' Massa and Missus.

One reason the switch from narrative dramas to chopped pastiche premiered first and primarily in New York at the Chatham (rather than, say, at the Bowery) may well have been that the Chatham endured the more persistent political pressure to control its space and signification. Pastiche form hits and runs, slips and slides, and is more difficult to pin down than narrative drama. *Dodgy* is the word for Dan Emmett's skits. As "Dixie's Land" subsequently showed, his work served conflicting purposes, from championing blackness to blazoning Confederate values.[34] This formal slipperiness was a way of tempering and deflecting the clanging political pressures imposed most programmatically at the Chatham. Guerrilla wit and moving targets were apt responses on the part of this new workers' culture to the heavy hand of authority. The inverse of this logic is that although moving targets remain hard to hit, they also do not mount a focused effect. And they are easy to misinterpret and disdain.

These turns conclude my checklist of blackface developments at the Chatham between 1824 and 1848. Armed with this thumbnail sketch of American blackface during its first quarter-century, as seen from the vantage of the Chatham theatre, I am now ready to look again at the way James and Eliphalet Brown turned the folk drawing of 1820 into a talisman of cultural incorporation in 1848.

The Brown brothers lifted from the 1820 folk drawing its entire commercial composition. They copied its balance, off-centered to our left. They reproduced its gestures down to its buttoning of blouses, the rake of its central attitudes. The Browns copied all the formal arrangement but they did not copy the stallholders' view culminating in backdrop masts. The theatre advertisement uncovered the point of view and smudged the rectilinearity. (In the curtailed version appearing on the poster, Figure 1.5, the lines have become horizontal. In the fuller version, Figure 1.6, Mose's right toe points at a few remaining boards and others survive in the shed to the right.) The Browns give us mingled space. The structural differentiations of the folk drawing have become internalized by 1848. They are now finer demarcations of clothing and class—but sifted throughout the lithograph, in the many differentiated details of hats and clothing. For the Brown brothers, viewers are consumers, not sellers, in the marketplace. These consumers have a ready appetite for plentiful details and can digest them well.

In closing off the distant masts, the Browns crowded viewers, including us, tightly in with the dancers. The point of observing the market activities as theatre—either actually in the theatre, or in the image of it—is, after all, to enter its world. Or at least the Browns and Chanfrau organized their forms to maximize this entry. By mingling viewers more and minimizing the folk drawing's privileged spaces, the Browns and Chanfrau increased the motley solidarity. When they added the heavy-flanneled observers, who did not appear in the folk scene and were cropped from the poster advertisement (but whose looming presence in the close-up, Figure 1.6, competes with Mose), they represent quite a different social distance. If in 1820 there was an implied separation between stallholders and dancers, the significant setting-off in 1848 involves these stolidly middle-aged and middle-class men, watching the dancers from their right. Their contrast emphasizes both the dancer's ragged calico and, more important, his loose and nimble motion—which the rest of the crowd, save only the newcomers, shares and seconds. And, peeking in from the background, the Brown brothers included a large wheel, placing its rim at Mose's left hand.

Certainly the 1820 drawing organized the 1848 play's advertisement. In the commercial prints, copies of gesture and grouping from the earlier drawing are too exact to have derived from the turmoil of either market memories or the play's dance episode. It is almost certain that Chanfrau or Benjamin Baker, musing on the drawing, organized their Catherine Market scene—and even Chanfrau's role in it—on the looming youth fascinated with the black dancers in the folk drawing. The proportionate sizes of the black dancer and his chief b'hoy admirer have certainly altered between 1820 and 1848. Whereas in 1820 the dancer was slightly larger than his white admirer, in 1848 the dancer has shrunk and the b'hoy competes for bulk and gravity with the interceding flâneurs. Chanfrau and the Brown brothers document the growth of class formation in the western Atlantic. These three related drawings show how the new cohort took its places next to the middle class; how they viewed each other; and how, in dancing round what they figure here as middle-class mass, lumpen youths came to recognize dimensions of their own magnetism.

Chanfrau's incorporation of street credibility had several other effects. His play transmitted knowledge of Bobolink Bob and the other dancers at Catherine Market, compacting them as "Jack, a Negro and Dancer for Eels" (see Figure 1.5). Chanfrau's use of Jack and his "Niggar Dance for Eels" also commented aggressively on the rampaging form and plantation content the Virginia minstrels had bequeathed the minstrel show. The staging was at least partially a corrective reminder of the local knowledge of black charisma: it came together here on Catherine Street, said Chanfrau and the Browns, so go stuff your sugar harvests. These accumulated changes tell an early story about incorporation of vernacular culture between 1820 and 1848. As I compare these three images I will search out characteristic traces of this inclusion. When black street gestures were brought into the house and marketed, what was wiped out, what persisted, and how?

The actors of this early popular culture were elaborating the gestures blacks made available when they danced at Catherine Market. Performers and congenial publics were struggling to form and hold cultural space that had an early instance and a smaller scale on the shingle in front of Burnel Brown's Chandlery. By the time James and Eliphalet Brown pictured this struggle, in 1848, it was twice nested.[35] First, it was picked up by the whites that we are watching in the folk drawing. Second, these youths had shouldered their way onto established stages from the Chatham, the Bowery, and other theatres west to Cincinnati, south to Charleston and New Orleans. Performers re-created those dances both as their own and as the gestures of others.

I want to watch that nesting politics invade and be absorbed in the Chatham Theatre. The Chatham was a site deliberately chosen for struggle by one wing of New York's middle-class power, the invading Codfish new money from New England. But another element of New York power also left its nested traces on blackface song and actions—the older moneyed style of the Knickerbocker elite. At a different theatre, they made their distinctive move to police culture rising from the Catherine Market crucible. The Knickerbockers focused on what ultimately came to be known as the Bowery, but the theatre reverted to that name only after the market's motley crew had rebuffed the Knickerbocker protocols.

The Bowery came slightly later than the Chatham, opening only in October 1826, originally as the New York Theatre. A consortium of gentlemen rebuilt it on the site of the Bull's Head Inn where a less organized cluster of mechanicals and butchers had been gathering to make their own rude theatre. Henry Astor owned this property, conveniently enough. He obligingly sold it to the gentle group for $105,000—a massive price to erase a saloon theatre, even with a massive polite theatre. Thus, the Bowery, as the

New York Theatre, was a fisted thump against the popular behavior of common labor. But this blow bruised its own knuckles, as might have been foretold by its first production, Thomas Holcroft's *The Road to Ruin*. Foreign fare did not slake the thirst salted in the local working public after they had enjoyed the Chatham and Bull's Head productions as their own. After only a few seasons, certainly by 1830, the grand audience retreated to the Park, "The New York Theatre" became the Bowery, and local amusements resumed. Chalk one up for the Catherine Market crew. The Bowery remained a working-class theatre, by and large, for the rest of its long and useful existence.[36]

Replacing the Bull's Head Inn with what became the Bowery was a classic Knickerbocker maneuver, even in its failure. It was a reflex spasm of the city's old elite. Characteristically, as in the massive payoff to Astor, they were trying to keep their money within their unbroken circle. This circle was the group that had commissioned John Searle to paint it in repose at the Park Theatre when it opened in November 1822.[37] The Knickerbockers were able to seal money within their class, but they could not choke back the rambunctiousness rising from the East River slips. This inability tokened their weakening position in the city. It is instructive to compare this Knickerbocker inability to maintain its intentions with the comparable reflex at the Chatham just a few years later on the part of the newly emerging Codfish entrepreneurs.

Both old and new elites were at least as eager to control the threat of working-class activity in the Five Points and Catherine Market area as they were to contain the far less socially potent activity of blacks, free or enslaved. This early in the century, blacks were still understood to be chained down tight. It was the newly roaming (for the most part, white) crew who were the most frightening. They were beginning to make theatrical interludes displaying their erupting unreliability. And they were doing so in terms of runaway slaves and insouciant black servants. That is, white working youths displayed themselves as blacks as part of their strategy to ward off just the sort of stolid surveillance that middle-class visitors to Catherine Market represent in Eliphalet and James Brown's lithograph. This unmoored white underclass learning how to represent itself was what scared New York's elites. And what frightened them most, as it had in 1741 when they hanged Hughson at Catherine Slip, was when this white and black lumpenproletariat merged into a common force with a distinctive consciousness.

There is some evidence that this commonality was again alarming elites at the end of the 1820s and into the 1830s. Among the merchants, leading governing families, lawyers, and doctors in the audience in Searle's painting of the Park Theatre Knickerbocker circle, for instance, is one James W. Gerard, a lawyer who incorporated the Society for the Reformation of Juvenile Delinquents. Gerard formed this society in anxious response to the growing youth culture. His anxiety developed as the manumission statutes ripened and as youths of different pasts, occupations, and hues swapped gestures and symbolic behavior at festive sites from shingle to stage.

When that swapping gathers momentum, we recognizably enter the world of popular culture, black charisma, and contending elites. These three—each with its subsets—have been struggling among themselves like boys under a blanket since the beginning of the Atlantic world. But the blanket comes off, and the wrestling reaches tag-team dimensions, from the beginning of the nineteenth century onward. This is when the term "juvenile delinquent" comes into use. Now, critical masses of free and runaway blacks—along with slaves on such holiday leave as occurred at Pinkster, Christmas, and cornhuskings—conjoin critical masses of sailors, rustics released and enticed from the country, and youths displaced from apprenticeship. All come together in cities.

These workers are between traditions, between controls, and between phases of their lives. The interludes they begin to perform, and attend, formally express their in-between stage, quite literally. All at once these mingled cohorts not only are between controls but very much more positively are *among themselves,* cuing on one another's moves—exactly as the folk drawing and the Browns' lithograph show. They are among themselves while they are also under scrutiny. Participants in this mingled consciousness enjoy and develop their own distinctive agency under the anxious eyes of elites, partially distinct from their many folk and ethnic pasts, ripe to express their own overlappings. They constitute a new blend, particular to the markets of the Atlantic world after the trade routes set peoples in circulation. Their self-discovery caused nightmares among their more settled onlookers.

The minutes of the New York City Common Council for 13 October 1823 show deep concerns that have given elites sour dreams ever since. The sheer number of theatrical performances in the city had increased so precipitously and the competition for its audience had become so vulgar, worried these Knickerbockers, that "the more useful pursuits of the Young are neglected for these amusements, an unnecessary expenditure of time and Money is incurred, and the baneful habit of late hours at night and neglect of business in the morning is the Inevitable Result."[38] Sleepy, sloppy workers were the bottom line. Leave leisure culture to the Leisure Class and let the Young sleep at night: that is what replacing the Bull's Head Inn with the New York Theatre was about.

Codfish elites shared with their Knickerbocker competitors this patriarchal attitude toward young workers. Henry Ward Beecher, a few years later, calls them alien, not settled, a "floating population." This is a surprisingly precise term for the crew mingled by merchant ships and plantation needs during the previous two centuries. The floating population those ships and needs set in motion has come home, but remains adrift, represented now by actors:

> A floating population, in pairs or companies, without leave asked, blow the trumpet for all our youth to flock to their banners! . . . the young men are ours; our sons, our brothers, our wards, clerks, or apprentices; they are living in our houses, our stores, our shops, and we are their guardians, and take care of them in health, and watch them in sickness; yet every vagabond who floats in hither, swears and swaggers, as if they were all his: and when they offer to corrupt all these youth, we paying them round sums of money for it, and we get courage finally to say that we had rather not . . . they turn upon us in great indignation with, Why don't you mind your own business—what are you meddling with our affairs for?[39]

Clear here is the dual and dueling sense of proprietorship over youth. Who owns the young—their elders or their charismatic peers? This question was real. Both Knickerbockers and Codfish leaders *were* losing control over "their" charges. As the apprenticeship system broke down, as rural and foreign youths migrated to the cities, they were no longer living "in our houses, our stores, our shops." They were finding lives, instead, in rooming houses, stews, and on the streets. They were populating neighborhoods that the plague doctors had documented in 1820. The fathers and foremen, owners and employers for whom Beecher spoke were, in fact, no longer their guardians. Instead, these youths were guarding and girding themselves. Blackface plays were one way they were finding they could go *en garde.* Acting out their condition as a "floating population" was important in that girding. It gave the youth culture its own web of fables and meaning. If the apprentice ship would not float them, then perhaps the blackface ship would.

Henry Ward Beecher, brother to Harriet Beecher Stowe and son of Lyman Beecher, was a second-generation agent for Codfish activism. The Codfish style would prove more persistent, much more effectively damaging to the rambunctious culture than its Knickerbocker predecessor. Codfish activists would also receive from the new popular culture, in return, the brunt of its hostile stereotyping, as we will shortly see when we look at the song "De New York Nigger."

One significant difference between the operative styles of the old and the new elites in the city was the new money's willingness to contest workers on their own grounds. If the Knickerbocker style alternated between massive thumps and rapid retreats, Codfish tended to hands-on slogging. Take the example of the Tappan brothers, Arthur and Lewis, come to New York from the Connecticut valley via Boston in stages, set up as silk merchants on Pearl Street, founders of the American Tract Society in 1825 and the American Abolitionist Society in 1833. Lewis and Arthur Tappan were ardent abolitionists, anti-Catholics, Christian fundamentalists, cloth importers and retailers, early creators of the urban credit bureau, founders of a frontier college (Oberlin) and seminary (Lane, where they struggled to rein in the independent Beechers). The Tappans extended surveillance and character checks into every nook of private life, regulating their employees' housing, leisure, and faith. They were extraordinary organizers and very difficult personalities. They came to Manhattan to sell their prints to clerks and *calicots* just as the Erie Canal opened and New York began its population surge. They soon saw that while this surplus population was necessary both as employees and as customers, it required bridling. While Knickerbockers formed societies to police juveniles, Codfish came among the juveniles and gave them a home—one of Lewis Tappan's earliest charities was an Asylum for Indigent Boys.[40]

Although they had more hubris than most of their group, these Tappan brothers were hardly alone in their prodigious energies, in their susceptibility to the magnetic pull of the black-white issue, or in their anxiety about social volatility. Allan Melvill, father to Herman Melville who was to reflect some of this charisma between outcasts and blacks as the intimacies between Ishmael and Queequeg, as well as Benito Cereno and Babo, also moved from Boston to New York. The senior Melvill came in 1818, just five years after Lewis Tappan fronted his younger brother Arthur thousands without interest to move from the Connecticut Valley and set up his silk business on Pearl Street. Lewis would not join him from Boston for another decade. These New Englanders gradually infiltrating New York merchant circles were moving from a relatively secure world of precedents into a "business world . . . less regulated and more volatile. To go to New York," Michael Rogin has shown, "meant to shatter traditional ties and place oneself on the wheel of fortune."[41]

When James and Eliphalet Brown copied the 1820 folk drawing to a lithograph advertising Chanfrau's play, they pictured that volatility with just this metaphor. They added the large wheel behind the urchin with the string of porgies. This wheel had almost as many allusions as spokes. One was to the dizzy life that the foundational song of blackface performance had by then sneaked onto the lips of all the Atlantic community in the antebellum years:

> For I wheel about an' turn about, an' do just so,
> An ebery time I turn about, I jump Jim Crow.

This wheeling about and freezing in upstart poses was itself a maddening embodiment of the stuttering unpredictability that the elites were determined, but failing, to stanch. And bootlegged onto *that* wheel were its transmitted connections back to Catherine Market at Catherine Slip, and the Catherine Wheel associated with St. Catherine, Mother Immaculate of volatility: when she touched the wheel upon which she was to be quartered, it exploded. That's the wheel which Mose had at hand, and before which the eel dancers gyrated.

High and low, on and off the street, the turns of fortune and the mingled realities which merchant ships, industrial production, and overlapped lores were bringing to Atlantic cities were creating mutualities of expression. These concerns displayed mutual struggle to understand and display anxious matters. Mose's hand on the wheel while he leans toward black dance at Catherine Market: that was a visual pun, a tableau about rising and falling at fortune's behest. It was iconography becoming secular. It was more or less available to publics of all classes. Everyone was involved in it. Part of that common matter, however, was a widespread awareness that matters were ripe to blow sky high. Images and terms turned and punned—especially about the anxiety-inducing nodes of volatility. Thus, while one might conclude that the Browns' litho is about the formation of a common, cross-class melting pot of Americana, that judgment would be a mistake. It would be mistaken because beneath the mutuality, competing ideologies continued to ripen in their separate ways.

It is not so much that there were new class consciousnesses emerging in the early nineteenth century, for there had been plebeian custom and proletariat consciousness since there had been big houses and merchant capital. What were new were the urban conditions newly providing places informal and formal for those persistent consciousnesses to display, even stage themselves. In that restaging not only did new middle-class publics suddenly discover that workers had cultural lives independent from their own, but so did plebeian actors renew the resourcefulness and complexity of their culture. In playing out their old gestures, actors elaborated and mixed them into new roles for themselves as for others. This reactivation is why it is important that previously unrepresented class points of view were roughly shouldering their way onto the stages of the Atlantic. The activity of the contest was helping people define themselves.

> I don't like de house; I wish it was bigger,
> 'Cause dey neber, hab rom to let in de nigga.
> I wind it up now.
> —"De New York Nigger"

At this moment for young workers in the markets and trades, in service domestic and commercial, as the 1820s grade into the Jacksonian 1830s, matters are winding up ever more tightly in New York. Unattached youths crowd the boarding houses. The system of learning a trade by apprenticing oneself to an artisan is breaking down as managed employment is incorporating more and more skilled work. This puts the squeeze on artisanal shops, and their owners are increasingly feeling edgy. By the simplest definition, artisans are middle class, for they own their means of production, and they understand that their interests lie with the merchants and an established order. But this alignment is tenser now because production modes are changing decisively. Artisans lose independence if they throw in with the big merchants, and their knowhow separates them from the young workers, sailors, most free or enslaved blacks, immigrant Europeans. The working class suffers another of its splits. Its potentially stablest members, its artisans, separate from it, and one sign of this separation is that artisans disproportionately engage in urban riots.[42]

In the 1820s and 1830s everyone is looking askance, trying to figure out where they stand in relation to everyone else. Merchant managers like the Tappans are improvising the piecing-out system of production, particularly developed in lower Manhattan. Many coordinations are necessary for this piecing out. So many parts of so many products assembled in so many sweat shops move via so many cartings across town through so many separate agencies that owners must inculcate predictable uniformity, clockwork, and well-seated behavior. From their angle of view, such managers as the Tappans are not simply sticking busybody noses in the lives of others. Paradoxically, they are trying to bring home to the metropolis some of the cooperation that the plantations and ships in Atlantic trade had pioneered.[43]

But this is also the period when New York fills with heterogeneity unprecedented even in European urban life. The challenges of different cultures living cheek by jowl, as along Catherine and Chatham Streets and in the Five Points, winds up by several notches the mixing of behavioral cues, making everyone the more conscious of gestures as signs, and of cultural presentation in general. Youthful workers run on their own mad clocks, unsettled in their hormonal anarchy, their syncopated sleep rhythms, and their stimulant habits.

The Tappans thus enter this story about the fascination of blackface action because they attempted to lead the containment. They wanted to straiten the youth culture that was then defining itself to itself by turning around black song and dance. Among all the reasons for this fascination, not the least for these young workers was to confound and contradict the simple, romantic racism that the abolitionist conception of blacks was broadcasting. It follows, in such a positional analysis, that the Codfish group achieved much of *its* identity from disciplining these dizzy energies of dissipation and recalcitrance.

There are good reasons why cross-racial folk mimicry pushed into professional practice at particular moments, beginning in the 1820s. Blackface was a distinct and, at first, minor part of a much larger stirring of race issues in the Atlantic world. Tens of thousands of runaway slaves were pouring through border and northern cities. Many merchant abolitionists like the Tappans were accused of promoting "amalgamation." This perceived aggression by the abolitionist movement upset the liberal-conservative alliance for African colonization and culminated in such violence as the July 1834 riot in New York City, which began at the Chatham and had one of its ends burning out Lewis Tappan's Rose Street home. So, blackface was one among several factions articulating responses to race issues. Blackface performance was, however, a *distinct* faction.

Although it is newly conventional to say that blackface performance contributed to white anger at blacks competing for jobs—that it constructed whiteness—in fact, this claim is methodologically weak. The closer one looks at the police blotters, the more they reveal that the people arrested at the riots were less often workers than artisans desperate to clarify their position in the economy. Also, the claim that blackface performance—as opposed to simple disguise—contributed to these riots is interpretively naive. The forms of blackface delineation are so complex and multidimensional, performed by so many different actors in so many different situations, that they worked generally to confound political action. Therefore, I argue that blackface developed distinct responses to "amalgamation"—not by attacking but by enacting miscegenation.

Blackface performers worked out ways to flash white skin beneath a layer of burnt cork, stage the pastiche grammar of a creole dialect, and recast traditional Irish melodies with fantasy images of fieldhand fun shadowed by violence and dislocation. As fear and fascination grew apace in different parts of the several newly urban audiences, so did minstrel shows proliferate, all the while compacting and compounding their motivating images. Their effects were as multiple, and as troubling, as the pressures they were winding up to keep in play.

Blackface minstrelsy was a much more complex attempt to understand racial mixing and accommodate audiences to it than either abolitionist propaganda or the counter-riots of the artisanry. These wrangling middle-class antagonists had specific intentions and policies to promote. To boost their intentions both these parties needed to reduce images to fundamental singularity and freeze matters there. Despite their internal dissensions, the abolitionists were gifted at creating firm tableaus—"Am I not a brother?" asked the kneeling slave that the Tappans were selling during the 1830s printed in four poses "suitable, perhaps . . . as a purse covering or lamp mat." Likewise, the artisan mobs in New York, Charleston, Cincinnati, Boston, Philadelphia, and elsewhere were winding themselves up with similar images of simplified blacks, but more grotesquely racist. Of all the parties to this argument who had access to the stage or other media, only one group broadcast complex and contradictory images of blacks. Only one saw blacks as people with an implicit intelligence evinced by explicit talent, irony, and capacious resistance. This singular group was blackface performers and their publics, still in their protean early phases during the 1830s.[44]

As befits the different and complex sources for their imagery, this first popular culture in the United States used blackface distinctively. In this popular culture, blackface was not a figment of illegal or sinful issues, as the merchant press or Christian pamphleteers understood it; not an arm either of abolitionist or proslavery propaganda; not a symbol of wretched animalism, as the Davy Crockett almanacs and earlier popular American imagery had conceived blackness. In this new popular culture, blackface was not the insipid blackness of romantic English abolitionist narratives, patronizing indigenous peoples in order to sustain imperial governance. Disempowered young workers applied blackface as a defiant measure of their own distance from those arguments among enfranchised interests. Youths in blackface were almost as estranged from the bourgeois inflections of the slavery quarrel as were the blacks whom they therefore chose to figure their dilemma and emphasize their distance. Blackface picked up steam exactly because it kept itself distinct from the arguments of the several ensconced groups and provoked their combined disdain.

In its early commercial stages, minstrelsy was one development young workers themselves could shape with their patronage, for what youths did not pay to see did not remain in the nightly posted theatre bills. Performers kept close tabs on their gate receipts and changed the skits and patter to keep the sales high. Sam Sanford (1821–1905), before going out on his own, was one of the early troupers with the Buckley Family Minstrels, who were subsequently incarnate as New Orleans Serenaders and then Ethiopian Serenaders. Sanford gives many instances in his unpublished autobiography of how closely he watched the gate receipts and played to the taste of the audience. His quintet appeared once in New Orleans at the same time as the Sable Harmonists, who had reached the city before them. Sanford describes their competition:

> The press gave us the preference and thus so dismayed the Sables, that they left in disgust starting up the river. I will here say the press did not do them justice for myself and old man Buckley both admitted they were

our superiors in singing—but they had no Banjo or jig dances, this negro element we had. And it was the most relished part of the programme. Again, their end men could not display wit. But their choruses and songs were given in a pure operatic style, having operatic singers in the company, they done justice to all their singing. It would be presumed they were the best if number should have an advantage, they having eight, and our party five. *Yes* only *five* and we took the rag off the bush.[45]

Thus the minstrel show was the first among many later manifestations, nearly always allied with images of black culture, that allowed youths to resist merchant-defined external impostures and to express a distinctive style.

Abstracting themselves as blacks allowed the heterogeneous parts of the newly moiling young workers all access to the same identity tags. Irish, German, French, Welsh, and English recent immigrants, as well as American rustics, could all together identify in the 1830s with Jim Crow, Bone Squash, and Jumbo Jim, then in the forties with Tambo and Bones.[46] Disparate ethnic and class groups could not come together like this over theatrical images of English figures from whatever class. Nor could they identify with rural American types, like the Kentucky Rifleman, Davy Crockett, or the Yankee Peddler, certainly not with anything like the same paradoxical fit that they could feel with the raggedy black figure. All the extant figures which preceded Jim Crow carved out their space by representing power or position that opposed the positions of the new publics. Plucking a chord close to home in this heterogenous cohort, the caroming jitters of the Jim Crow figure nixed the bluster of his western competitors. Precisely because middle-class aspirants disdained the black jitterbug in every region, the black figure appealed all across the Atlantic as an organizational emblem for workers and the unemployed. Hated everywhere, he could be championed everywhere alike.

In such early blackface acts as the entr'acte dances and the initial narrative skits, white working youths, many of them Irish immigrants like a portion of their audiences, were identifying with blacks as representations of all that the YMCAs and evangelical organizers were working to suppress. Whether their songs were inaccurate pictures of African-American culture is not the point. Until the cows come home, we might debate how well or ill minstrels copied black culture. But that is a fruitless task and always to be followed by such further imponderables as, What is authentic black culture? Is any authenticity there? What is "black"? Therefore, no matter how racist the resultant crude stereotypes became in blackface performance during the 1850s and afterward, one must neither miss nor forget the less obvious uses that proletariat youths were even then making of the material. They were flaunting their affection for these signs of akimbo insurrection against the conventions of control.

When the formal minstrel show developed after 1843, these youth publics were on the side of the spontaneous Tambo and Bones rather than that of the middlemen. The middleman's correct speech and elaborate attire represented protocols which the Tappans and other merchants hoped to inculcate. It was no accident that the middlemen, who came later to be called "interlocutor," began every show addressing the endmen with the exasperated dictum: "Gentlemen, be seated!" From beginning to end of each individual show, as well as over the extent of the entire blackface lore cycle, the minstrel show has displayed struggle over the seating of chaotic energy. Youths have projected themselves as blacks partly in order to rouse and engage just such commitments in their various fundamentalist opponents.

The expressive union between perceived black performance and young workers occurred when industrial capital was reaching dominance on both sides of the Atlantic. But neither this motley class nor its expressive union lasted through the 1850s. After that, the momentum of their coded images carried their original union disturbingly deep within blackface performance, but not in the narrative form that had emerged during the 1830s. This early blackface narrative drama unmistakably expressed fondness for black wit and gestures. But it did not last long in the cauldron of entrepreneurial pressure leading up to the Civil War. To sustain its sentiments, performers had to chop them up into the pastiche effects of the minstrel variety show. And this minstrel show survived seemingly to serve new interests. That is to say, the industrial economy of the Atlantic world and the microeconomy of minstrel theatre producers reversed the original Jim Crow engagement. As blackface minstrelsy gathered momentum in the 1850s and afterward, gathered stereotypes and gathered power, it expanded its public beyond the culture of rogue working youths. Entrepreneurial control absorbed and damped the implicit critique youths in blackface were making of upright mercantile style.

Merchants seemed to rein in insurgent expression, but what sort of success did they have? When the white minstrel's engagement with black charisma seemed to be contained, even turned inside out to derogate that charisma, the identification was still there in fact, but encoded. Apparently controlled and debased, it had a momentum of its own. Apparently deflected and defused, blackface was nevertheless raising Cain autonomously. It would be quite a while before any of this became apparent in history. However, I shall foreshorten history and take up these issues in the next chapter.

"Dancing for Eels *1820* Catharine Market" pictures the birth of a young, ragged, cross-racial culture nobody knew what to Do With. It was a force that surprised the old elites, the Knickerbockers and their equivalents in other cities, too. In some instances they were surprised into bitter retirement from the lists. Their places, however, would be taken by others. Rising elites would prove their mettle by entering the lists with those who danced for eels—not to dance, too, as we have agreed to do, but to tamp the dance and stifle the song, rechannel the manpower and housebreak its energy. It is not difficult to imagine that those two well-fed interlopers standing stiff as their sticks at the left side of the Browns' 1848 lithograph represent just these stifling elites. Arthur Tappan was one of those aspirant elites who thought he Knew What To Do.[47]

Arthur Tappan gave $5,000 for the purchase of modern steam presses when he helped found the American Tract Society. These merchant tractarians were willing to invest heavily to impose their Connecticut creeds on the surging populations of the Fourth, Sixth, Seventh, and Tenth Wards of New York City. The cultural lists were moving slowly toward the center of Manhattan from the edge. They all came together where Catherine Street met the bottom of the Bowery at the compound joint of Chatham and Division. Indeed, the tractarians and the youth culture were going to kick heels and lock heads wherever they went, edge or center of the city, edge or middle of the country.

Working for the clampdown, Lewis Tappan and colleagues handed out tracts. They "roamed the wharves of the East River; they entered the dingy stores and taverns of Five Points; they stopped in the countinghouses of Wall and State Streets. To each person they met they gave a tract, or, if rebuffed, perhaps a word of warning. By May, 1831, Lewis Tappan and the other distributors in the wards of the city had dispensed six million pages."[48]

At this point, too, the Tappans worked particularly to clamp everything down on Sunday, including the Sunday mails, saloons, whaling ships. This

Sabbatarian impulse increased their conflict with the Catholic working class and with the Jacksonians. "Treating" to rounds of beer was a customary rite of democratic sovereignty. Bone Squash, one of the early blackface theatre's most popular workers on the lam, sings of this custom:

> And ebery Nigger dat I meet,
> I'll stop him in de street
> And I'll up wid a penny,
> Head or tail for a treat.[49]

Bone literally sells his soul to a Yankee devil (modeled more than a bit on Arthur Tappan), in order to participate in this fondest rite of democratic brotherhood.

Sunday was often the one day free for this bonding. Therefore it was also a serious contradiction of democratic custom when Arthur Tappan founded the New York *Journal of Commerce,* in 1827, to rival the theatre and liquor advertising gazettes of the city. By the 1830s Arthur Tappan had become the scapegoat in the dispute between New York's clamped and their clampers. The *Working Man's Advocate* said that his name was "a running title to volumes of recorded sneers and sarcasms." Satirical poems on the streets mocked the American Tract Society by inserting its founder in street poems as "St. Arthur de Fanaticus" or "A. T. Burgundy" for the grape juice Arthur Tappan permitted at communion.[50]

This give-and-take went on for years. Increasing layers of codified anger piled on the black stereotypes of minstrelsy and the white stereotypes of the meddling clampdown. In the early blackface song "De New York Nigga," Arthur appears as "Massa Arfy Tappan." He is stepping out with Miss Dinah (as in Someone's in the Kitchen with Dinah):

> His Dinah walkin' wid Massa Arfy Tappan.
> Old Bobolition Glory, he live an' die in story,
> De black man's friend, wid de black man's houru.

It is a mistake to read, or to read off, even these most apparently vile songs in the minstrel songsters too quickly. This one sets up Tappan as Massa on an urban plantation, replete with sexual hierarchies. The punning on *houru* is complex enough to throw the point of view up for grabs. A "houri" implies a mixed-race person, specifically a white-skinned black-eyed person, a mulatta perhaps, or an actor in a mask. This wordplay indicates what I assess as a fairly typical self-consciousness about the performance.[51] The pun on *whore*, additionally, shows aggression about Dinah's betrayal of the speaker that is part of the larger song's stirring together of conflicting attitudes. The song provokes so much clashing that I present it whole to show its shocks at once:

> When de Nigger's done at night washing up de china,
> Den he sally out to go and see Miss Dinah,
> Wid his Sunday go-to-meetins segar in his mouth a
> He care for no white folk, neder should he ought to,
> His missy say to him, I tell you what, Jim,
> Tink you gwan now to cut and come agin.
>
> He walk to de Park, an' he hear such mity music,
> A white man he did say enuff to make him sick,
> He turn round to see who make de observation
> An de sassy whites laugh like de very nation,
> Jim was in de fashion, so he got into a passion.
> Cause de damn white trach was at him a laffin.
>
> Jim cut ahead an tink he never mind 'em,
> White folks got de manners—he tink he couldn't find 'em
> He walk a little furder an tink he die a laffin,
> To see his Dinah walkin' wid Massa Arfy Tappan.
> Ole Bobolition Glory, he live an die in story,
> De black man's friend, wid de black man's houru.
>
> He gwan to de Bowery to see Rice a actin,
> He tink he act de brack man much better dan de white 'un,
> Only listen now, a nigga in a operar,
> Rice wid a ball an' brush tink much properer
> He cut de pigeon wing, an' he do de handsome ting,
> Wheel about and turn about, an' bring de money in.
>
> De little house now, what is called de Olympic,
> Wha massa Geo. Holland makes de people grin,
> Ching a ring, Pompey Smash, an, ride upon a rail, sir,
> De little house coin de cash, while de big ones all fail,
> But I don't like de house; I wish it was bigger,
> 'Cause dey neber, hab rom to let in de nigga.

I wind it up now, I tink you say 'tis time, sir,
You got no reason, but got plenty ob rhyme, sir,
I'se gwan to go away, but first I leave behind me
What ebery brack man wish, in dis happy land of liberty;
Here's success to Rice, to Dixon, and to Lester,
May dey neber want a friend, nor a hoe-cake to bake, sir.

Spoken.—Rice, Dixon, an' Lester, de proud supporters ob de brack
drama, may dey neber want de encouragement de greatness ob de
subject demands.[52]

This song was still current in the year of the Emancipation Proclamation.
It had a performance cycle of a quarter-century, from before 1840 until
some years after its 1863 publication. T. D. Rice had died in 1860, his
performances had lost popularity since at least the mid-1850s, and he had
been notoriously acting *Bone Squash Diavolo* (signified by the "ball and
brush" reference) in the early 1830s, opposed by a Yankee Devil. When
Arfy walks out with Dinah, he culminates a quarter-century's insinuation
that those Codfish elite were all Yankee devils. They came at first for the
soul of working youth. They returned for the working women.

My supposition here supplements the critique of blackface performance
since the 1960s. It looks to me that the singer and his public are *identifying*
with "De New York Nigger" at least as much as they are distinguishing
themselves from him. The New York Nigger is us, Sir or Missy—says this
song—may we Jims neber want a friend nor a hoe-cake to bake. In songs
like "De New York Nigger" a popular culture is discovering for its public
who they are, what alliances are possible for them, who is betraying them,
and why.

This song only more clearly than many others is about its own packaging,
playing on mixing and prostitution, and the eagerness in various groups
to slide up and down social hierarchies leaving traces of their having been
there. The main thrill and pain of the song is over the double-edged capacity to cut and come again. This is a masquerade capacity made possible
by urban closeness, material sufficiency, symbolic surplus, and egalitarian
excitement. Jim can cut out with his cigar jutting in front of him, leaving
behind his mistress with her intimate wink of his coming again. She's used
to his interruptions. When he sallies out, the military verb nicely balances
a martial eruption through a gapped fortress with the contrary mincing
embodied in its feminine tag. He can sally nightly to the theatre to see and

be seen, but in the passage he runs a gauntlet of manners and abuse. "Jim" is already a come-again figure, the truncated return of Jim Crow, with the crow associations cut. That he used to claim he was fresh from frontier regions like Kentucky and Virginia is conveniently censored for this New York variant.

The fourth line of "De New York Nigger," constant in all the variants I have seen, is worth emphasizing: "He care for no white folk, neder should he ought to." These declarations of sympathy for Jim's black pride, and, more, the justness of this sympathy, are what the outraged critics of minstrelsy programmatically ignore in order to make the songs seem programmatically racist. In fact the song is as wholly on the side of Jim as it can be, given that it also laughs with his plight, which is the plight of the song and the plight of its public. Laughing in this song is laughing at one's own male plight, black or white.

The song repeatedly sympathizes with Jim's foiled attempts to find dignity commensurate to what the urban parade offers others. In one of its several sly rhetorical expansions, the song makes the "sassy whites" persecuting Jim's sartorial efforts expand so that they "laugh like de very nation" at him. This then is a double intensifier, laughing hard, yes, but also laughing in national unison, which has a political bite. But the image defuses itself, too, when challenged. That is, the political bite can also be denied by the simple intensified meaning—the singer might say he did not mean the whole nation was laughing, just that people were laughing hard, Whatsa matter, you don't understand street talk? So it feints and retreats, dodging. Maybe the singer just means that people will laugh at strutting youths of every hue. Jim and Dinah *are* every hue, whiteness beneath blackness in his case, blackness beneath whiteness in her case. Even the "missy" of the first stanza is ambiguous. She is probably a white woman, a middle-class employer. But the diminutive Jim uses for her is part of a common pun in these blackface songs on *mistress*. Public laughter at Jim humanizes his reaction in the next stanza when he sees Dinah also cutting out on him, as he implicitly cut out on his employer, "missy." Whether Dinah and Jim will come again, and with whom, is still an open question for these youths of New York, newly understanding themselves as distinctive, newly understanding themselves, too, as "niggers."

This identification of many ethnic groups under the banner of "De New York Nigger" is tainted through and through. It is a Gordian knot of acknowledged taintedness. Their identification displays their condition as that of the lowest and least powerful in the city in order to shock and confound the middle-class proprieties. They identify with blacks to bring themselves together and to explain to themselves how others disdain them. They do so in order to score blows against others of their class—"white trach"—who are cruel to blacks. But *white trash* is not a northern urban term; it is a southern black name for poor whites, which intensifies its usefulness as a marker of northern urban black/white affinity: we integrate, they segregate. Another reason to profess this low bond with other youths is to complain and gird themselves against female betrayal. Dinah is the butt in this song because she fancies rising sexually beyond their class.

Those are some of the tainted strands tied up in this song, but they are mild, and I believe are meant to seem mild, when they are understood in relation to the cable that is the song's real armature: the racist context which tangles its many strands and to which they allude. A specific master rhetoric contains this song even while it allows the actor to play out his resentments.

O den I goes to New York,
To put dem rite all dare;
But find so many tick heads,
I gib up in dispair
Weel about, and turn about, And do jis so;
Ebry time I weel about, I jump Jim Crow
For dare be Webb he tick upon,
De paper dat he sell;
De Principal, wat he say good,
I tink him worse as hel.

> —Jim Crow, "as sung by all the comic singers," Harvard
> Theatre Collection

James Watson Webb, on 3 August 1835, complained in his paper the *Morning Courier and New York Enquirer* that "The air in all our public conveyances is poisoned with the rank effluvia of . . . aromatic damsels, who . . . always challenge the favorite seats . . . dressed in silks obtained from the munificence of Arthur Tappan."[53] Webb wears on his sleeve, for all to see, the same possessives ("our" public spaces) that Henry Ward Beecher used to possess white working youths going to the theatre, that Thomas De Voe used to describe Manhattan Negroes dancing at Catherine Market. Webb feels aggrieved challenge when anyone else sits in a seat he assumed was his prerogative. Here, then, in this aggression, is the master rhetoric, as published by the Tammany editor James Webb, whom Jim Crow thought "worse as hel."

Both song and editorial were doubtless bandying images circulating orally at the time. While Webb's editorial clearly had the most immediate clout, nevertheless minstrel song had wiles enabling its destabilizing effects to last the longer and work the sneakier. That's what interests me about "De New York Nigger" and its taintedness. It does not picture Webb's power versus worker powerlessness; it does not show one discourse mastering another. Rather, it admits imbalance of power but displays the resourceful ways that vernacular culture marked out its position within the taint of this imbalance.

Did Webb dictate terms to blackface performers? Probably. Certainly his heavy hand indexes the dominant racist reality. The class disdain and racism expressed in Webb's editorial remark drive the omnibuses in which all the "floating population" must move. Webb did not invent the terms, but he employs them forcefully. Workers with no access to presses or to boardrooms had to resort to minstrel songs and shingle boards to sing and dance their positions. It was that or float in the flow that Webb spewed. Carried nested in the poisons that elite politics broadcast, it is no wonder that songs like "De New York Nigger" are tainted. Their soiling is the condition of culture in the unsettled space of the early industrial world.

"De New York Nigger" is not free art. Its performers are not free agents in some never-never land of free self-activation. The song attests to a thoroughly nested cultural struggle. The imagery in such struggles is shared, but the power is not. The power remains unequally dispersed. This is not to say that the singer has no power. Rather, what power he has manifests itself in different ways than Webb's. Webb is upfront, so sure his prejudices reign that he need not hide them. The singer is forced to be downback: sneaky and two-faced, which is one possible definition of "blackface."

Webb's editorial and the song's recalcitrant disturbance of "his" imagery both struggle to control a mutually engaged energy. They share terms, but it is perfectly clear they do not share intentions, and they are not alone in this fight. There are additional parties—more bodies wrestling under the blanket. The Tappans fought this master rhetoric more directly than proletarian self-activation could. The Tappans bought physical space to preach their rhetoric, paid for presses to churn out tracts to disseminate it and a newspaper to second it. Gentlemen of property and standing like Webb and his Tammany rump had their own newspaper, the *Courier and Enquirer,* to broadcast their side. These vicious fights about who was controlling urban ideology revolved around questions of who would draw the limits of civilized behavior. That's what was really going on when Webb talked about "aromatic damsels" and the Tappans strove to keep free Negroes in New York rather than ship them, colonization-style, back to Liberia.

Here is Webb again, in an even more abusive and telling remark, directed once again specifically at the Tappans:

> The egis of the law indignantly withdraws its shelter from them . . . when they debase the noble race from which we spring,—that race which called civilization into existence, and from which have proceeded all the great, the brave, and good, that have ever lived—and place it in the same scale as the most stupid, ferocious and cowardly of the divisions into which the creator has divided mankind, then they place themselves beyond the pale of the law, for they violate every law divine and human.[54]

This middle-class struggle to locate the edge of the community as the "pale of the law" is what contaminates the world of "De New York Nigger." The reverse of the same token shows just how radical and threatening to that internecine bourgeois conflict a song such as this can be. These songs mock that struggle by determinedly crossing and recrossing, tirelessly tangling and looping that border line. Jim has imaginative access everywhere. But he has sovereign access nowhere: "dey neber, hab room to let in de nigga." In lines like this, we see declared that old Catherine Market spirit. Bobolink Bob and Jim Crow survive, nested in "De New York Nigger."

What is remarkable about this song, like much of minstrelsy behind it, like all lore with legs, is its *compaction.* It winds up so many references and conflicting attitudes in Jim that he proves unreadable, irresolvable, backing one agenda or ideology only if he is excerpted in fragments. He is a working-class flâneur strolling through swamps of disdain, and he knows it. Looking wryly on as the abolitionist leader walks off with his lover, Jim remains on the outside, scorned by whites whose manners are undiscoverable. He is a man with no home but a place to scrub other people's china. Arfy and Dinah surpass him. The opera house that represents him prohibits his entrance. But no one else in the world of the song shares his modicum of dignity: he tells plain truth. And plainly his audience is meant to feel the unfairness of his betrayal and exclusion. While the storied actors and pretenders of both genders enrich themselves at his expense, he retains his put-upon, Chaplinesque dignity. He still hopes that the black drama will have success, because that is the one place that his story can peep out, in its way, between the cracks, hoping there will be auditors to hear its codes.

Nevertheless, "De New York Nigger" criticizes the racism of its own minstrel form: the exclusions of some of the theatres, the laughing at blacks. This is one of the ways it shows its awareness of its own genealogy, to which it alludes in snatched phrases ("Ching A Ring Chaw" and "Pompey Smash," in stanza 5, are both early minstrel songs that themselves blend lines from a storehouse of minstrel-song couplets). That these references cohabit with the phrase "ride upon a rail" shows that the singer is aware of the broad connection between shivarees (charivari, Skimmington rides, rough music) and the social function of blackface performance as vernacular struggle. Much of the fullness of the song, as in other blackface actions behind it, develops from holding together this conflicted gene pool. A cynicism and a humor cut every which way unpredictably in this song, including at the end against itself—though it has more "reason" than it admits. And the doubleness of the spoken end is also a tough nut—"de greatness ob de subject" is undoubtable even within the self-mocking terms of the song, even without the Civil War, Reconstruction, the civil rights movements, and subsequent liberal empathy to validate it. The singer knows the seriousness but reasonably suspects that little people will always be paraded about even while they are barred from the very institutions that represent them. In actions like this song, the spirit of Catherine Market escaped the containers in which New York's elites, of all sorts, were trying to catch it.

"De New York Nigger" is a small skit which samples dance and vocal gestures from earlier performers. It replays the integrated fascination of the neighborhood as a distinct consciousness. It shows itself separate from and harassed by more powerful ideologies. It finds wiles within this unbalanced power to mount nightly sallies. We can think of "De New York Nigger" as dancing out the codes of Catherine Slip as the Chatham incorporated them. When it could, the Chatham gave hospitable space to the spirit of the dancers for eels; it was, after all, the closest of the theatres (whose productions have come down to us) to Catherine Market.

The struggles waged over the Chatham's stage instruct us about the importance of vernacular gesture and its persistence. The Chatham enclosed the rudimentary performance space that truck farmers, slaves, free blacks, butchers, sailors, carvers, navvies, and other roustabouts of every color, all exploring their conditional stages of freedom, and its lack, parceled out at Catherine Slip. But the Chatham housed a good bit more. Because it was giving venue to these gestures, it too became a contested space. As soon as it became a recognizable determinant of the popular mind, this dancing, this popular lore, became something to promote and to stifle. When these forms of popularity stepped on stage, and drew audiences, a wrangling consortium of politicians, editors, reformers, and religious tractarians began their oppositional moves. They were not subtle. They were direct.

An inventory was done of the goods at the Chatham when the Tappans leased it. Two of the musical items listed among the properties to be transferred were "Incle & Yarico Score & Parts" valued at $3.50 and "Padlock bound score" valued at $2.50. In July 1833 these and the rest of the music in the theatre were summarily taken to Franklin Square to be sold off "to the best advantage."[55] These staples of the Atlantic community's budding opposition to race slavery, sentimental division, were just more detritus to the earnest Tappans. But throw them away? No, sir. Sell them. Turn scores and lyrics to tracts. Opened in 1824, conventional theatre until May 1832, evangelical chapel for more than seven years, pressure cooker for the early classic minstrel shows in February 1843, Chanfrau's stage to present eel dances for the widening proletariat public from the spring of 1848, and the first Manhattan home to *Uncle Tom's Cabin* in 1852: the Chatham was a thorough example of the push come to shove between the many forces of propriety and the various arms of the western Atlantic's first proletarian youth culture.

Now the Chatham is gone. Knickerbocker Village squats at the site of Catherine Market. The whole city has grabbed the butchers' and the Codfish strategies of taking and occupying the territory. The East River with its Slip at the end of Catherine Street hardly seems a membrane of Atlantic culture any longer.

But the eels, those cultural eels for which we have danced: they lasted longer. They were coded in turning gestures. The eels have it.

2

The Blackface Lore Cycle

Fugitive Culture

Given that North American blackface musical performance goes back at least to 1815, probably in Albany first, why is the minstrel show said to begin in 1843 in New York City? Given that the minstrel show has seeped well beyond its masked variants into vaudeville, thence into sitcoms; into jazz and rhythm 'n' blues quartets, thence into rock 'n' roll and hip hop dance; into the musical and the novel, thence into radio and film; into the Grand Old Opry, thence into every roadhouse and the cab of every longhaul truck beyond the Appalachians—why, then, is the minstrel show said to be over? Cultural beginnings and endings constitute a series of problems I will deal with throughout this book. This chapter shows what happens to these matters in their middle, after they have begun and before they seem to have disappeared.[1]

I approach the problem by observing two points. One, blackface minstrelsy, as a characteristic lore cycle, is separated and set spinning within specific low groups. Two, tracing the texts of a lore cycle can help us approach again the consciousness of its precipitating publics—and distinguish who these publics were.

Already a harlequin mask in the late eighteenth century, bald pate
and brows disguising the individual beneath, the visage of labour
by the 1840s could be somehow rendered grotesque and faceless;
a mass unrecognizable to capital as human thus became subject to
the most extreme form of discipline.

—Peter Way, *Common Labour*

In one of its simplest forms, the argument about the beginning of the
minstrel show revolves around whether its initial instance was in late January or early February 1843 at the Chatham Theatre when Dan Emmett's
Virginia Minstrels first performed. Emmett remembered the preliminary for
this coming together in a letter: "I was residing at No. 37 Catherine Street,
and one day, while playing upon my violin, and accompanied by Billy
Whitlock on the banjo, the door opened and Frank Brower entered." Eu-
reka, Frank Brower walked fully formed through a door to play the funny
bones on stage. When the door opened again, and Dick Pelham brought
them his tambourine and dancing, the Virginia Minstrels would be complete. A few more days of practice and they would go to the Chatham
Theatre for the first formulaic minstrel show—a benefit for Pelham, a boon
for the depressed New York theatre, a defining wedge for the construction
of whiteness, and an albatross around the neck of black culture that has
yet to be lifted. That's the way the story still goes.[2]

But there are many reasons *not* to consider this the beginning either of
minstrelsy in general or the formulaic minstrel show in particular. Why
should the Virginia Minstrels be said to have started things when Micah
Hawkins, George Washington Dixon, T. D. Rice, and many performers imitating them had been delineating "Ethiopians" in the western Atlantic for
more than a quarter-century? Perhaps, you might say, because these fore-
bears did not call themselves minstrels, and the bands in the early 1840s
did. Naming is hardly beginning, however. It merely emphasizes one dimension of the whole.

A better reason is that there was a difference between creating an entr'acte
character, inserting a blackface performer into a melodrama, or even writing a farce as a vehicle for his specialties, as Dixon did in the 1820s and
Rice did more elaborately in the 1830s, and aiming to organize a whole
evening's entertainment around songs, dances, and patter purporting to be
the behavior of southern plantation field hands. That is what the minstrel

troupes tried to do in the 1840s. Dixon and Rice were still operating within the framework of the compromise conventions worked out in the English "illegitimate" theatres. Those warped conventions had translated largely intact across the Atlantic to the popular theatres of Chatham Square and the Bowery, Louisville and Cincinnati, Pensacola and Mobile. In the west Atlantic their forms were enforced by neither the same class system nor its entrenched privileges, so were ripe for modification if not supplanting.

It is a commonplace that the depression of the late 1830s crippled the American stage, opening up possibilities—by the early 1840s—for ever more vulgar acts. But this partially plausible argument does not account for either the lag between the depression in 1837 and its effect in 1843 or the fact that the vulgar acts were targeting precisely those people with the least capacity to pay for their seats. The depression argument ought to explain why poor people, who could not afford theatrical luxuries, were filtered out of the audience. It ought to account for a performance tradition refined toward literate standards. But that is not what happened as the 1830s became the 1840s. Instead, while literate drama held its own, the most surprising growth occurred in the poor audience—who were spending their money to discover their identity on the stage. Blackface was the first Atlantic mass culture.

Too, its performance was shifting from scripted toward improvised theatre. The former mayor and lifelong diarist Philip Hone confirms these trends when he notes that while the Park Theatre did well during this period, the Bowery drew full houses "with Jim Crow, who is made to repeat nightly almost *ad infinitum* his balderdash song." Moreover, in the 1840s American performers trained in the circus rather than in English theatrical conventions successfully shouldered their rougher performance tradition into the established patterns of tragedy, entr'acte, and farce. Adding to the paradox, in the western Atlantic this possibility for circus acts in theatrical spaces had London precedents. The same tendency had been under way in England before it appeared in the Americas. Thus even the form taken by the 1840s minstrel show was in part a variant of imperial practice.[3]

The depression was important, therefore, not for its affordable theatre tickets but because it so drastically increased the critical mass of people aware of their community and their lack of cultural franchise. The depression focused the formation of a new working class that would seek images of itself chiefly on the stage. On both sides of the Atlantic theatrical producers underwrote novelty that would quench the apparently fickle—but perhaps simply unknown, perhaps gargantuan—appetites of the new populations in the rapidly industrializing Atlantic economies. That's why, in London, at the Royal Surrey Theatre in the summer and fall of 1836, T. D. Rice's Jim Crow alternated in the bills with "The Real Bedouin Arabs," a North African acrobatic troupe imported via Paris, who had a run of some ninety nights.[4]

Why has blackface performance lasted? Why has minstrelsy produced a lore cycle with legs that have run and run, while tumbling Bedouin Arabs no longer have currency in Atlantic culture? Because the Arab tumblers were imported as novelty, while blackface was built up in the Atlantic markets and other working places where men and women rubbed against each other under the stresses that produce cultural form. This blackface form was a long time coming. It grew out of the way actors copied and adapted the dances of New York markets and plantation frolics. It grew out of the way they proved those gestures in theatres across all regions of the United States and, across the Atlantic, from London to Dublin. It grew out of the way the blackface figure always resisted, or did not easily fit into, other peoples' forms—and so gradually forced a form that gave it room of its own. The Real Bedouin Arabs did not produce that interest in the nineteenth century.

Yankee Peddler, Kentucky Rifleman, and Jim Crow—Constance Rourke's comic trio—had all been pushed into European drawing-room dramas. And each of these produced a flurry of further formal activity—the Sol Smith plays, the Davy Crockett almanacs. But it was only Jim Crow who disturbed the culture enough, and was sufficiently seized as a broad champion of metropolitan working spirits, to create a genre of his own. Looking back on the 1840s, one sees an apparently independent *form* taking shape on the western Atlantic stage as early postcolonial consciousness. Despite its international parallels in circus trends, its apparent independence is the reason cultural historians keep trying to validate the Virginia Minstrels' claim of beginning their pastiche. But the Virginia Minstrels were not the only and not even the first assemblers of this bricolage. The troupe of Emmett, Brower, Pelham, and Whitlock were not even the first to take the name "Virginia Minstrels."

Just as T. D. Rice did not first dance Jim Crow in New York City but in a score of provincial theatres from Pensacola to Pittsburgh, so the first minstrel show was not in New York City but in provincial Buffalo. That's where E. P. Christy formed his band and gave his first concert in June 1842—six months before the Emmett group in New York City. As reported in its earliest clippings, Christy's band was originally three performers: E. P.

Christy, George Harrington (who later changed his name to Christy and became a favorite endman, bones player, and female impersonator); and T. Vaughn. They called themselves, then, the Virginia Minstrels.[5]

The size of the minstrel band, supposedly fixed by either of the troupes calling themselves the Virginia Minstrels, was always a sliding affair, in fact. For all the years since Rice's grand successes, accompanists and companions had augmented the dances of the single blackface performers, as in Figure 2.1. Theatre bills from the Franklin, Chatham, and Bowery theatres all show there was nothing fixed about two, three, four, five, or more performers.[6]

Therefore, the minstrel show that appeared in the 1840s was not a New York City form, as such. Nor was it fixed at four performers. It did not have specific instrumentation. It did not have a fixed format. It did not yet have an interlocutor. It did not yet have the endman convention. All that was in continual flux. Certainly a commercial minstrel show with distinctive postcolonial features did appear in the 1840s. But we have to find features other than number, format, or fixed roles to define the form.

> Freely depicted in his own vocation . . . the Canaller would make a fine dramatic hero, so abundantly and picturesquely wicked is he . . . A terror to the smiling innocence of the villages through which he floats; his swart visage and bold swagger are not unshunned in cities . . . Nor does it at all diminish the curiousness of this matter, that to many thousands of our rural boys and young men born along its line, the probationary life of the Grand Canal furnishes the sole transition between quietly reaping in a Christian corn-field, and recklessly ploughing the waters of the most barbaric seas.
>
> —Herman Melville, *Moby-Dick*

A big part of the problem in the history of minstrelsy is the triple prejudice in favor of New York City. The meager records have often been kept there, are about there, and have been analyzed by writers there. Buffalo as a goad to minstrelsy? The idea is outrageous to anyone believing in either a plantation or a metropolitan concept of blackface origins. Being neither a plantation nor (in the early nineteenth century) a large metropolis, Buffalo is well worth a pause as we consider this sliding beginning of the blackface lore cycle.

How and why did the gestural elements of minstrelsy travel from plantations and such postcolonial markets as that at Catherine Slip, to be reas-

2.1 Eliphalet Brown's lithograph of Whitlock playing the banjo and John Diamond dancing at the Bowery Theatre

sembled with panache in remote heartland places like Buffalo? How is it that the early minstrel show could seem to emerge at the same time in two places well over five hundred miles apart, connected by water that could be traversed no faster than five miles an hour?[7] In one word: canals. In two: canal laborers.

Canallers and the conditions of their work underpin both Buffalo, as a city, and minstrelsy, the first popular culture along the Lakes. During the 1820s, when the Erie's construction was climaxing, population grew more rapidly in the canal region than anywhere else in the country: "Albany gained 96 per cent, Utica 183, Syracuse 282, Buffalo 314, and Rochester 512."[8] After they dug Clinton's ditch, canallers became sailors, plying the waterways and the Lakes.

The early canals in North America, including the Erie (1817–1825), were dug largely by unfree labor. Slaves built southern canals. Slaves working alongside indentured laborers bought from European boats docking in Philadelphia, Baltimore, and other eastern ports, shoveled canals in the mid-Atlantic and northern states. In the early days of canal work, free workers also contracted to work alongside the slaves and the indentured workers. But that changed during the years of the Erie's construction. "Increasingly, the work became stigmatized as the roughest of rough labor," writes Peter Way, who has looked at canal work from the point of view of the workers themselves. Their work was

> performed by the lowest of the low, Irish immigrants and slaves. These two pariah groups, pushed into the worst kinds of work as the most disadvantaged of labourers, pulled canal construction further down in the estimation of potential workers from the late 1820s. Republican freemen soon lost their appetite for canalling, making it one of the first truly lumpen proletarian professions in North America. In sum, the various "Corktowns" and "Slabtowns" were hardly Lowells, Lynns, or even St. Clairs. They were environments that left little scope for self-determination.[9]

There is a fissure in the history of work in the Atlantic community that corresponds with the completion of the Erie Canal in 1825. After this break, the world of work had a distinct schism between navvy and republican, apprentice and artisan, slave and freeman that had been less marked in earlier dispensations. Until this schism it is possible to generalize a mutuality in common labor. The schism can be overemphasized—I think *has* been overemphasized. But there is much less danger of pushing the mutuality too hard, because its story has hardly been broached.

The mutuality of miscellaneous labor is a virtually untold story in the cultural history of the Atlantic world. What I call *mudsill mutuality* is the shared experience of sweating at hard material work, digging and cleaning, cutting and cropping, sailing and herding, while all along being stepped on and despised for the work others disdain. Mudsill mutuality existed alongside, and in vivid tension with, the gradually increasing internal opposition along ethnic lines. Although an internal schism becomes quite pronounced in the Atlantic world around 1825, this break does not mean that the shared experience of despised labor disappeared. On the contrary, its consciousness increased proportionately with its increased embattlement. Ethnic divisions and mudsill mutuality are not necessarily in a hydraulic relationship, one rising as the other falls. They can increase or decrease together. I believe they hyped each other.[10]

I do not deny the racism that also increased along with the schism. The racism is a fact. It had real costs for the life of laborers, and particularly that of black people. It became an intra-class distinction of tragic proportions.

Even as we learn to reconstruct and admit this working class racism, however, we need to remember that there were virile instances of it more than a century before the earliest blackface performance. During worker and slave revolts in 1712 and 1741 in New York, public authorities appealed to "white" unity to try to divide workers, and workers themselves used "white" in a very different cant sense to refer to "privileged" or "rich" people.[11] Details like these remind us that no class is one-dimensional, that not everyone was pushed into or chose the same route, that change was gradual, fitful, and lapsing rather than immediate, monolithic, and steady. Multiple fissures remain in the course of labor consciousness. Not only inter- and intra-class arguments exist, and not only black-white animosities, but also white on white and black on black, generation on generation, gender on gender (just to point at the gross cracks). In this reassessment the difficulty is to hear and score all the tones. Many of those tones are blue notes, sliding uncertainly between their fixed notations.

The dominant historiography describes the poignant decline of artisanal labor, and its struggle to organize into trade unions. But what of the mass of workers who had no trade and no license, the journeymen and their sisters, the diggers and haulers, cleaners and cooks, navvies and slaves, pressed sailors and convicted soldiery, the *hogler* (or lowest field laborer) of England who became the *hoggee* digging the canal? What about Melville's "piebald parliament," that unacknowledged but surely ultimate legislature of history? What about that *lumpen* stir from which all culture springs?[12]

The *lumpen* stir is the mass which even Karl Marx disdained, feared, and memorably defined in 1851, the same year Melville centered it as castaway culture, calling it the "Anacharsis Clootz deputation" in *Moby-Dick*.[13] Rightly conceived, blackface performance gives us more clues to this suppressed but ultimately powerful force than we have yet traced. The blackface lore cycle is what held together in useful tension the conflicted voices of this class.

The rule of thumb is that rough laborers did not then and do not now organize. They left few records of their own in the eighteenth and nineteenth centuries and they do not leave many more now. For they have never been warranted by a "moral economy" providing them a safety net of traditional protocols.[14] The comments made about them by journalists and diarists are dangerous to take at face value. What cultural creations they have been historically allowed to claim have been either oral or so cheaply produced that they long ago sifted to smudge. There is a long looping logic of disdain that makes rough labor seem to have no discrete consciousness. If rough labor is not rooted as artisanal toil is, according to this logic, if mudsill work does not manifest inherited organizational forms and customs, then it has not had cultural existence. But what if its tracings are more fugitive than sturdy? What if these light-fingered, light-footed tracings have more ultimate staying power than those middle-class phenomena thought to be "permanent" because they stand erect to be counted? What if, as Ralph Ellison's narrator noticed in *Invisible Man*, your castaway population is characteristically found "running and dodging the forces of history instead of making a dominating stand"?[15]

What if the lumpen alliance of rough labor has found ways to propagate itself as a parasite precisely on those acts and cultural marks that oppose it? To understand the dispersal and survival of a rough culture that leaves no monuments to itself that can be attacked or buried, it helps to think of it as burrs attaching themselves to the passing pants of the very planter who would stamp them out. Vernacular culture circulates and survives like weed seeds. It obeys no boundaries, personal or state. It sifts its way across the abstract fictions of borders as readily as it stays put. Going and staying are the same to the burrs of rough culture. They combine with whatever keeps them going. That's the way vernacular history really moves.

Despite these biological images, there is of course real difference between cultural and biological ecology. One important difference is this: extinguished species are rare in the ecology of culture. Vernacular culture adapts rather than disappears. It hangs on the very acts that seem to erase or efface it. Because of these mutations blackface performance has been able to survive past its apparent initial containment. Thus despite the few records mudsill labor has left behind, tracing its genealogy back through the adaptations of minstrelsy is one way to return mutuality—along with schism—to our history of the formation of the working class in the western Atlantic.

The movement of men and capital, and the stories of their engagement up the Hudson River, then massively west from Rome toward Buffalo, and from Rome east toward Albany, between 1817 and 1825; the digging of 363 miles of canal by pick and barrow; the hardening of attitudes toward the hierarchy of work and those who would do it; the industrializing of the old rural tasks of moving soil and water—all this was ripening in the lyrics and gestures and especially the mask of minstrelsy a few years later.

Peter Way notes that foremen commonly shaved marks on those diggers who fled their labor. Shaved eyebrows and bald strips and crosses on the skull: these traditional harlequin signs were becoming by the 1840s "the visage of labour." Repeat offenders had iron collars forged around their necks.[16] These details suggest a mutuality among disdained workers extending from the stooping work they did, digging and picking, to the way they were marked. Employers marking men they owned or rented across race is important.

The self-marking of blackface minstrelsy—a mark we are still learning to *see*, rather than look through—had one of its beginnings in transfiguration of these historical marks. Minstrels on the move as performers mark their solidarity with journeymen by accepting the marks born by the journeymen in the minstrel audience as the theme of their own acting. Employers marked the visage of labor; minstrels made a sign of that visage. And it is not just the face of labor or the face of Jim Crow that they thereby made meaningful. The whole stooped posture of the hoggee, permanently bent by the shovel and barrow, and still evident in day laborers to this day, is caught in Jim Crow's gimp. Jim Crow embodies common labor, face to foot.

Finally, when I say that canalling experience shows up in the lyrics and mask of minstrelsy, I mean that the songs of this formal minstrel period of the 1840s and 1850s are everywhere about the distance from *home,* emphasized in its characteristic rhyme with "roam." The lyrics are about the daily scramble that gave journeymen their name. It was no accident when the Christy Minstrels sang, "Old Massa gave us money / And sent us on our journey."[17] George Christy (né Harrington), who performed this song, was a multiply masked man from Buffalo, who had changed his name, performed blacked-up and cross-dressed, and here negotiated the in-between problem of licensed-but-enforced roaming. Slaves and other workers forced to middle passages without their families for war, for sugar, or for canalling were characteristically caught in this quandary. What too often has seemed like sentimental rhyming is also a way of declaring within the surveillance of the minstrel theatre the terrible exhaustion, loneliness, and privation forced onto the lowest workers of the Atlantic.

It makes a gnarled sense that the cultural song and dance representing back-stooping labor of shoveling and carting dirt, of building locks and being uprooted from family and home for long periods of time, should appear at the same moment on Lake Erie and along the Atlantic coast. What looks like polygenesis, simultaneous generation of the same form in more than one place, is really the appearance of that form at about the same time at both ends of the waterway whose making matured the symbolism of the labor.

The activity that became known as minstrelsy was largely the cultural symbolism of this mutual labor. The fate of this symbolism is a lore cycle. The fate is not fixed. The cultural symbolism of blackface performance, like other contentious cycles of lore, is sometimes disdained, other times fetishized, sometimes buried, other times enhanced and elaborated. Along the way it has absorbed its warped interpretations, folding them also into its effects.

> INGREDIENTS: Dried Potato, Vegetable Oil, Potato Starch, Salt & Vinegar Flavour (acidity regulators E262, 262; Flavour Enhancer—621, Malic Acid, Citric Acid), Salt, Emulsifier (E471), Colour (E160c). Best Before 27 May 95.
>
> —Rippled Potato Snack packet, dustbin, British Museum, 1995

The forecourt of the British Museum, lunchtime. I am among schoolchildren. They are spilling, tossing, swapping crisps, that most processed of contemporary foods. The British crisp, eaten in the United States as a potato chip, is one far-gone fate for the western Atlantic potato. The crisp has several functions in these circles as an individual and group indulgence with a short shelf life, indoor frisbee, token of trade, and trash feed for sparrows and pigeons. These many unintended effects constitute a parable for other slicings and deep fryings on equally casual display here in the broad border area between the street and terminal curation.

Italian, German, French, Hindi, and Dutch vowels are caroming among more local consonants from the Old Kent Road south of the Thames to Kentish Town on its north. I have spent the morning deciphering Jim Crow plays in the manuscript room. Now, drinking tea and unwinding with a sandwich, I am wondering, Why are these plays locked up here on Great Russell Street in London? Why not in Pensacola or Pittsburgh or New York, to which places one might plausibly trace their definitive coming together and their apparent erasure from history?

The Jim Crow scripts are curated here in this place, and in no other, because of accidents of disdain in the west Atlantic and, in the east Atlantic, accidents of arrest. In North America most associations with Jim Crow were long ago suppressed. (But not of course expunged. The gross effects of Jim Crow cartooning linger in a sub rosa half-life. Some private collectors perversely prize its grossest emblems as camp artifacts: the ceramic Jemimas whose grins functioned as ashtrays, the stamped-tin Uncle Bens that advertised rice on roadside fence rails.) Across the Atlantic in London, the Lord Chamberlain's censorship, imperial collections, and a Victorian confidence that all details may someday fit the grand jigsaw—these have united to keep manuscripts of Jim Crow plays from the 1830s locked up with mummies, Parthenon friezes, and a few lyrics scrawled in John Lennon's hand to McCartney's "Yesterday."

Such are the thoughts possessing me while I avoid these kinetic children, their shirttails akimbo, flushing one-legged pigeons in my direction. Frowning Chinese couples photograph each other before the steps rising toward the polished brass in the Museum pediment. American students come and go by twos and threes, with their hightop sneakers and flat vowels, buying postcards. Scholars hurry, guards search for bombs in bags, vendors hawk faux scarabs in "Egyptian" blue wash spread on tarps at their feet.

In all this crowd a group of young Japanese arrests my eye. These tourists are more assured and urbane than others. They clearly have the means and liberty to elaborate themselves as they will. Men and women alike are dressed casually in jeans and pastel running shoes. Some wear baseball caps backward betokening favored mascots from far edges of North America: Blue Devils, Seminoles, Huskies. These Japanese tourists have carefully assembled their signs of who they would be. But their caps and jeans are not what hold my eye. The meaning of their hair is what produces my double-take. Even such a rooted entity as hair has been routed.

These flourishing young Japanese have tightly curled and matted their formerly shiny straight hair into varying forms of the dreadlock. Ragamuffin question marks tumble topsy-turvy on some. Cornrows plait symmetrical patterns over others. Beaded dreadlocks, tied in African scarves, drape yet others to their shoulders. These Pacific young men and women have closely studied the variety of black Atlantic styles.[18]

In the early summer of the mid-1990s they are lifting those styles from across the world, as they have increasingly listened to Charlie Parker, Little Richard, and Prince. Their liftings are not brazen or aggressive, but routine. Their seamless absorption of the Atlantic strange into the Pacific conventional, but with the simultaneous persistence of blackness—that's what focuses my double-take. I register this global circulation and continuity, and it all seems appropriate. I am wondering, Why haven't these visitors tied their hair in tea-lead or eel skin? Such details, I realize, are obscured by the paradox of curation: what's kept inside is kept from circulating outside. But had these eastern visitors penetrated the inner chambers of the West's archives, had merchants with the right labels marketed eel skins with sufficient cachet, surely these youths would have blazoned them gracefully and proudly.

Returning inside to the manuscript room, to *Bone Squash Diavolo, Jim Crow in His New Place,* and *The Peacock and the Crow,* I am reinforced in my conviction that these plays traced a moving force older and newer than the scripts I am reading. Like those Japanese dreadlocks outside, Jim Crow plays are waystations for lore circulating ever wider. What I noticed in the forecourt of the British Museum was the extension of routes: the black Atlantic gone global.

There are important sights on both sides of the walls of the British Museum. Sights like the Jim Crow manuscripts, on the inside where "infinity goes up on trial," as Bob Dylan sang, are set in the amber of public warranty. On the outside, the sights still "flow like de seeds ob de squash," as Dan Emmett used to preach in his stump sermons.[19] Constantly rechosen, they are continually reanimated. If we were talking about folktales, we would call this reanimation "tale maintenance." But I seek terms for a process that, although it parallels folktales, is more furtive and difficult to trace. My topic is the choosing and the enlivening of gestures and style signatures. So I call it lore maintenance. These choices constitute the fundamental practice of identity. In this practice, identity finds its proof and reproof.

The door opens and Bobolink Bob comes among us . . . alive as you or me . . . but this time he speaks Japanese and he rides a tour bus. These are late turns in the minstrel lore cycle.

What Is a Lore Cycle?

Lore composes the basic gestures of all expressive behavior, from moans to narratives, signs to paintings, steps to dances. Part of this lore acquires a special status. Certain of these gestures separate from the others. These particular motions of the hands or mouth represent a group to itself and to outsiders, and they are recognized for their representation. Groups do not acknowledge all their gestures in this same way. Rather, they choose to emphasize some gestures as abiding tokens of their membership. These key gestures the group promotes, centers on the stage (and other media), and makes talismanic. These are fetishized gestures. They are continually embedded in further activity. That's how the stance of the dancers for eels became Rice's "Jump Jim Crow" and later became part of the basic architecture of hip hop. This grit, gradually surrounded by more nacreous material, hardened through blackface performance into the minstrel show.

This transfer of dance steps from blacks dancing in the market to whites and blacks dancing on the stage illustrates a further point about talismanic gestures. They are a group's informal cultural capital that can travel. They are those elements of a group's emphasis about itself which are not so much surplus as they are groomed to be separable from the group.

Some examples would include, one, the motifs of the Tar Baby (the farther he rambles the more he talks about his briar patch); two, the way the dancers at Catherine Market raised hands over head and wheeled about to encode their complex conflicts about liberty and work; three, the apart-playing among the cornhusking performers. In each of these cases the lore encodes a particular place and time. However, when lore has wider meaning, appealing beyond the initiating group and the conditions it has registered, as do all these examples, lore also circulates. It becomes available to others. Like special export beer, bottled for distant consumption, or like postcard scenes of the beach, talismanic lore is separated from its local scene and sent forth for others. Only the very naive would mistake the export for the locally tapped brew, or find the postcard an acceptable surrogate for the surf. But when one is thirsty, or needs a reminder of sun and sand, the tokens have their satisfactions. These tokens form a currency. They are transferred, when others choose them, to betoken aspects of other peoples, other locales in their times and places.

Why say *lore* rather than "folklore"? Because groups that are not embedded in traditional, oral cultures also use it. "Folklore" has historical associations with peasants and provinciality. Drop this associative baggage, and the concept of *lore* becomes a tool to recover emotional histories of groups who have left few conventional records. We are ignorant of the fugitive culture of common laborers mostly because it is difficult to find its records, but partly because it has fallen between the valued stools. Important groups who are not "folk," who have been excluded from the folk concept, also use lore. There is a reason why the study of folklore began in the same years during which the classic minstrel show formalized.[20]

This arrival of this first Atlantic mass culture, and the anxiety it roused in polite circles, clarified—scared up—the important affinity between folk and high cultures. The surprise of mass culture made high culture revalue its connection to passive, nonthreatening folk ways. Modern theory developed ideas that began to conceive the "folk" anew and to show that elite and folk cultures both have deeply rooted and highly elaborated forms of community. But there are important bodies of cultural material that neither exhibit these roots nor produce elaborate patterns in cultural monuments. Whole groups of people are left out of expressive history if we do not learn to interpret the lore cycles that are in these gaps between the traditional peasantry and franchised modernity.

What Does a Lore Cycle Do?

Lore does in culture what stereotypes do in discourse. Both lore and stereotypes hold current beliefs together in highly charged shorthand. Lore expresses a group's beliefs so that the group does not need to weigh and consider all its ramifications at any given moment. Especially is this true of talismanic lore. It keeps a running tab on all the prior consideration and negotiation that has brought a group's beliefs to their current balance.

Since actions follow from belief, lore thus eases a group's actions, licensing and modulating them. Lore serves, also, to bond the group together. There is an important circularity in this: individual actions, as they are in concert, form the group; the group silently formulates a member's actions and style. One is a member of a group if one successfully participates in its lore; using the lore increases its self-authenticating "truth"; and the limits of the group are indicated by how completely its members relate to the lore. This reciprocity is what makes group lore function so effectively. But this circularity can also make the efficiency of lore seem inescapable at any given moment. The reciprocity of talismanic lore can look like a forever-closed circle, just as stereotypes act like self-fulfilling prophecies. I will shortly show Herman Melville analyzing these apparently closed circles in his novella "Benito Cereno."

But understand this: lore's circularity is only apparently closed. In fact the circle of lore works like a valve to regulate the entry and exit of content. Because one group's lore overlaps and catches on another's, the turnings of lore are not smooth. Its ends do not meet exactly, and it spirals, ovate and lopsided in time. Because its axis wobbles when it turns, lore never returns to the same place. Every group's members must adjust their lore cycle constantly. They prop it up. They adjust for its slippage. What they sustain is alive in its stresses and constantly moving, always becoming something else.

Lore moves in a cycle, therefore, not a circle. Lore moves and returns. Patterns of lore rise and fall. They sustain complex meaning over time, but they do not enforce the past exactly. Rather the turns of a lore cycle convert the dead hands of the past into living presences that deviate from what went before. There are surprises in living lore.

Be it a nuclear family, a neighborhood association, butchers in a market, fugitive workers learning to recognize their distinctiveness, or some transnational alliance seeing itself as a class—in every group, some members query their group's lore.[21] They may share belief in competing lores. They may understand themselves as being between groups, between lores. For instance, brides and grooms are between family lores. In traditional societies, religious and state ceremonies anticipate this troubling transition while the individuals' lores are upset and merging. Carefully ordained rituals exist for just such interludes; vows and patterns of behavior are prescribed to coddle novitiates through their liminal stage. After a while the bride and groom withdraw their reliance on these artificial, intermediary formulas. They build up their own, new, family lores. They stop thinking of themselves as novitiates partly because they accumulate their own stock of identifying stories. They are among themselves.

Right across its membership, therefore, a group's lore is always adapting, changing. This has surely always been the case, even in peasant societies, although there the rate of change is remarkable for its imperceptibility. But the Atlantic world was created out of turbulence in populations, in manufacturing and agricultural organization, and in urban layout. No one experienced more unsettled life than the mudsill workers of the Atlantic. We discover their consciousness in the traces they left in blackface minstrelsy. Except in the 1840s and 1850s, when white males dominated the minstrel show, blackface was cross-gender.[22] It was transnational, trans-"race," significantly cross-class, and it was certainly turbulent.

The requirements of merchant and then industrial capital formations spread fugitive and rogue populations—as workers and slaves, as runaways, as drafted soldiers, as pressed and willing sailors—all across the coastal areas of the Atlantic. New markets in the sense Adam Smith meant, as well as the old face-to-face sorts of market, new theatre stages and newspapers and broadsheets and songsters, new lithography and forms of advertising—all these made the mediating functions of lore relevant and visible. During the half-century that began about 1825, a promiscuous culture was required to explain to a radically mixed working population who they were and how they might sustain themselves.

They fashioned a popular culture that worked. It is this promiscuous capacity of lore to meld the spicy aspects of apparently distinct cultural strands that brings together baseball caps, ragga dreadlocks, and Japanese young professionals just as its commercial counterpart joins reconstituted potatoes from the Chilean coast with the vinegar and salt of Scarborough Fair.

This continual recombining of disparate motifs makes lore cycles important within the instigating group. The reasons for their importance underwrite one another. First, lore cycles enable and regulate collective agency. As their practitioners make the many small choices that affirm certain clusters of gestures, dances evolve that are distinctive. Other gestures gather into narrative (taking form variously in skits and songs, jokes and toasts). Other gestures combine into graphics, as the examples of dancing for eels at Catherine Market have shown. Other gestures gather into distinctive costumings, which minstrelsy gleefully caricatured in its extreme collars, long-tailed blue coats, and endmen's rags. Thus, this first function is determinative. It culls and enforces a style.

A second function of this combinatory practice is adaptive. The group's daily small choices fit it by degrees to the changing pressures and challenges in the environment. The carters, riggers, and printer's devils who paid 6¼ cents to see white men in black masks act out the charisma of blackness at the Chatham, the bricklayers and sweeps in London who jammed the sixpenny gallery at the Surrey to see T. D. Rice jump Jim Crow, were adapting the proletariat's sense of itself to their depressed conditions. They were choosing to see themselves in terms of blackness and to align themselves with ciphers of rootlessness and transgression. They were adjusting the sense of life that had been bequeathed to them. They were bending it toward blackness. They were weaving African elements, not worrying about their diluted authenticity, into the life rope of a new expressive culture. They were forming an alliance that gradually accreted great power in Atlantic life. They were nominating their piebald parliament.

This power encourages me to see equivalences between the lore cycle and the *habitus* Pierre Bourdieu has articulated in his study of peasant societies. Indeed, with important exceptions, his habitus works much like a lore cycle. Although Bourdieu allows minimally for glacial change, he wants most to explain social behavior that is famously stable and continuous across eras. The habitus accounts for North African peasant cultures that have persisted through the punctuations of Atlantic change. Bourdieu's peasants have not so much bridged these eras, however, as they have quite aggressively, even violently spurned the modernization that fiscal and technological structures have gouged into Atlantic experience. Lore cycles differ from Bourdieu's habitus in mediating both continuity *and* adaptation.[23]

Atlantic diasporas and the creation of the Atlantic world set workers flowing. This traveling proletariat is quite different from any stay-at-home peasantry, and these distinctions illustrate what sets a lore cycle off from the habitus. Herman Melville saw the distinction as it was first forming. Melville's meditation in *Moby-Dick* on Atlantic lore and its emergence contrasts the western workforce of "meanest mariners, and renegades and castaways" to the "outlandish strangers" Ahab secreted on board to power his boat. Melville distinguishes the mariners and castaways by the way they adapt not only to hardship but also to the monomaniacal abasements of their captain. His narrator, Ishmael, contrasts this western workforce with Ahab's secreted "five dusky phantoms" brought on board from "the unchanging Asiatic communities, especially the Oriental isles to the east of the continent—those insulated, immemorial, unalterable countries, which even in these modern days still preserve much of the ghostly aboriginalness of earth's primal generations, when the memory of the first man was a distinct recollection."[24] On both sides of this division Melville doubtless exaggerates. His distinctions display, nevertheless, the conscious excitement at change already full-blown and enlisted as an Atlantic feature in the instant that the blackface lore cycle rounds its first bend into formulaic minstrelsy near the middle of the nineteenth century.

Lore cycles, therefore, describe features of those groups which begin to appear with merchant capital, come to self-awareness within industrial capital, and continue into the industrial aftermath. Melville's early term—"castaways"—has proved exact. The logic of development that has presented us with Brixton and the Bronx is now confirming that rogue and castaway peoples have all along been funneled like so many waste products of capital and modernism: slaves and a working class treated as disposable.

These groups, which most concern me as they increasingly did Melville, and which lore cycles most help us track and understand, are ever emergent, always fighting against their funneling. They have not often been able to stop it. But they have understood the drift of things. They have represented it with irony and humor that exasperates those who control the channeling. Castaways are always finding themselves. They are always figuring themselves out in lore cycles like that of blackface performance.

Sometimes, at propitious junctures (like the 1830s and the 1950s), castaway groups try to step onto the stage of history. (Sometimes they are *not* seduced into joining the struggle for dominance; sometimes they do not desire to compete within the main frame. Shakers are one example, and indeed the many-faceted communitarian crafts movements—those which went off by themselves rather than adapt to mass production—from the eighteenth well into the twentieth centuries would qualify.) There are then at least three reasons why the groups that most concern me here give fugitive and fleeting rather than monumental form to their expression. First, they are continually emerging. Second, they are excluded from the technologies of representation, curation, and production (all three of which purport to enable permanence). Third, they reject this technology.

Thus the cultural landmarks of fugitive groups are different from those of more privileged and curated strata of culture. Sometimes these castaways may find partly sympathetic champions like Dickens and Melville, Whitman and Pynchon. But the internal masterpieces of lumpen culture are its performative ethic and its performed experience.

Performance attributes are most frequently associated with the African diaspora. Even today, when black vernacular performers do have access to artifactual sophistication, many still prize the making and remaking of the experience over the ostensibly "finished" product. Some scratch the record itself. Some remake the song in improvised performance, emphasizing the lyric's orality rather than its written text. By dubbing and other encouragements they foster supplemental levels of meaning to be added in the audience's reception.[25] But these are not solely black hallmarks. They have spread beyond black culture to other, admiring, agreeing publics. One of the places that spreading began was in the compact of blackface imitation that became the minstrel lore cycle. Those groups holding these days to this performative emphasis are still judged with the same critical disapproval as were the early black vernacular performers. White or black, these factions are said to be subliterate, naive. These are just the sort of groups who have dropped out of and will continue to fall through the net of history unless we learn to read *their own* signs independent of the middle-class disdain that has cloaked them in external interpretation.

Lore cycles gather momentum in improvised contest. As their gestures winnow into repeated narratives, they help people understand themselves as a distinct group. Incorporating those stories, the people explore their own capacities and assign meanings or explanations to their tales. To the extent that the explanations prove useful to a larger culture, these self-clarifications combine into commanding narratives with closely watched conventions. This is what happened to blackface performance as it became increasingly popular through the 1840s and 1850s. It hardened during the countdown to the war between the states, as class became so significant in midcentury life. As one way the working class knew itself, minstrelsy became very useful, not only to its precipitating alliances of black and white common people, but also to those who would police these precipitating publics. That is, minstrelsy became a complexly contested field. As a consequence, many more publics were trying to map meaning onto it and, after about 1845, to use it, than had been involved in the early improvisations among its core publics. Rolling stones may gather no moss, but social forms gathering momentum certainly do attract policing attention.

Blackface performance became a social rite that elites wanted to harness and gradually did. What had begun as a way of registering cross-racial charisma and union then became *also* a way of registering racial separation and disdain. As a maturing cultural form, blackface places into compact tension, at once, both charisma and disdain, in a continually adjusting but never completely erasing process. The meanings pile up. Their priorities change, often drastically. As groups change power, adjusting their grip on the cultural franchise, what then changes is the way they and their contending groups map the cultural form. The way we represent terrain can emphasize some features and hide others, but the actual terrain remains largely the same. So, too, in lore cycles, one group may try with its reading of images to control the way other groups are perceived. But unless a dominant group actually annihilates subject groups, the subaltern features remain coded in the performance, even if no one recognizes them for a long time. Effacing occurs, but not erasing.

The most apparent parts of a lore cycle are now visible, and I can summarize them. Lore cycles begin in the casual gestures of ordinary life. Their parts become tokens of transfer in marketplaces and other informal theatres where stress is stirred among miscellaneous populations meeting each other. Publics come to recognize themselves by their clustering of gestures into stories and signs that can travel, both among themselves and among others who also desire their tokens. These currencies are performed, competed for, and contested. That is, all the groups that participate in a lore cycle try to turn its gestures to their own uses. Thus as black gestures are taken up by white workers at first, then attended to, or policed, by more powerful whites, the uses of the tokens will alter in the transfer. But the original uses of the tokens will also remain in the absorbed gestures. The lore cycle will now have compacted (1) the original gestures along with (2) the early desire from another group to appropriate the gestures, and will have overlaid these eager spirits with (3) the patina of disdain that inevitably stamps the mix. That is what happened to minstrelsy by the 1850s, when it had become popular among groups beyond the workers who initially energized it. In the 1850s blackface became the product of entrepreneurs eager to tame it, to bring it into alignment with political allegiances already rehearsing strategies for the coming conflict between the states.

But we must not mistake the segments of this cycle, turning from desire for black gestures to disdain for black gestures, to be either separate from each other or complete. Rather, the parts turn together and they cycle on. Disdain is not their conclusion; replacement of one with another attitude is not what happens. The desire continues even if it is now covered over with disdain. The middle-class control is only an early crest of the lore cycle. It then moves into the afterlife of control. That's when the lore circulates covertly.

Moving Ratio, Moving Target

The early lore cycle of minstrelsy is an arc of insouciant gestures rising toward containment and control. It follows the fate of a potent fascination. The developing curve shows over time the growth and lapse of that fascination, its separating out and deeming of formal meaning to gestures. To follow this curve is to observe how gestures become meaningful, how they gain increasing interpretive complexity, how they gradually slough, and how they sometimes, by turns, increasingly enforce that complexity. The developing fate, and developing power, of lore over time is a "moving ratio."

Paul Rabinow uses the term "moving ratio" to describe how self-consciousness and self-presentation increase as anthropologists doing field work rely on local informants.[26] I believe similar changes rise at home, in one's "own" culture. In home work, too, the agents of group identity acting as informants to other groups come to realize their self-interest as they shuffle knowledge tokens. The moving ratio that Rabinow found operating in the field also applies when a modern culture increasingly understands, and continually reinterprets, its own selves at odds with one another.

In thinking about lore cycles, I think about modernity understanding and using its own internal otherness. The economy of modernity requires that radically different social, ethnic, and class cohorts fit together. Short of force, modern society achieves this integration by recognizing, interpreting to itself, and acknowledging as its own many constitutive parts that non-modern states do not countenance. The tricky thing about modern society's capacity to hold together substantial differences is that it begins by declaring them "other"; then it frequently sets up cultural patterns that license crossing the barriers to join the others. Modern society builds in these contradictions that define groups both as pariahs and as charismatic attractors—attractive because pariah, and vice versa. Such entities as a "folk" are often doubly signified, shunned and commercialized.

The blackface lore cycle is surely one of the earliest sustained cycles that go through this transformation from folk to pop and commercial gesturing. In that way, it forms a plinth course of Atlantic modernity. It inaugurates the features of media-saturation that distinguish the developed and over-developed Atlantic world from traditional and peasant societies in its own and other basins. The lore cycle of blackface performance negotiates the uneasy and never clean separation of modern culture from its earlier self.

Talking about moving ratios in media-saturated societies allows two things. First, it points at the gradual shifts in understanding and agency that allow a culture to stay together, if not "whole," while its parts modulate their relationships. Second, it fingers the residue of contradictory coding that maintains dynamic irresolution at the center of a culture's self-definition. Achieving this dynamism is the main function of lore cycles.

This scab-picking irresolution of the basic issues in modern culture is less present in folk or peasant societies, which exhibit more unanimity. Lore cycles do not solve this modern irresolution. Rather, lore cycles are what keep social contests open and at odds. The trajectory of lore cycles presents the way cultures (do not) solve problems.

Performance of racial masquerade neither solves nor resolves the issues it addresses. Instead, the conventions of minstrelsy keep its troubling parts grinding against one another. But the achievement of this nor any other lore cycle is not that this slippage grinds out the grit. Rather, performance grinds out ways to live with perceived cultural difference. This grit rubs identity raw enough so that we who are abraded can feel who we are and are not, what we do and do not share, and what we might use together. The study of lore cycles looks at the mediational process of culture that allows people to fit themselves to the stimuli and irruptions of their eras.

To follow the history of a lore cycle like that of Atlantic minstrelsy is to trace the control of multicultural gestures. But control is no one-dimensional concept. Not only its policers but also, of course, its everyday performers have acted on their awareness that the control of lore is a negotiable, political entity. This shared awareness drives the struggles to authorize knowledge, to install or expand or shrink some canon, to license religions, to warrant or outlaw chiropractic or homeopathy as medicine, to privilege critical attention to one kind of performance over another.

This struggle to include one's stories within the cultural franchise and to maintain the lores that explain groups goes on at every level of power. People will protect their capacity to act out their expressive culture. If they do not manage to house it in museums, print it in anthologies, or have it taught in curricula, still they write and rewrite it in gestures and everyday practice. They inscribe it in cultural performance. This constantly remembered and performed culture of everyday practice is, after all, probably a more lasting shelter than any anthology can give its texts or any museum give its artifacts. Even when an important story is curated in museums and curricula, people still perform its continuing variations and move its ratios. Even after Joel Chandler Harris and Walt Disney and the Golden Books froze a few of the tar baby stories, the underlying motifs of those stories continued to circulate orally and separately.[27]

Groups may not tell others or even themselves they are advancing their politics when they link their gestures together ceremonially, as when white youths like Rice and Diamond imitate shingle steppers, one hand up, the other on hip. Indeed, they usually deny any political meaning to these linkings. Nevertheless, cultural performance is a way of maintaining the corpus of their gestural signals without talking about it, and whether or not critics continue to pay them or their lore attention. Both the performance and the conscious denial of its meaning is how groups maintain and protect their lore. Since all culture is a tussle both inside and outside the gesturing group, the very process of performance is inevitably political and oriented around struggles for survival, mutation, and destruction of gestural forms. I use this life-and-death vocabulary here because my experience is that many audiences grow wary at the idea of vernacular culture as a place where lines are drawn. I believe that is where they are drawn most determinantly.

Lore cycles have middling longevity. They are neither so ephemeral as period-bound contingencies nor so grand as the destinies of discourse. Lore cycles perform a mediating function. They keep culture traveling and mutating even while they monitor the positional relationships in the originally textualized scenes. Once a taboo line is fixed and challenged, the lore cycle that accrues around it may move the line back and forth, accepting or proscribing behavior; or, the allowable play along the line itself may broaden or attenuate. But its own inertia tends also to maintain the line.

Lore cycles exist to draw and redraw the line. A lore cycle gives itself power by moving the line slightly. This is cultural gerrymandering, and it is quite political. There are exact illustrations of this in minstrelsy, which has repeated motifs of *walking the line,* reinforcing the image with such vivid vernacular as "walk chalk" and "walk jawbone."

The historian's ability to trace gestural genealogies is dependent on the outcome of these gerrymandering struggles, on their chance suspensions, or on both. That's why filling in the gaps of these genealogies, finding the

spots where their lines twist and knot, and twist and shout, trying to recover the reasons and means for these knots and shouts, and generally
levering up the story of mudsill mutuality is so important.

How Does a Lore Cycle Turn?

Who ever heard of a white so far a renegade as to apostatize from
his very species almost by leaguing in against it with negroes?
—Captain Delano in Melville's "Benito Cereno"

At some points the ratios or lore cycles suddenly reverse. Their meanings
invert. The world goes upside down. The politically correct goes belly up.
Blackface goes volte-face. The minstrel antics and fright wigs that coded
blacks as risible in the second half of the nineteenth century suddenly
become the charismatic dances and hairstyles of rock 'n' roll in the 1950s.
Then they become Afro hairdos in the 1960s. They become tokens of es-
teem for Asian tourists to achieve and brandish in the 1990s. This dramatic
about-face produced and accompanied massive changes in social policy in
all corners of the Atlantic world.

Where do such large changes come from? Micro-inversions inhere in the
codes of gestural performance throughout a lore cycle. They record the
differences and perturbations, the adjustments and fittings that people have
made in their lore over time. To those who read them from the inside, the
fetish texts of a lore cycle are full of oppositions and cancellations. Like
stereotypes, which only seem stable, the timely clusters of meaning in lore
cycles are necessarily unstable. They suddenly kink like excited eels. Unlike
the habitus, lore cycles unsettle, even upset, their conventions at startling
moments.

These moments when the meanings shift are political and cultural crossroads. One instance when these reversals occurred was in the 1850s. Minstrelsy apparently coarsened then into the stereotypes for which it is infamous. A second inversion happened a century later, when white popular
culture suddenly had great sympathy for the conventions of black performance, as in the work of Lloyd Price, Chuck Berry, Little Richard, Fats
Domino, Ray Charles, Elvis Presley, and many more performers who were
still working the blackface cycle. The two turns went in opposite directions.
The early turn hardened white attitudes toward blacks and enforced gross
racist stereotypes. The second was still animated by the same images and

worked the same forms. But it released a liberatory sympathy that contributed to the Civil Rights movement. It negotiated the much bigger breakthrough into the mainstream that black culture achieved in the middle of the twentieth century than it had even in the Jazz Age of the twenties. It achieved these ends by trading the gross racial stereotypes for smaller or finer, perhaps therefore more pernicious, stereotypes. Cycles mediate these shifts. Their tangles direct and map our journeys.

The power of lore cycles comes from their compression. Stereotypes and lore cycles are packed palimpsests of meaning. They have been written over but not erased. They are like the graffiti on metropolitan passage walls: posters for rock concerts against racism, scrawled over by growing Janes declaring their lust for rising Jacks, these layers again obscured by spray-painted signatures of gangs in rapid generation. Each successive layer aims to efface the previous strata. But the hurry of their postings, the uneven erosions of time, as well as the erasures of weather and ultra-violet fading, cause the earlier strata to peep through. The old signatures, postings, and markings remain encoded on the wall, packing considerable tension into popular culture's palimpsest, reminding those who pass of their histories.

The passage wall I have in mind here leads to a concrete bridge over a railway line into a park in North London. I first started paying attention to this place as a text when I photographed its surfaces to record the punk slogans ("No Heroes!") of the mid-1970s. At that time, a neighborhood group gathered to redecorate the walls. Children painted over the punk anger with a sunny mural of flowers, rising suns, mothers pushing strollers, fathers spading vegetable allotments.

Point, counterpoint has gradually given this wall the rough texture of petit-point knotting and the flair of a mural. Soon cheap paper posters advertising reggae bands covered the recent family scenes. Super glue on these posters inhibited both casual removal and painting over. Poster fragments still float on the surface like stamps on a sea of messages. Gang signatures in fat dumpling script have appeared: GIRL EVIL CHOP, New York modulating to Euro Wild Style. These blanketing letters have successfully spraypainted over the bollocks-to-you anger of the seventies, the social rock of the eighties, the repressive bliss of the community activists, and the individual name-writing: "Sam C. 4 Richard A. 100%," "LUKE4LUCIE," "Nigger Scum," ". . . Writers United," "Snooze," "I Love Life," "Dare 92–93," "Rain B4 Rust," "Toxic Heaven."

My relationship with this metropolitan passage spans just a short interval in the long memories this bridge elicits. Older residents of the area recall at least one previous bridge, wrought iron, bombed in the Blitz. When older people cross the newer bridge, their eyes sometimes glaze over. They are filtering out not only the smells and dog excreta, and me watching them. They are also focusing on flashbacks that screen all the times they have walked through this text. All the signs they have passed on this bridge punctuate their memories in private ways that I cannot approach. This graffiti grit mingles with memories to provoke a sponge of responses that holds forth against obliteration and hierarchy. We move through inscribed time in daily rites of passage that are literal and visceral, hardly metaphorical.

These passages through which we flow have infinitely coruscating aspects. Most of their infinity goes unused. We enforce just one of the many meanings in the wall's text. We paint over and block out what irks or offends us. When I try to read the mural, I find that I must focus on only one part of it at a time. Nowhere can I step back far enough to see it whole. And when I go to the other side of the passage—far enough to see it segment by segment—I am already too distant to make out its smaller notations.

Images or sayings become stereotypical, and a narrative becomes commanding, when one contending group in culture has sufficient power to repress all but one of the historically accumulated meanings that these cultural talismans carry. Stereotypes and commanding stories, however, are located within culture. They rely on the always altering ratio of power among its many publics. When this ratio shifts, remaining counter-traces (which may not be apparent to audiences unfamiliar with the original contexts) excite and necessitate the stories' reiteration—this time not to repress but to reveal the residual meanings. Talismanic stories, like stereotypes, are instances of packed overdetermination; they have energy and endurance well beyond their apparent resources. They carry hidden reserves.

A good example is the way Melville founds "Benito Cereno" on minstrelsy. The levels of this story that concern us here show how prejudiced perception can paradoxically extend and protect, even enable, the cultural effectiveness of revolutionary action. This problem comes to focus in the remarkable shave which the seeming slave, Babo, gives to the slaveship's ostensible captain, Don Cereno.

It is still not clear at the moment of the shave, either to first-time readers or to their personification in the story, the visiting North American Captain Amasa Delano, that Babo has achieved a violent slave rebellion. Cereno and Babo are both playing to Delano. But neither of them can speak his real needs aloud. Cereno is powerless in his captain's role. And Babo's quandary is that he cannot take his otherwise successful mutiny to shore. He is in an Atlantic limbo of Euro-American clichéd prejudice. He does not have navigational skills. He does have a highly practiced African-American capacity to perform complex masquerade—extraordinary cultural navigation, as it were. Because the rebels cannot show their power in any of the colonies that forbid their victory, Babo is directing a decidedly ambiguous form of theatre that really matters.

The shaving scene simultaneously displays and hides this situation. Looking on, trying to decode it, is a variously knowing, variously complected set of publics both in Babo's immediate audience and in the story's much larger reading audience. The "idea flashed across" Captain Delano's imagination, Melville says, "that possibly master and man, for some unknown purpose, were acting out, both in word and deed, nay, to the very tremor of Don Benito's limbs, some juggling play . . . But then, what could be the object of enacting this play of the barber before him?"[28]

Indeed, the purposes of this play are multiple. The chief intention must be for Babo to discipline Don Cereno with the razor. Under the cover of man coddling master, Babo will bloody and terrorize Cereno so that the Spaniard will not answer the questions Delano is putting to him. But Melville is also calling attention to the many further significations that his actors are juggling. Like Captain Delano, but perhaps a bit more quickly, we readers are gathering suspicions about the unknown purposes in the passage. Melville's shaving scene is a brilliant manifestation of the way a disciplining authority tries to curb the associations surrounding communications. It tries to enforce one meaning out of the juggled many. The audience is vaguely aware that the many meanings exist, but there is a customary collusion among the participants to stay with the limitation. Babo knows this and manipulates it.

That this scene is theatrical is unmistakable. Less obvious to twentieth-century readers is that it relies on the specific theatrics of minstrelsy. Delano has absorbed, as if they were true, clichés that are by the mid-1840s associated specifically with the conventional reading of the minstrel show. "Most negroes are natural valets and hair dressers," Delano explains, "taking to the comb and brush congenially as to the castanets." And: "God had set the whole negro to some pleasant tune" (p. 716). But the story is going to upset these conventions, I insist, without ever "transcending" minstrelsy. It can do this because Melville did not just rely on these surface clichés. The whole scene comes directly from the minstrel theatre in a way that recognized depth in its lore. Melville tried to fulfill, not contradict, blackface lore.

In Dan Emmett's unpublished papers is a holograph script for an "Ethiopian Burletta" titled "German Farmer, or, The Barber Shop in an Uproar." Emmett's model for Babo is one Pompey Smash, who shaves an officious country farmer, a German immigrant, come to the city to chair a jury. Pompey has an apprentice, Slippery Joe, to whom he is teaching his trade, just as Babo is teaching his watching black crew some new ways of relating to white authority. While the cutting continues, Emmett's German farmer laughs when black Pompey tells how he has suffered exclusion and prejudice from the whites in his church. Consequently, Pompey commits much pratfall violence to the farmer. As the German sits down, Pompey pulls the chair out from under him. And "Pompey chokes him with the towel." The farmer says he has a toothache and wonders how Pompey would cure it; Pompey replies, "Fill your mouth full ob sour-crout an set de fire till its cooked." Pulling out huge shears, "Pompey . . . accidently gets them around Farmers neck (business)." After the haircut, Pompey offers the farmer his choice of shave, "de French, de Garmon an de old Warginny styles." Supposing it is cheapest—although Pompey fools him even here—the farmer chooses the last. Pompey performs the old Virginia style by stropping his razor on the farmer's shoulder, then on the floor, scraping the farmer's "oakum" off his face, and smearing the gore on his clothes:

FARMER: Auch! murter! how dat razor pulls.
POMPEY: It pulls does it? What ob dat? De beard am bound to come if de handle dont break
FARMER: Te Furchinny style makes tam pad hurt on mine face (writhes).[29]

Thus Babo's aggression in "Benito Cereno" is hardly Melville's invention. That aggression had been playing to mechanics at Chatham Square and along the Bowery for years. What makes "Benito Cereno" brilliant is not literate culture's reversal of stock simplicities in the popular culture it draws on but the way it follows out popular culture's suggestions. Emmett's script is just that, an unfinished series of notes on which he and his blackface colleagues improvised. Melville specified and committed to print what the parenthetical "business" was when Pompey placed his shears round the farmer's neck. The sympathy toward the black-on-white violence that Melville extends (and hides) was robustly foreshadowed in Emmett's burletta. There is no doubt with whom the Chatham Square audiences sympathized and identified in Emmett's shaving scene: the black barber who suffered prejudice in his white-folks, middle-class, church. "Benito Cereno" is not in opposition to its popular origins but further along in a blackface lore cycle that was already complex.

In Melville's tale the American captain's statements about blacks' fondness for bright colors, castanets, and song demonstrate what I have termed micro-inversions. When they are embedded in a lore cycle, such statements hold compactly together the opposing perceptions of the core groups— taste and distaste yoked in each image. Eventually they heap up into the macro-inversions that can kink the direction of the cycle's meaning. During Delano's time his statements seemed truisms to the bulk of Melville's contemporary readers. Indeed, they remained "true" for many American readers for another century, into the 1950s. But for other readers, all along, they also flagged racism, even while they may also have flagged their own taste. That is, to these readers, such statements as Delano's naive mistaking of his own view for universal truth were clichés of class and race. Melville's shrewdest achievement may have been to inoculate his readers with germs of their own residual bias.

Whose racism do these clichés tag? Delano's alone? Do they show that Melville, too, was caught up in the dominant beliefs of his time? Or, as I think, do they indicate that Melville was exploring the sliding fate of racism's markers? Certainly his story narrates the fate of conventional meaning insofar as Delano's knowledge could encompass it. The history of the story's reception goes on to map that fate's lore cycle.

What is going on in "Benito Cereno" is what goes on also in *The Adventures of Huckleberry Finn* and *Pudd'nhead Wilson,* and indeed more covertly in much American literature: the world of brotherhood and freedom can take place only in the oceanic fiction (Poe and Melville and Delany and Heller) or on the river (Clemens), in the woods (Hawthorne and Hemingway), qualifiedly in the slave quarters (Jacobs and Twain and Faulkner), or in the drugged imaginary (Pynchon). Fulfillment can happen in performance of writing or dancing or singing, but these are momentary arcs toward transcendence. They flop back to the ground, "too good to be true," said Leslie Fiedler about such images in 1955.[30]

Nowhere in American literature do fictions about social actuality sustain a sense of liberatory possibility. Nowhere is there a sense, even, of a near miss. Nowhere a liberated life that *might* have been lived were it not for some accident of history, some fatal flaw of character. Some of the nations of the Americas were founded to pursue profits in sugar and cotton. Others recommitted to pursue happiness. But the literature of the Americas frustrates happy endings. The fairy tales that ended "And they lived happily ever after," the eighteenth-century fictions that ended "Reader, I married him," these are stories belonging to eras when matters came to completion. Novels like *Moby-Dick,* which ends with a drowning Indian reaching above the waves to nail a red flag and an eagle to his sinking mainmast, are a different story. Boys like Huck lighting out to a disappearing territory of dubious freedom, are also a different story—as if an end can only be a new problematic beginning. Slave revolts uncompleted, as in "Benito Cereno" and *Blake,* are stories of this new dispensation. American literature is afloat in an Atlantic matrix of such massively and frequently shifting force that happy completion is not to be imagined. These Atlantic fictions end awash in orphans and dubiety.

In this appraisal of what lore and fictions can tell us, it is not sensible to *complain* that "Benito Cereno" is the story of an uncompleted revolution. Yes, Babo's actions are de-fused in "endless layers of ironic containment."[31] But these layered ironies are not only inhibitory. They also diffuse his meaning. As protective swaddling for Babo's actions, Melville's ironies float those actions out into the bullrushes of another era, perhaps to be unpacked anew.

The immediacy of Babo's revolt is one entity. It took place months before the day of reckoning narrated in the story, the day Amasa Delano visits the *San Dominick* and wonders about what he sees there. But the issues present in "Benito Cereno" turn on how Babo's former actions are perceived and received among the whites who enslaved him and whom he forced to try to understand him. Delano does not understand. But then the story is not named "Amasa Delano." The story is named "Benito Cereno." And Cereno does understand.

Cereno understands so much that it kills him, too, indirectly, three months after Babo's trial. Cereno's imaginative immersion in the experience disables him to live on the corrupt shore with the legal simplifications of the events. The sure aspect of this ambiguous ending is that it fits well with the logic of Melville's career. Throughout late Melville, the concept of a fixed tale is most mocked in his work. The idea of a lore cycle as something that keeps turning, ever more ambiguously, is the story's end result. There is no escaping this thought as the last words unfold and we are told that "Benito Cereno, borne on the bier, did, indeed, follow his leader" (p. 755).

Which leader? At this point, the syntax is unmistakable. Cereno's leader has become not Christ, not Christopher Columbus (the ship's first figure-head), and not his friend Alexandro Aranda whose slaves Cereno was transporting (and whose skeleton Babo had installed to replace Columbus). Cereno's leader is Babo himself, "that hive of subtlety" (p. 755). If the story is about revolutionary action, then Babo's activity has proved unsustainable in his time. If the story is about the lore cycle in which revolutionary activity is kept alive in narrated reimaginings, then Babo's effect remains continually resonant. In the switch of Cereno's leaders, Melville has evoked the Atlantic world's swapping of lore cycles from top-down aristocratic order to bottom-up lumpen charisma.

Babo cannot transfer his revolution from ship to shore. There is a plot sequence in Martin Delany's *Blake,* a novel set in the very 1850s in which Melville wrote his story, that is exactly the same. Martin Delany, an African American, coedited Frederick Douglass's anti-slavery newspaper, *The North Star,* until he could no longer condone Douglass's approval of *Uncle Tom's Cabin.* Delany's *Blake; or, The Huts of America* is the first black nationalist novel published in the United States.[32]

By the middle of the novel, Henry Blake, a runaway slave and a revolutionary, has gone to Cuba to find his wife, who was sold away from her family. Blake has, further, hired himself out as a black sailing master on a slave ship in order to mutiny, recruit the Africans to his mission, and capture the ship's heavy guns. "We must," he proclaims, "have a vessel at our command before we make a strike" (p. 198). But when the time to strike arrives—the slaves in the hold armed to the teeth with sugar knives and billhooks, the white officers preoccupied fighting a tempest, and the ship just a day's sail from Cuba—Blake is paralyzed. "Blake during the entire troubles was strangely passive to occurring events below" (p. 236). Instead of seizing the slave ship, with its guns and cargo, he contents himself with an altered plan. He will spread rumors of the mutineers in the hold, thus reducing their cost enough that mulatto conspirators in port can afford to buy them and recruit them to the cause. This, Blake achieves. However, his planned revolt remains a dream deferred.

In *Blake,* blacks plan revolutionary acts but white-on-black violence dominates the prose. We see only traces of Henry's self-protection—in the trail of dead dogs and overseers' bodies that Henry leaves on the ground as he passes through plantations. The text of the novel itself is truncated before the actual Cuban revolt which Blake intends will incite, in its turn, a general American slave revolution. Readers see none of this. Delany, perhaps our most revolutionary American author of the nineteenth century, leaves the future that did not happen in an ellipsis . . . Revolutionary actuality cannot be landed in most of the Atlantic world as then constituted—despite the successes in Haiti and the long history of marronage and violent resistance throughout the Americas.[33]

Whether Delany's and Melville's judgments constituted pessimism and defeat, or real assessment, I leave for others to argue. I emphasize instead how Melville documents revolutionary hopes cycling through and *beyond* defeat. This secondary resonance of action is what "Benito Cereno" deals with most interestingly. The day's events in "Benito Cereno" take place on a ship called the San Dominick in 1799. The name of the ship clearly evokes the slave revolution on Santo Domingo, later to be Haiti; the year evokes the moment, 13 June 1799, when Toussaint signed his first treaty with Britain and the United States, clearing their adversarial forces from the island. But those details inform readers, not the story's participants. When the story opens for them, time and change seem to have settled: "Everything was mute and calm; everything gray. The sea, though undulated into long roods of swells, seemed fixed, and was sleeked at the surface like waved lead that has cooled and set in the smelter's mould" (p. 673). Filtered through the consciousness of Captain Delano, this imagery is tainted with his fatuous complacency. This is the way the present frequently seems: inevitable and steady. People do not wake every day thinking, Today's the day the world turns. Melville, though, is using the language of lore cycles: swells *seem* fixed even though momentous change is in fact building. The pencil's, or printer's, lead of narration can seem to smelt a permanence that enforces a particular conception, even when that understanding will be overwhelmed.[34]

This imagery continues periodically in "Benito Cereno." Another smattering comes just after one of the few surviving Spanish sailors has risked tying a fantastic Gordian knot, thrown it to the puzzled Captain Delano, and urged him to "Undo it, cut it, quick" (p. 707). This celebrated symbol in the story represents the knotting into each other that all the ship's groups have achieved. In one of the story's best puns, Delano holds it "knot in hand, knot in head" (p. 707). But even this knotty representation of the ship's tragic involutions cannot dislodge Captain Delano's fixed picture of order: he cannot undo it. Delano sees the "grayness of everything" and declares "the leaden ocean seemed laid out and leaded up, *its course finished, soul gone, defunct*" (p. 709, my emphasis). Even after he experiences the revolt, and has gone through the inquest in Lima, Captain Amasa Delano returns to the fatuous conclusion that nothing is different. This return to stasis is a primary predicament for literature, as Ralph Ellison realized when he chose these lines for his epigraph in *Invisible Man:* " 'You are saved,' cried Captain Delano, more and more astonished and pained; 'you are saved; what has cast such a shadow upon you?' " What Ellison does not cite is Benito Cereno's reply: "The negro" (p. 754). Amasa Delano clearly is one of those bachelors on whom the experience of others does not register.

Delano has not traveled far enough under Babo's razor, nor long enough in the radically anguished social space of the *San Dominick*'s cuddy, to imagine the effects that the Spaniard feels.[35] Cereno imagines Babo's reality more wholly because of his "collusion" in the "juggling play" of the shaving scene. Babo wraps Cereno in his Spanish flag to be shaved, making him proclaim his "harlequin ensign" (p. 720). In playing out his role as a partner, Cereno has entered Babo's experience. It has forced him out of his privileged ideology and joined him mortally to the inside of the Atlantic lore cycle of castaways.

As Delano is the reader's agent in the story, his callous refusal of Babo's "shadow" is a problem for those who want to believe that the story furthers social change. But it is not a problem for those who watch how the roods and swells of lore cycles mediate change—because there are no day-trippers in lore cycles. Members of lore cycles are in for a long journey. They go through the events in full, some more than others; but when the cycle kinks, they come along. Cereno had that Gordian knot in his head, whereas it was *not* in Delano's head.

But Delano's heirs, American Atlantic readers, have eventually come along, too. The meaning of "Benito Cereno" has changed for readers since Melville first published it in 1855. For a century after its publication, many readers believed the story studied the gullibility of Cereno's diseased Catholic sensibility. Or, they thought it displayed Melville's racism. Or, those who were impatient with Melville's aborting of Babo's revolt thought it showed his liberal despair. Today we are more likely to see it as a profound analysis of a dupe and his racism, of perception and the swells of change.

There are thus two answers to the question, How does a lore cycle turn? The answers ultimately meet in the middle and become one, but they start separately. A lore cycle turns from the inside, by inversion of its very popular, very compacted meanings. And a lore cycle turns from the outside, when it is pummeled by new forces making demands on it or policing it.

They meet in the middle as the lore cycle mediates people's adjustment to the stimuli and pressures of their time. A lore cycle transmits the terms by which groups understand themselves in relation to others. Its turning tends less to volte-face inversions, however dramatic they are as illustrations, than to *adjustments*. The main reason cultural inversions do not effect social revolutions is that they are knotted up with so many other ameliorating factors.

Raymond Williams has written of the triad of residual, dominant, and emergent ideologies always operating at any given moment in a society. Jonathan Dollimore has refocused this triad as the work of consolidation, subversion, and containment in art.[36] I mention these useful categories in successful recent attempts to understand ideology because lore itself, preceding and paralleling ideology, also works quietly in the same ways. Ideology is the intentional wing of the lore cycle's inadvertent work. Negotiation is their business.

Trains' Actions

> Take your real pal
> Go down to the levee
> I said, to the levee
> And join that shufflin' song.
>   —Young Jakie Rabinowitz in *The Jazz Singer*

To provide a picture of the negotiating adjustment that is the characteristic work of lore cycles, I am going to conduct a train of scenes spanning the century from 1820 to the end of the 1920s, from vernacular presentation to theatre, through literature, to mass film. A whistling sound flies into the city as a bird and steams out as the "sign of the train." It is a locomotive drawing freight around the country.[37] Motifs enter the market and become signs of value. The elements continue, but they feel different because their ratios are moving.

I follow this *changed same* by tracing the whistling song from its folk instances to those already formalized in popular early performances of minstrelsy. Stowe will pick it up and center it in *Uncle Tom's Cabin*. Similar samplings of minstrelsy appear in Martin Delany's *Blake,* but he is also using them overtly to negate Stowe's representations. Finally, Al Jolson summarily deploys whistling signs in his improvisations during *The Jazz Singer.*

Every motif or gesture is embedded in a train of previous such gestures which pull it to the present. I want to suggest that we conceive the "exchange" of cultural tokens as *transactions:* they do not replace the parts of one's identity but, instead, compound who one is. Although the cultural market grew out of actual material markets and although the crossings in material markets are prerequisites for cultural flows, the transfer is different in the two spheres. When people dance for eels in a market, two separate transferences occur, one at the material level, another at the cultural level. Although they are often designated by the same word, "exchange," these transfers produce discrete results.

At the material level, a performer gives steps (or enjoyment) for food and a buyer gives food for steps (or enjoyment). A crude replacement occurs. I give something I have for something you have. At the same time, another transfer occurs—the passing of cultural gesture, or identity tokens. This is quite a different sort of transfer and cannot be analyzed by the same calculus as the exchange which it seems to emulate. Why not? Because in cultural exchange, the transfer is not of one good *for* another, but a compounding of goods, one *onto* others. When I pick up a cultural gesture, it need not bump out a corresponding gesture I already practice. Rather, I graft it onto who I am. Perhaps even more important, when one group passes its gestural practices onto another group, there is not a loss of those practices. Nor is there a unilateral ownership on either side. Instead, there are mutual transactions. Sharings and cross-connections prevail, with both groups continuing to practice those gestures so long as they seem to be useful blazonings of identity.

These transactions, or trains' actions, are continual, but uneven in their flow and spread. These transactions are the ways people gradually negotiate their fit to their times. The train of motifs that I conduct here is one thing when I first join it and changes to another during its century of reiteration. First it is a folk whistle, then it becomes the whistle of steam locomotives.

This modulation is what I want to slow down and peer at, for it turns out that the folk whistle is still carried in the sound of the train.

The mechanical whistle does not erase or replace the earlier whistle. The trains' action is to compound and overlay and *pull along* the earlier signs even as the locomotive whistle may erroneously seem to replace them.

Whistling was already a formal part of the self-representations black performers were selling at Catherine Market when they danced for eels in 1820. We have seen Bob Rowley, come across from Long Island as Bobolink Bob, cashing in with his specific imitation of furtive field birds putting on blackface to breed. I am now in a position to suggest a bit more in Bobolink Bob's transaction.

The whistling metaphor exactly enacts the contradictory needs of black-face performance. The bobolink's whistle is perforce both furtive and brazen. The bird must simultaneously escape his predators and forthrightly mark his territory for propagation and genetic transmission. The blackface whistler performs the same dilemma. He has had to mark his territory for propagation and cultural transmission within a space controlled by those who would feed on him. He, too, has blazoned his working-class culture within an antagonistic surveillance.

The whistling bird is an image of competence that penetrates and over-laps other activities hustling in the same space at the same time. Anyone waking to the dawn chorus is hearing these many sufficiencies. Likewise, anyone moving through urban space is experiencing the hyped equiva-lence, these days, of the dawn chorus: boom boxes, pagers, cellular phones, stylized bumpers on autos, stylized coats on people, brand insignia, literally flashing heels, screaming alarms—all aggressively marking territory, all poignantly claiming their sufficiency in crowded space. The young men turning contorted in crowded Covent Garden and relentless Times Square, shouting into phones with short antennae bristling, stamping like Rum-pelstiltskin at contacts on the other end of cellular connections—these are cousins-german to the whistlers of Catherine Market and the Chatham Theatre. These men mark space, performing like birds their own imperti-nent communications under the angry eyes of urbanites crowding the same space. But the anger was not always so intense. Surely, anger increases as the overlays and crowdings exponentially surpass the urban and human carrying capacity. At first these impertinent sufficiencies were welcomed to the market and desirable. Everyone was learning to be a denizen of sur-veillance.

The urban whistler performs an impertinent completeness in the midst of hurry and fragmentation. In an urbanizing context, to watch a rube whistling is akin to watching a human go naked among others who have girded their loins. Human whistlers pretend to be as free as birds to perform their lives under human scrutiny. This whistle performed in city markets has come to stand for a seamless personality. The whistler in urban space does not differentiate between a private and a public self. Such a whistler performs a seamlessness that was being lost to those in the urbanizing audience who put on faces to meet faces. New Yorkers at the beginning of the nineteenth century would pay to see blacks come across the water as rubes and recall for them their prelapsarian confidence. What the subsequent nestings of performance clarify is that the early whistle already had a taboo feel. Its public felt they were peeking at a naked, forbidden completeness.

When in the late 1830s and early 1840s white performers in blackface spread the imitations of black performance that T. D. Rice and George Washington Dixon had inaugurated, they included whistling. But it was whistling with a difference, whistling yanked into a new context. At first, whites in blackface carried over the folk whistle blacks did as a marker for their authenticity. Thus a newspaper reviewer of Rice's London performances cited his "strange whistle" as part of the performance's "extraordinary reality." As blackface delineation gathered momentum and its own conventions, its most popular whistling came to be imitation of locomotive whistles. Here is the way Billy Whitlock advertised his famous fascination with steam power in London, 19 June 1843: "A locomotive lecture on de machinery ob de globe by Mr. Whitlock, who will give an imitation of a locomotive in operation, with the steam-whistle accompaniments, and also relate the full particulars of his first love with Miss Lucrezia Snowdrop, and of their visit to the wild animals, to a ball, etc."[38]

By 1843 the nastiness of racist expropriation is taking further turns. The white performer in blackface, like Whitlock, does not abase himself to perform human seamlessness. Instead the appetite of popular performance has driven the performer to aggression. This "locomotive lecture on de machinery ob de globe" seizes on the vulnerability of the folk whistle in an urbanizing world. Whitlock and others are overlaying naiveté onto the earlier image's brave nakedness. What had been a token of self-sufficiency in a contested space is becoming a joke that assumes it is ridiculous for blacks to describe the world's mechanisms. Jerking blacks through a rapid sequence of disjointed and apparently unusual contexts (courting, a ball, the zoo) was funny in itself to Whitlock's audiences, on both sides of the Atlantic.

In order to satisfy this nasty appetite, however, the performer depends on his audience knowing the history of the target and the pattern of hits on it. Locomotive imitations became a staple in the minstrel show. This enjoyment puzzles us today the way marathon running puzzles the couch potato. Like a fondness for Marmite on toast, humans impersonating locomotives was an acquired taste, unimaginable to those not raised on the stimulus. To enjoy Whitlock's stimulus, his audience had to conceive "blackness" as including particular conventions that bespoke seamless enthusiasm for nature. These conventions represented the opposite of urbanity. The humor depended on the performer being a rube closer to bobolinks and the natural world than to steam technology and its flattening force. Thus when Whitlock burlesqued a locomotive the setup necessarily pulled Bobolink Bob along as part of its train of associations.

Every performance of the image continually excited an invisible penumbra of meanings that extended and qualified the event. Furthermore, this locating of the purported black rube in these odd locations was in itself odd. These trains, zoos, and balls, after all, were locations where white working publics would themselves have gladly lingered. They'd liked to have been strolling with a finely dressed partner. They'd have welcomed a *frisson* with a caged tiger. They'd liked to have ridden on that train pulling Whitlock.

Billy Whitlock and the other minstrel whistlers of the forties, then, are performing a characteristic move. They are lifting a folk gesture. They are lampooning it with a racist abasement that distances them from their target. But they are also using the target as their fantasy agent. The agent takes them places that stretch or surpass their reach. Each opposing side of the move enables the other. The more ridiculous the black agent, the more incongruous is his penetration into forbidden zones of luxury life. This goes the other way, too. The more power the agent is given, say by identifying him with a locomotive, the more risible he becomes. Thus the more fun, and the crueler, it is to imagine him in some further forbidden scrape. I believe that audiences are aware in varying measures of all these conflicting affects.

Let's follow this train on a detour, trusting this train's actions to return us in a trice to Stowe, the next station down the line. The repeated fascination with noisy locomotives in these performances is a sign of the cross-roads popular culture was both mapping and threading. This playing with locomotive power linked it to similar attractions in the culture of other classes. This locomotive imagery was rampant enough in political cartoons at midcentury to became famous, in Leo Marx's phrase, as "the machine in the garden."[39] The middle-class inflections, however, were different from those playing on the most popular stages. At the Bowery and Chatham theatres, the sound of the locomotive evoked the sexual dimension that always lurks in Eden. On these stages was made manifest the transference popular sexuality was making from rural eels to urban trains and steam power.

The locomotive pulled behind it a series of adolescent metaphors of sexuality, as in "Julianna Phlebiana Constantina Brown," a comic song of blackface love that is a characteristic document of the youth culture's cocky furtiveness. The boasting singer dances, he sings, "wid locomotive might." He flirts enough with the wives of others to rouse jealousy. He does the polka. The song turns around its duet line, "Den up an' down my darkies, oh! gently up an' down," which rhymes with Miss Brown, the love interest of the title. This up an' down might refer to the swaying of the dance. But to the youth public, whose congeniality called it into being, the motion is sexual, confirmed in the double entendres of the last stanza:

> I lemonaded home wid her; by gum she ax'd me in
> De way I went it darkies, wid Pheby was a sin
> She played on de piano,
> My feelings quickly riz,
> My heart got cold, my gizzard shook,
> My eyeballs nearly friz.[40]

As the singer's blood deserted his head, the chorus was doubtless enthusiastically sung by the entire audience in the theatre:

> We're all here, here, here, in this happy throng,
> We're all here, here, here, in this happy throng.

This chorus reinforces the audience's unity with their singer's actions. He is their man, performing their fantasies for them. But the chorus is chaste. It is part of the double power of the blackface move to have the trickster agent, the minstrel performer, do the penetration for the throng that stays chaste. Their agent enacts their private fantasies in public. He gives them the erotic seamlessness that Bobolink Bob had performed, but now he does so with all the subtlety of a locomotive. Maybe it took "locomotive might" to do the unifying cultural work that "all . . . in this happy throng" were demanding their rituals achieve. Let's not forget this throng unifying with blackness, however crudely constructed, however safely enacted. Let's not forget, as our detour returns to the further sequence of whistling scenes in blackface performance, how much momentum and libidinous power these performances had generated during the decade of the 1840s. Let's wonder where that power went.

So far as we know, Harriet Beecher Stowe never attended a minstrel show. Finding her at the Chatham or the Bowery or some traveling show in Cincinnati would have been far more shocking to her public than when the castaway crowd glimpsed Billy Whitlock's blackface character lemonading Lucrezia Snowdrop to the zoo or the ball. I raise this comparison to emphasize that middle-class proscription of down-class mixing was far more stringent than lower-class proscription of cross-racial dallying. Stowe spent little time on plantations and, before she wrote *Uncle Tom's Cabin*, never went deeper south than northern Kentucky. But her innocences did not stop her novel from anatomizing slavery. Nor did they stop her from lifting minstrel staples, including its whistles, for several of the novel's most famous scenes.

Indeed, Stowe's novel was able to move such heavy cultural baggage— turn a thing into a man—chiefly because she was in so very many ways, if certainly not all, confidently integrated with the dominant assumptions of her time. Her era's orthodox Christianity and racialist assumptions, its dominant political accommodations—all these she endorsed, but pitched them with spin. She likewise accepted abolitionist tableaus as roughly accurate representations of black-white relations. But she invested them with great power by nesting them in ambitiously detailed contexts. More specifically, she sluiced into abolitionist tableaus some of the power of minstrel conventions.

She adapted Frederick Douglass's question "What to the Slave is the Fourth of July?" to "What is freedom to George Harris?" George steps beyond being a complaining action character into being one who can make a cultural difference, however, when Stowe tricks him out in dandy costume lifted from the Jim Crow plays of T. D. Rice. She confirms the allusion by giving George a servant named Jim. To readers in the late twentieth century, it seems an almost inexplicable paradox that George frees himself by using the minstrel dandy's gloves and facial darkening: "A little walnut bark," says George, has turned his "yellow skin a genteel brown."[41] But within the proscribing protocols of Stowe's era, the liberatory power of the minstrel show was a given. These protocols made George smart when he was yellow and dangerous when he was walnut.

Eliza is interesting enough as an abolitionist's stereotype—mulatta madonna crosses Ohio River with child to freedom. But what made her legendary was Stowe's addition of minstrel leaps and contorted twists. Stowe wrote that "blood marked every step" Eliza took. Stowe turned the scene into such a ritual dream that e. e. cummings later rewrote it as "whirlleaps toward an outmost brightness." To create this ritual intensity, Stowe tied abolitionist and minstrel conventions into a bowline. Her knot tied together two lore cycles into one tableau whose contradictions ensured it would toss and turn all night. Eliza's bloody crossing became the cover image for the book, the scene featured on posters for the subsequent Tom plays when it went back onto the minstrel stage, and the central image of the Tom movies.[42]

Stowe's relation to the minstrel show was an intervention that went both ways. Minstrel material profoundly shaped her writing; and her writing, in turn, bequeathed figures to the working-class stage. The train of associations that we have been following, the whistling performer's merger with the locomotive, as performance shifted from folk to popular culture in the Atlantic, permeates *Uncle Tom's Cabin.*

Topsy does the Billy Whitlock locomotive whistle better than the professional. But Eliza and George Harris's four-year-old boy, little Harry, is also tellingly involved with the main features of this transaction. When Shelby whistles him into his song-and-dance routine at the novel's beginning, Stowe is invoking one of the most famous of early minstrelsy's talismanic performances. It is a Philadelphia story. While traveling toward his triumphant Manhattan arrival from the Ohio Valley and Deep South stages where he had put together his Jim Crow dance, T. D. Rice improvised a routine in Philadelphia in 1832. He danced out on stage carrying a gunny sack over his back. At the second verse he intoned:

> O Ladies and Gentlemen, I'd have for you to know
> That I've got a little darky here that jumps Jim Crow.

And out of the sack tumbled four-year-old Joseph Jefferson III, dressed in minuscule ragged imitation of Rice. Exactly the age Stowe assigned Harry, young Joe Jefferson danced and sang a junior version of "Jump Jim Crow." The tall man and the small boy traded verses while the audience threw coins to reward the boy.[43] Harry's performance at the outset of *Uncle Tom's Cabin* replicates Jefferson's and pulls behind it, in its train, Rice's Jim Crow.

Stowe's Harry is a signature character at both ends of the novel. As Harry Harris, at the opening, he is specifically hailed as "Jim Crow." Powerful men pull him through a short catalogue of stereotypical black roles (a rheumatic Uncle, a pious Elder) the way Whitlock yanked his black character through grotesquely fractured personae. Having crossed the icy Ohio at Eliza's breast, at the end of the novel Harry crosses water again, accompanying his mother and father's costumed reach for freedom. After Canada their third crossing will be the Atlantic, eventually to Liberia. This return emblematizes Stowe's colonizationist sympathies at the time of writing, which she later regretted. It also emblematizes one mystery of Catherine Market— that authenticity resides beyond the water. If George and his family are to settle in a place of authenticity their minstrel-educated author will keep them going back across water until there is no more to whirlleap. Tipped off that slavery agents watch for them at Lake Erie, Eliza shears her hair to dress as a man. She cross-dresses little Harry as a girl, rewards him with sensible seedcakes, and renames him Harriet, Stowe's own name.

Throughout *Uncle Tom's Cabin,* Harriet Stowe has been identifying with Harry Harris. Harry is a well-formed quadroon well situated to perform caricatures of his people. Stowe passes him across water to be borne again as a fugitive through the kitchens of the underground railroad. At the end of her novel Stowe shows how her characters were bound to minstrelsy from the beginning, as was the novel itself—indeed, as was her own imagination. In its quest for liberty, this novel has had to transform the performances its culture commands to another sort, still commanded, still rewarded, but less demeaning. As a partial dramatization of these implications, the author of *Uncle Tom's Cabin* projects herself into one of its least powerful characters. She portrays his plight—and escape—as her own. Harry is rewarded for playing at blackness with being sold down the river. Then he is rewarded for playing at femaleness with being delivered to Canada, finally a free person.

If these signature namings suggest what I suspect, they show Stowe's confidence that she controlled her material even as it projected a dream— or nightmare—imaginative space. She believed it possible to transcend some if not all the forced patterns. Escape was partially a choice one might make to cross into another identity. Harry could be delivered from blackface impersonations by his father, who had used them as the first step in his own escape. Harry's "last passage on the lake" traverses the territory opened and colonized by the rough labor on the Erie Canal that the Christy Minstrels transmuted into blackface minstrelsy. Harry-as-Harriet, George, and Eliza cross to Canada by traversing the imaginative and real Lake Erie that blackface opened.

Martin Delany's novel *Blake* was composed just across Lake Erie in Canada. Delany wrote to counter Stowe. Nowhere does Delany display his countering more than in his bitter, brutal rendition of plantation owners commanding the performed whistle. It is the cruelest scene in an often grueling novel.[44] Delany's footnote announces "This is a true Mississippi scene" (p. 67), which may be correct, but the passage nevertheless is precisely modeled on Harry's dancing for Shelby and Haley in *Uncle Tom's Cabin*. Delany intended to detonate the eventually happy conclusion that Stowe was dreaming as authentic.

Delany introduces this scene by having his Mississippi host welcome white guests to his black show with the conventional minstrel opener, "Gentlemen! Be seated." They move to the "pleasure ground" behind the plantation house and call in a consumptive slave youth named Rube. The host acts as "a ringmaster in the circus":

the command was imperative, with no living hand to stay the pending consequences. He must submit to his fate, and pass through the ordeal of training.

"Wat maus gwine do wid me now? I know wat maus gwine do," said this miserable child, "he gwine make me see sights!" when going down on his hands and feet, he commenced trotting around like an animal.

"Now gentlemen, look!" said Grason. "He'll whistle, sing songs, hymns, pray, swear like a trooper, laugh, and cry, all under the same state of feelings."

With a peculiar swing of the whip, bringing the lash down upon a certain spot on the exposed skin, the whole person being prepared for the purpose, the boy commenced to whistle almost like a thrush; another cut changed it to a song, another to a hymn, then a pitiful prayer, when he gave utterance to oaths which would make a Christian shudder, after which he laughed outright; then from the fulness of his soul he cried:

"O maussa, I's sick! Please stop little!" casting up gobs of hemorrhage. (pp. 66–67)

Unlike Harry, whose performances lead finally to his escape, this boy, Rube, dies that evening: consumed. His lashed glossolalia is his legacy.

Delany shows these planters enforcing the narrowly permitted performance of the black repertoire: "whistle, sing songs, hymns, pray, swear like a trooper, laugh, and cry." Blake's own rhetoric of rebellion, or any of the language of complaint and anger that the novel has already shown in the quarters, or the more revolutionary calls to arms that we will later see in the novel—Rube performs none of those, of course. This is a spectacle not of an unconscious trance but of a conventional theatrical repertoire that Rube and our host to this scene have worked out: "I know wat maus gwine do," says the boy. Thus the limited list and the lash are significant in the passage. Also significant is the methodical effect of authentic emotion Rube projects "from the fulness of his soul." But most important is the phrase "the whole person being prepared for the purpose."

The whole person is prepared by the whole society. Rube is far along in a train of performers that the visiting English comedian Charles Mathews early projected after his 1824 scrutiny of North American types. He started the *polymonologues* which Billy Whitlock, then Harry Harris and Topsy in *Uncle Tom's Cabin,* and now Rube in *Blake,* are varying. In each case, their audiences had been "encouraging," or lashing a new kind of spectacle that demonstrated not a firm personality but the ranging of which character is capable. In one man, in one evening, in one "at home," Mathews showed a spectrum of types in one society. Mathews seems broad, but his range is crucially limited to the risible and it excludes serious anger or resentment. Delany's Rube brilliantly renders the ruthlessness of this consuming spectacle.[45]

Rube was not allowed to voice, and Mathews never displayed, any black role that was challenging or even worthy of respect. The performances are called up by a particular sort of audience looking for resolution. But the obvious grotesquerie of the spectacle can for some audience members have disparate effects. It is a rite of passage that deforms Rube, as it will later deform Jakie Rabinowitz as Jack Robin. We need not cop a superior posture toward this material from our late-in-the-cycle vantage. We are not the only people to whom the material has signaled its deformations. It was potentially a deforming influence on the contemporary public it (dis)pleased, also. Note Delany differentiating the responses even among the cavaliers he convened for Rube's forced display:

Franks stood looking on with unmoved muscles. Armsted stood aside whittling a stick; but when Ballard saw, at every cut the flesh turn open in gashes streaming down with gore, till at last in agony he appealed for mercy, he involuntarily found his hand with a grasp on the whip, arresting its further application.

"Not quite a Southerner yet Judge, if you can't stand that!" said Franks on seeing him wiping away the tears. (p. 67)

Their capacity to acknowledge what they are seeing ranges from Colonel Franks's stolidity, through Armsted's powerless sympathy for blacks, to Ballard's involuntary tears at their treatment; and, of course, Rube is fatally powerless under the lash. But even this scene of Rube's forced whistle will turn inside out later in the novel, when such ritualized festivities as King's Day are used as cover to plan and stage the fictive Cuban revolution.[46] Indeed, Delany's use of festivity in the second half of his novel is the most conscious exploitation of subversion in popular culture that I know about in the nineteenth-century imagination. Against all the odds, Blake has proceeded toward his goal. At the end, however, his focus fades. Why?

This deliquescence of revolutionary intentions may be exhaustion and it may be the flawed narration of a beginner. But interesting complications and self-doubts may also be creating Blake's indecisions. Such inverse sequences as Blake's failed mutiny on the slave ship may be Delany showing, and his character Blake realizing, the horrific scope of what they are trying to achieve. There is no evidence that either Delany or his hero doubted for a second the need or the rightness of revolution. But maybe the revolution's hemispheric scope is why Blake becomes so curiously passive. When he is chosen "General-in-Chief of the army of emancipation of the oppressed men and women of Cuba," Blake responds knowingly: "In bondage again! Well, I suppose those who are bound, especially when they seek it, must obey" (pp. 241–242).

At this point in the novel, well into the Cuban plot, another scene is linked symbolically to Rube's whistling performance. It thus becomes part of these trains' actions whose effects I am tracing. Piece by piece, Blake has assembled the elements of his planned revolution. He has brought runaway slaves, activated Havana's educated blacks and Creoles, and enlisted a few sympathetic whites. Blake has brought one former slave boy, a lad named Tony, to Cuba to work for a married couple of converted white revolutionary sympathizers. The wife has sent Tony out to play for a few hours. Tony returns with "an orange sprig well strung with a variety of birds; many among them of the choicest warblers," and tosses these corpses at the foot of the white woman. Horrified by the slaughter, she asks the boy how he could kill the birds. "Da was singin' an' did'n see me," he says, "an' I jis sneaked up an' popt 'em . . . dat ain't nothin' to kill a bird!" (p. 240).

At its end, *Blake* is impressive for such ambiguous scenes. It is as if the playing out of the novel has delivered Delany to realizations he never anticipated at the plot's beginning. Callous children playing at killing off songbirds throws light on the simultaneous reticence of the revolutionary general. Youths are taking violent actions easily while the older Blake is becoming more and more hesitant, more and more aware of the long-reaching trains of consequences of one's actions. The novel trails off inconclusively, not unlike history.

> The birds are singing the day that you stray.
> —Al Jolson, "My Mammy"

The most remarkable human warbler in the twentieth century was Al Jolson. His performances are a potpourri of gestures gone akimbo. His hands fist up, clasp, reach wide. His fingers graze his waist and hips, snap and clap. His rolling eyes and octopus arms surround oedipal longing like a wet blanket, and camp it up. Other times, maybe just a line later in the same song, his eyes demur downward, appeal on high, then rake his audience ahead of his trailing head and shoulders. He rocks on his heels and taps toes. He swivels, pumps, and pulls his hips. His knees march. He flaps his elbows like a fledgling crow struggling to fly. He sticks his tongue into his cheeks like Chip and Dale, sucks his molars like The Thinker too wired to sit down. His face broadcasts attitudes that bump into one another documenting his lyrics and seconding the conflicts in his emotions, adding visual quaver to his tremolos.

In Jolson's performances, uncertain gender sympathies cohabit with regional locutions, mingling his class origin with his class aspiration. One hears him clipping Cherry Street's growled vowels and exaggerating California's pep. He busily rags songs already syncopated. There are recordings of songs associated with him, as "Alexander's Ragtime Band," in which his spoken introductions banter colloquies that were far-gone clichés of street-corner jive. He exaggerates the slurred suffixes that whites and blacks, too, had thoroughly cartooned into "coon" songs. Jolson's performance has constant, colliding intimacy with familiar remarks and customary gestures. His originality is located in a plenitude we already know.

Jolson seldom grades into a gesture or hints at nuance in a word. His thoughts are sudden eruptions, like a robot whirring to programmed stimuli. The result is a heap of primary feelings and elementary movements all jostling for their place in the song. There is no resolution. The scores of the past do not settle. They are all present at once in his work, without hierarchy, without erasure. So many pressures show themselves converging in his performances that Jolson clearly culminates the line I have been following like a caboose—locomotive drive overlaying the minstrel whistle.

Jolson produced and survived a thorough conjunction of folk and industrial lores. His excitement at their possibilities, however, did not stop him from posting their costs:

> the Birds are SingIN' the DAY THAT you Straaay.
> but Wait unTil you Ahh fURRther aWAAY.
> things woan Be so LAHve LEE when you're ALL aLOaaan.[47]

Jolson assembled a fable of membership to fight the aloneness of Atlantic migration. He performed this assembly, however, as if he were reinventing the wheel from others which were themselves demonstrably well greased and load-bearing. He abstracted the core of membership fables by watching earlier fables turn. "My Mammy" is all inadvertent parody of every plantation song from the late 1840s onward—Henry Russell, Dan Emmett, and Stephen Collins Foster included. Jolson extracts their rhymes on roam and home, their longing for Missus and Massa, their wounded manhood, and boils them into one condensed syrup. Jolson's far-along version of the fable was surely self-conscious and camp. It was at the bottom of the waterfall of gestural identity each earlier wave of immigrants had concocted. By Jolson's time in the teens and twenties of this century, his churning gestures were both a thorough register of actual historical pain and thoroughly conventional. His acting was a template of legends and winces and winks. What was unusual was his openness to these conventions and the way he encouraged them to cluster in his work. I find his work nakedly earnest and poignant.

Al Jolson was an eager conduit for the collective force of blackface lore in *The Jazz Singer*. With helpful spurts from Vitaphone's synchronized sound, the lore Jolson enacted was overwhelming. It took over the film's weak screenplay and filled the vacuum of its weak direction. Jolson's semaphore gestures were luminous with all the meaning communal practice had packed into them during the century since blacks danced for eels on the very streets filmed in the opening of the movie. As Warner Brothers transformed the source material to coincide with the career of their star, they put together a film that would convey even to provincial theatres much of the urban, secular ritual of assimilation that was its topic.[48]

In *The Jazz Singer* (1927) all this compaction, overlay, turmoil, and peeping-through shows cannily in the tableau Warner Brothers filmed in one six-minute take on 16 August 1927. The set and soundstage were in downtown Los Angeles, but they imitated a San Francisco cellar called Coffee Dan's. This tableau would be the first Vitaphone sequence they used in the movie. It was also the first scene in which Jolson appears in the film, its first California scene, its first in which Jews do not predominate, its first scene where women appear independent.

The film focuses everything to emphasize these differences as a jump cut to a new possibility. Rather than his disapproving father yanking him offstage, here approving peers cheer on Jack Robin, for he is no longer Jakie Rabinowitz. Here, Robin poses before a backdrop of pagodas and sequoias—Pacific Rim icons—instead of the Catherine Slip sails that framed dancers Bobolink Bob and Jack at Catherine Market and in Chanfrau's play or the plantation scenes behind dancers at the Bowery (see Figures 2.1 and 4.2). Associating blackface performers with the Orient was not new. It continued an old excitement. Harriet Beecher Stowe had shown that giving black gestures an oriental overlay was conventional by the mid-nineteenth century. When St. Clare brings Uncle Tom to his New Orleans mansion, Stowe says its "Moorish arches . . . and arabesque ornaments, carried the mind back, as in a dream, to the reign of oriental romance." It "looks about the right thing" to Tom (pp. 141–142). Before Stowe these remarks and their spirit had appeared in T. D. Rice's farces. In *The Virginia Mummy* Rice's character Ginger Blue referred to the Queen of Sheba as the "She Nigga."[49]

Meanwhile, back on the West Coast, at Coffee Dan's, people eat and drink with gusto, like early birds grubbing spring worms, but more so: caffeinated. They too imitate the spirit of Ginger Blue in *The Virginia Mummy*, who drinks and eats today like there will be no tomorrow. Jake Rabinowitz has become Jack Robin—but so has Jim Crow. Jack Robin is a bobbing variant on that old carrion predator whose assimilation problem began in the same neighborhood where Jake Rabinowitz first danced and sang.

The movie had opened literally looking down from high camera angles on street markets in "Jewtown," as Catherine Market and Cherry Street were called in the 1890s. This is the neighborhood where Irving Berlin fantasized blue skies as a boy, the neighborhood where Jolson, né Yoelson, would have found lodging had his father, Cantor Yoelson, crossed to New York rather than to Washington, D.C.[50] Now, when Jolson rises as Jack Robin to sing on the Coffee Dan stage, the camera is looking up. The crowd has asked him to sing. He is rising in the underground. He will bring with him the accumulated gestures of Jewtown, but he will also caffeinate all the gestures that had developed on those Lower East Side streets before they were Jewtown—when they were the territory of the Chatham, where T. D. Rice and Frank Chanfrau, Dan Emmett and Billy Whitlock worked over the Tappan brothers and Charles Grandison Finney.

"Wish me luck, Pal," says Robin to his partner at their table when he rises to sing at Coffee Dan's. His intertitle echoes the words choked off when his father had earlier dragged him, legs swinging like a spasmodic puppet, out of the saloon theatre. "Take your real pal," young Jakie had then been advising his audience, "And join that shufflin' song." The first words of the first song the mature Jack is about to sing at Coffee Dan's announce that "Wonderful pals are always hard to find." (Pals letting him down will drive him back to his Mammy in the film's final songs). After his impromptu appearance in the cellar is done, he will sit again at his table for a minute amid applause before Mary Dale will summon him to join her across the room. As soon as he stands to leave his table, even before he turns his back, his "wonderful pal" will reach past their ketchup bottle to wolf down Robin's eggs.

The first song Robin sings is "Dirty Hands, Dirty Face." It is about a father coming home to find his boy waiting for him at the gate. It is also about blackface: dirty face. By oscillating between the two registers, the song accommodates the Lower East Side sequence that began the film and bridges it to the Broadway scenes that will end the film with Jolson singing in blackface mask. These multiple assimilations are what are important in the song, as in the larger theme of the film. In fact, multiple assimilation is exactly the theme of the film, and the song centers it.

The father Jolson impersonates in "Dirty Hands, Dirty Face," limping home from his labor with his collar rolled up, is hardly the cantor viewers just saw in the New York tenement. The father in the song is not withdrawn to protect his beliefs, giving music lessons and singing in Temple. This father has been taking his knocks in a working world. He has been absorbing its codes. The song inverts everything Cherry Street, everything that the opening sequence of the movie has given us. Jolson sings:

> And [*hands drop in exhausted gesture*] when my work is done, coming home [*marching gait, jerks his hands wide open, palms out, then reclasps them*] to the setting sun,
> From d' GATE he'll startta rrrrun, 'n' THEnn aWWLL [*eyes roll; voice goes soprano*] KEEuss my Boyyyyyy [*wrenching his shoulders to his right, cuts off the phrase by slicing down his left fist*]
> Dirty hands [*fists clench waist high*], dirty face, little DEvill, That's Whaaat they say
> Baat, t' me [*splays palms at his breast*], he's 'nanGELLL [*clasps hands earnestly, leans forward*] ovvahh JOYYYYYYYY [*operatic*].

"Dirty Hands, Dirty Face" condenses the earlier Lower East Side scenes into a two-minute, forty-seven-second jumble of gestures signaling a father waxing sentimental about his cute-bad boy. Jack Robin is reclaiming his youth and chastising his father, rebuilding both from another angle. The way this father tolerates, even cheers, his boy's dirt shows Robin remaking his past. These negotiating revisions are the beginning of assimilation.

"Dirty Hands, Dirty Face" broaches the film's attitude toward blackface masking as transgressive dirt. But it also places that dirt as childish. This is strategic domestication. When Jack later makes actual what is kinetic in this performance, when he blacks up for the dress rehearsal in the film's protracted climax—by dirtying his hands then his face—one may read this turn as fulfilling his gritty boyhood. He is blacking up to live out and face down, as it were, the paternal rebuke. The consequences for the film are that it enfolds blackness in childhood's dirty capers:

> Making noise, breaking toys [*opens his hands wide, rocks his hips, and whips directly into an egg-eyed, in-your-face counterpose, fists clenched*]
> Always fighting the boys

The gestures and delivery here are tiny tableaus. Jolson is not singing but speaking. He is not an integrated personality but a mob of conflicts. He impersonates one character, then another. He is frankly speaking the contradictions within one self. He is giving the stock poses from popular theatre on both sides of the Atlantic that many blackface songs had absorbed, modulated, and relayed for nearly a century. We have traced them in the poses struck by each of the three Harrises in *Uncle Tom's Cabin* and in Rube's fatal repertoire in *Blake*. These are not static poses.

The midcentury blackface clown Dan Gardner, for instance, sang "Jack Rag's Statues" to the tune of "Jump Jim Crow" in the 1850s. As Jack Rag, Gardner crowed that he would "give you the Grecian statues, in my own peculiar style; / To see Anderson or Forrest, you would not care a mag, / After you had seen them done by me, Jack Rag." At the end of each verse he struck statues of Mr. Hercules and Mr. Ajax, Mr. Cincinnatus and Samson, all of whom "stood just so." Like many black and blackface performers, Jack Rag included the primal crime of Cain and Abel:

> There was Cain and Abel, fell up with one another,
> So Cain to be revenged, thought he'd kill his brother;
> He took him up, and threw him down, and gave him such a blow,
> And when he'd done a whopping him, he stood just so.
>
> . . .
>
> And when or where his brother was, he said he did not know,
> And when they all ran after him, he stood just so.[51]

Freezing bug-eyed and fisted, Jolson is giving us something of this Cain in his tableau: "little Devil, that's what they say / . . . Dirty hands, dirty face, leaves the neighbors a chase." But the sentiment inverts him to an angel of joy. Both sides are present, neither is erased. As I will demonstrate in Chapter 3, this is often the patent business of blackface songs, to mask Cain's rage in domesticated and licensed guise, thence to smuggle it into niches, even Hollywood's sets, where one least suspects it.

This canning of blackness within insouciant capers contradicts one ready interpretation of the film: that it is about eager replacement of ethnicity or Jewishness with whiteness. "Replacement" is simply insufficient to describe what is happening in any of these black or blackface performances. Rather, they all stage continual transactions of assimilation. Desire to join a dominant group is only one of the many attitudes staged in any given skit or sketch, song and dance. Equally frequent attitudes are repudiation of the favored class and group and revenge against it. These skits do not resolve to *replacement* of the past.

Jolson's filmed tableau, in "Dirty Hands, Dirty Face," like others in its associative line, is a continual compounding or jamming of the present by the accumulated pressures and gestures of experience. It compacts generations of experience, cycles of lore, layers of formation. Even here in figured San Francisco, the present does not replace the past but both connects to it and pulls it along. Jack Robin sings out an identity that has his experiences with his father as its template. Although Robin effaces his Jewishness, although he does not mention his father's forbidding disdain, the cantor's disownment of his son is clearly visible in the song. The cantor's presence and the singer's conflict with him are factors for viewers to ponder not despite the son's reinventing them—but *because* of it. Both aspects of that conflict are there at once. The reconstructed one sparks the repressed one. This far in the film—and certainly this early in the six-minute Vitaphone sequence—Robin's reinvention of his earlier dirty-faced self and his patent construction of fatherly forgiveness seems incredible. But wait. The film will validate it when the ghost of Cantor Rabinowitz accepts the previously disowned son singing *kol nidre* toward the end.

During this Coffee Dan sequence no visible agency yet symbolizes the message of compoundment. There is just the Vitaphone process stammering shadows and sound together in one coordination. The film has not yet found a visual symbol for its assimilative action. The particular figure that negotiated that overlay in Atlantic culture for more than a century between 1820 and the 1950s was *blackface* performance. When Jack Robin blacks up toward the end of the film he will be able both to realize and to combine the various senses of himself, the pressures from his mother, his father, the kibitzer Yudelson, from Mary Dale and the show's producer, all these pressures simultaneously. He will be able to sing *kol nidre*, star in *April Follies*, and go on with his life.

Too many discussions of films and books and paintings about assimilation make "replacement" the issue.[52] A former self is exchanged, goes this argument, for another self or identity. But assimilation is not a clean erasure of one identity substituting another. It proceeds, instead, by combination and transaction, dirty hands and dirty face. Assimilation is negotiated in a moving ratio that always retains traces of the previous identity. *The Jazz Singer* shows this process in exceptional detail. The film figures it by the act of blacking up. Indeed, blackface is the means by which a good bit of Atlantic acculturation has negotiated a compounded identity, fuller than replacement. Enabling this fuller identity is one reason blackface continued to operate, even when it was so ostensibly awry from its originating impulses, even after it was embarrassing its practitioners.

The Jazz Singer shows Jack Robin trying to rise in a denatured modern future, but also longing to return to his Mammy, and eager to placate his unjust father. He is doing all this even while succeeding in a world that has tried to remove religion from its calendrical rites. *The Jazz Singer* celebrates *April Follies* instead of the Jewish springtime ritual of *kol nidre*. Nevertheless, the traditional rite of penitent, reaffirmed faith pervades the film. Certainly *The Jazz Singer* sustains continuing parallels between its own era of diluted tradition and earlier eras of forced assimilation. *Kol nidre* is a prayer specifically about reaffirming Jewish identification after inquisitions forced conversions. At the end of the film, Robin is torn between opening in his blackface revue and singing *kol nidre* in place of his dying father in temple on the Day of Atonement. Although the producer of *April Follies* insists that if he ducks out on their opening night he will "queer" himself "on Broadway," in fact Robin does nothing of the sort. Rather, he reaffirms his tradition against an insistent secular inquisition. Moreover, the dreamlike end of *The Jazz Singer* has his name in huge lights on the Winter Garden's marquee—the theatre's name suggesting all by itself the merged contraries that Jack struggles to realize. He compounds both tradition and stardom. The Warner Brothers thesis is that, really to succeed, a man must first acknowledge his ethnic self.

While he sings "Dirty Hands," down the cellar stairs into Coffee Dan's comes Mary Dale, arriving precisely for the lines about fighting the boys which set up Robin as a cute, latter-day Cain. Mary is visibly arrested. Fanfare indicates she is a star further up the assimilation ladder than our fledgling Robin. She sees him. He sees her. Her lips twitch. Slow cuts back and forth like freeway signage: Next Turn to Love Interest. But Jolson never takes the off ramp to Mary Dale. He sticks with Vitaphone in the middle lane. His first song took less than half the required six minutes. He'll sing "Toot, Toot, Tootsie," and he will adapt it to everything converging on this moment.

"Wait a minute! Wait a minute!" Caroming like a pinball, Jolson is doubling everything. "You ain't heard nothin' yet! You ain't heard nothin' yet!" This phrase is the title of another of his songs, lyrics also by Gus Kahn (1918) three years before he wrote "Tootsie" (1921). "You wanna hear 'Toot, Toot, Tootsie?' All right, hold on! Hold on!" Here, Jolson ricochets on tiptoes, elbows out as ailerons, back to instruct his musical director, Lou Silvers, at the piano. "Lou, listen. Play 'Toot, Toot, Tootsie!' Three choruses, ya understand, and on the third chorus, I whistle. Now give it to 'em hot and heavy. Go right ahead."

In "Toot, Toot, Tootsie," Jolson plays with what Hazel Carby notices has become, by the 1920s, the "sign of the train." Writing out the basic lyrics of "Toot, Toot, Tootsie" at the decade's beginning, Gus Kahn lifted his imagery (but neither his structure nor reality) right out of the blues. By then, of course, blues practice was thoroughly mixed up with minstrelsy. Both Trixie Smith and Clara Smith, the blues singers Carby was discussing when she coined this term, traveled in the early twenties in minstrel revues. So did Ma Rainey, Bessie Smith, Ida Cox, and, indeed, most black performers. They themselves may not have blacked up (although some did) but they sang to crowds that blackface capers had animated. The minstrel show was the conduit connecting all this material, as I have been arguing throughout, just as the whistle overlaid locomotive sound to provide internal copulatives. This mixed heritage is what Jolson's improvisations on Kahn's lyrics relayed, and, in some ways maximized. "Toot, Toot, Tootsie" was a blackface song even though Jack Robin was not yet in blackface when he performed it. The Vitaphone sequence moves to "Toot, Toot, Tootsie" after the hints of blackface in "Dirty Hands, Dirty Face" for the same reason that the whole film builds toward the blacking-up scene at the dress rehearsal. Jack Robin needs the blackface mask as the agency of his compounded identity. Blackface will hold all the identities together without freezing them in a singular relationship or replacing their parts.

In Carby's "sign of the train," blues-singing women have grabbed the train's power and claimed their own capacity to ride. And much the same power is in Mary Dale, although she is aggressively bleached. As the story develops, she will mentor Jack Robin. She will take the train to New York, migrating ahead of Robin. She will set him up in the *April Follies* revue that will provide his big break, and she will make the sexual overtures in the dressing room when he is blacking up. He will follow all her leads until the last, to which he responds that he is thinking only of his performance: "There's only one thing on my mind—to make good tonight."

Multiple mergers were Jolson's single-minded achievement in "Toot, Toot, Tootsie," as in other scenes in *The Jazz Singer*. Jolson jittered the most profane and tawdry Tin Pan Alley core lyrics with generous infusions of Atlantic gestures, physical and verbal. He compounded the girl and the train in the sound of the title. "Tootsie" is a double metonymy that substitutes the toe for the woman (tootsie) and the steam whistle (toot) for the immense force that the physical engines have as they roll into the provincial stations of the movie, larger than the frames which try in vain to contain them. The title and lyrics Jack Robin sings pretend to master both the independent woman and the awesome might of the train in a single verbal stroke. This is an even more fanciful trick than the way he reconstructed father and son in the previous song. This control was part of the ongoing effort of popular music and popular culture in general, of every hue, to democratize all the emerging excitements of technology.

We can place this effort and the way it was commenting on the class and race line in America if we juxtapose "Toot, Toot, Tootsie" to another song in a similar vein recorded eleven months earlier. Jelly Roll Morton's great "Sidewalk Blues," recorded in Chicago in September 1926, begins with a minstrel whistle, wolf-whistle subfamily. Morton interrupts it by overlaying the whistle with a klaxon horn, then with dialogue between an interlocutor, playing streetcar conductor, and a pedestrian endman:

> Hey, get on outta the way. Whadya tryin' to do, knock the streetcar off the track? You so DUMB you should be the President of the Deaf and Dumb Society.
> I'm sorry, boss, but I got the sidewalk blues.[53]

The music that follows is a pedestrian's reproof to those who administer technology. Part of the pride in popular music, white and black, is to keep up with and democratize all the whistles of technology. If one cannot ride, then one can face them down, as Morton's sidewalk star does. This strutter dusts off his pride, tentatively, at first. But soon his stride is swinging a rejoinder to the conductor's abuse. His music is eloquent answer to the conductor's klaxon, the very opposite of "dumb." Every time the streetcar's rude noise intercedes, the strutter whistles his own little undertune. He picks up his swing, extending the dialogue which began the recording, but he makes the terms his own. He reclaims his right of way, building his own momentum.

At song's end, the conductor's voice is still trying to break through, still stalled, but not silenced either. He is shouting out ambiguously and perhaps converted to the strutter's swing, "Let 'em roll." The music of the margin, of the sidewalk, has talked back to his klaxon command. Anyone who listens to the records of both Jolson and Morton can hear ample evidence that more subtlety is made on the margins than in the downtown sound-stages of Hollywood minstrelsy. My argument for Jolson's, and Warner Brothers', achievement hardly claims Jolson's superiority to his sidewalk sources, of Hollywood "jazz" to Jazz. I simply want to admit that what Jolson does manage to include is plenty.

I have not yet even reached the reason for including Jolson's performance of "Toot, Toot, Tootsie" as the summary of these trains' actions. That reason is the remarkable whistle that Robin promised his pianist he would produce. Jolson had learned to whistle with his thumb and forefinger in his mouth from Al Reeves. In the 1890s, during Jolson's prentice years, Al Reeves was a white man doing blackface banjo comedy known as the most risqué on the circuit.[54] It was Reeves's whistle that Jolson deployed in "Toot, Toot, Tootsie" (and as an aural signature throughout his career). Reeves's whistle was a talismanic holdover from black performers such as Bobolink Bob more than a century before. It was transmitted in the trains' actions of blackface performance, coded within the very overlays that seemed to obliterate it.

In a parallel development, the folk whistle was still being alluded to, asserted, and revivified by such black performances as Jelly Roll Morton's "Sidewalk Blues." But Jolson stretches out for thirty-five extraordinary seconds what was generally shrunk to a talisman. Like Morton, Jolson locates the whistle in a dialogue with the dominant sound of their respective modes: Morton's klaxon, Jolson's train toot. For Morton the klaxon is rudely ugly and associated with prejudicial abuse ("You so DUMB"). For Jolson, however, the train sound is a tame toot, and associated with his lover, whom he can take or leave. Morton extended the whistle figuratively with his clarinet arrangements. Jolson whistles directly, not figuratively. That's when Jolson's delightful, stubborn atavism bubbles up like a mad Jolly-in-the-box, like nothing so much as a blackbird.

I could never get a grip on Jolson's whistle while listening to it in North America. It is no bobolink's call. There is little of the mockingbird's repertoire in it. It is zany. Its phrasings end with ebullient, surprising trills. It is competitive, successfully besting the orchestra that it fronts. One must spend a spring in the eastern Atlantic to understand that Jolson's whistle is like that of the European blackbird (*Turdus merula*) marking its territorial bounds. As soon as the days start to lengthen, continuing until the solstice, dawn and dusk, from Russia to Ireland, blackbirds startle and amaze anyone with functioning ears. The European blackbird is closely related, in everything but song and color, to the American robin (*Turdus migratorius*), after which Jack Robin has changed his name during his own migrations. The blackbird breaks into song even when humans whistle to it. Jack

Robin's whistle is an Atlantic crowing—a record of minstrel performers crossing and recrossing the Atlantic. Its frame-breaking sequence in the film—Jolson's head bobs beyond bounds several times during the whistle, and only then—visually and orally documents the European origins of so many blackface performers, including Jolson.

This whistling sequence also refers to the raw orality of low cultures across the Atlantic. Jack's fingers in his mouth and his other hand pumping across them while his head jerks in and out of the frame are a strong realization of Bakhtinian carnivalesque orality. It images appetite, gusto, bodily penetration. Clearly, it alludes to such minstrel acts as the great Billy Kersands performed when he danced with two billiard balls wholly in his mouth, or when he proudly showed W. C. Handy how he could insert an entire cup and saucer in his mouth at once.[55] These contortions are usually now described as racist grotesques, whether they are performed by African Americans, like Billy Kersands and Pa Rainey, or by Euroamericans like Jolson. But this disdain addresses only part of the picture. The oral gusto of Jolson's whistle in "Toot, Toot, Tootsie" is part of the oral excitement at large in Coffee Dan's, where eating and talking are rife. Jolson's whistle condenses and radiates an Atlantic working-class orality that is trans-ethnic. It brings people of all sorts, and all classes, together in a way that enlists earthy vitality positively.

Jakie's father hauled his rebellious son out of a Lower East Side saloon for performing a levee song, "Waiting for the *Robert E. Lee*." The boy had consequently fled the future his father imagined for him as a cantor. He became instead a blackface vaudeville performer. That way he would hobnob in a troupe with other pretend WASPs. My premise here is that the other Anglified names in the vaudeville troupe, like that of his love interest, Mary Dale, are as transparent as Jake Rabinowitz's switch to Jack Robin, and more so than Asa Albert Yoelson's compaction to Al Jolson. Mary Dale is played by an actress with the celtic stage name of May McAvoy. She is a brunette when we first meet her during "Toot, Toot, Tootsie," and in rehearsals, but blonde or cloche-covered in public and befeathered on stage. Mary Dale and Jack Robin are names that wink at authenticity like Florida radio DJs naming themselves "Sandy Beach," or critics trying to palm authority by truncating their forenames to initials. Mary Dale's WASPness is no more certifiable nor genuine, no less a performance, than blackness or Hausaness, whiteness or Englishness. The vaudeville troupe in *The Jazz Singer* is a patent mockup of American arrival.

Of the several possible reasons for the unsexed quality of Jack Robin's interaction with Mary Dale, perhaps the most useful is that they are less lovers than brother and sister in a sodality of making it. The obligatory feathers on the female dancers are expressly parallel to the requisite black-face Jolson dons to act out his acceptable identity. Both the male and female leads are willing to abstract and mask their specificities to represent larger patterns. The process is racist, misogynist, and abasing. But it also affirms the gestures it relays. It does not have one effect, but many.

When Jack Robin blacks up in the film's most sensuous scene, he puts on his wig with Mary Dale in tandem close-ups—she with her own feathered skullcap as a bright match to his curly wig. He looks on her as a new member of a desirable club who has passed in her own way before him and can grease his own admission. He looks to her for help and advice about how to jack up his career from Salt Lake City (where he says he first caught her act) to Broadway.

From the moment he first sees Mary Dale, Robin looks to her for answers literally about how to construct his identity. The version of "Toot, Toot, Tootsie" in the film is most noticeable for its long whistle. But other times Jolson performed the song he suggestively expanded the lyrics and included a telling question at the end. Instead of the declaration of "Good-bye Tootsie, goodbye," we do not need headphones to hear Jolson belt out, "What-am-I, Tootsie? What am I?"[56] Both in the film and in Jolson's career, the song constructs and questions identity. That's what makes it such a vivid case of gestural trains' actions.

The Jazz Singer asks these identity questions throughout. Its answers are not resolutions, but process. Its conclusions are political but not binary, so they irritate those who expect exchange to be complete. Jake Rabinowitz does not solve his problems by naming himself Jack Robin and having others call him that. He is still anguished and still longing even in the film's final blackface image, whitened hands outstretched to his mother and the rest of the audience: Am I not a brother, too? This image finally successfully supplies the visual agency of compaction and overlay that earlier sequences needed. Its blackface reinforces the jostling physical and oral gestures of folk and industrial practices meeting. The final gesture appeals to the mother, of course. By its copping of the abolitionist pose, however, it appeals also to his peers and pals. It compresses the various anxieties of the film in one tableau.

The last light fading on the screen as the scene and film go dark is the tight white collar round Jolson's neck. It is brilliant bricolage of success and failure, of blackness championed and choked. The image continues unto darkness the anxieties and irresolution in Jolson's fable of membership that must extend so long as heterogeneous groups and classes try to meld in the Atlantic and, now, global economies. We will continue to require the sorts of transactions which *The Jazz Singer* brazenly supplies.

3

Blame It on Cain

When the farmer Cain and his younger brother, the shepherd Abel, made offerings, God preferred Abel's meat to Cain's grain. Cain "rose up against Abel his brother and slew him." The face of the earth did not swallow Abel's blood, but voiced it to God. God marked Cain "lest any finding him should kill him." God sent Cain roaming, "a fugitive and a vagabond" (Genesis 4).

This bottomless parable humanizes external authority and naturalizes the way people propitiate authority with offerings. The biblical parable of Cain is fundamentally conservative: it proposes and nestles a story of external power punishing and controlling humans; it stabilizes ideas of preference. But this parable is also moderate: although Cain murdered his brother, God made sure Cain lived. God marked Cain against vengeance. God disciplined Cain to rootlessness. Cain's story keeps issues of fraternal strife always in mind. The parable explicitly protracts Cain's troublemaking and licenses its painful consideration.

Because Cain's actions are more severe than God's judgment, the discipline bequeaths interpretive puzzles. Blackface minstrelsy associated itself with this quandary and used it to great effect as a cover.[1] Both whites and blacks in blackface have repeatedly cited Cain as the figurehead for their own inoculative doses of this troublemaking. They have taken God's marking of Cain as the first blackface marking. They have appealed to uprooted

116

farmers, wanderers in cities, costermongers and others who looked sympathetically to Cain.

Over time, blackface actors worked out one of the parable's most productive recodings. By claiming Cain and playing out his fugitive vagabondage, white and black performers inverted the European legend's conservatism without erasing it. By playing out their nomadic license, blackface performers probed the conditions and efficiency of discipline over spectacular vengeance. They wove a radical fabric in a regressive narrative frame and within a repressive social context.

A major paradox of blackface theatre is that its unprecedented popularity was apparently so effectually contained and disdained. From the beginning, polite white observers scorned its attitudes. They permitted but disdained its plentiful texts, the pocket-sized songsters which appeared in hundreds of editions. And polite observers turned the barbs, by which minstrels pricked the power structure, into ridicule of the powerless. This deflection and apparent containment pumped blackface into a compression chamber. It tamped the jokes and conventions of minstrelsy into much tighter contrariness than they seem to have had at first. This compression, like the steam that figured in so many blackface performances, gave them a staying power that has not been obvious.

A first principle of any analysis of blackface, then, is that it has always existed in a pressure cooker of disdain. Raising cain is a response to that disdain. Raising Cain by referring often to his story is a way to license minstrel practice and to establish minstrelsy's cardinal theme as the constant struggle between resistance and its discipline. The theme particularly draws out Cain's fugitive implications, underlining their self-consciousness, just as the mask's exaggerations, the cartooned motley attire, and the dialect conventions point subversively at the serious degradation behind the humor. For instance, just after referring to Cain in one of his stump sermons, a preaching Dan Emmett asks his congregation: "Who talks soft sodder an gibs de wimmin allamagoosalem? Who makes de chickens leab darr roos, and hide under de barn when dey see dem comein? Who eats you out ob house an home an gibs you no tanks for it, but comes foolin roun yoa wife and darters when you back am turned? Now, who does all dis, an moa too? It aint de culled preacher-man, not by a gourd full! Who am it den? It am de straight harr'd fraternity."[2]

Although this performer is masked and talking in dialect, although he is a comedian dressed in rags, he could hardly speak more directly. Powerful white men rustle your grub, mess with your women, unsettle your roost, "an moa too." In short, this sermon brilliantly uses its masked mark of Cain, its dialect, and its querying logic to license biting commentary on oppression within and beyond the straight-haired fraternity. I want to argue that Emmett's "preaching" was talking truth to power, as idealized fools did in Elizabethan drama. Alas, however, the audience for Emmett's sermon was not usually powerful. Instead, it was powerless youths within the straight-haired fraternity. Their plight was imaginably black. Their coops were raided by the same raiders that sent the preacher's chickens scurrying under the barn.

At every phase of blackface performance, the Cain trope was present. This presence extended back into the black folk performances that white performers imitated. Before new-world whites donned blackface there was a long tradition of blacks imitating whites, putting them on (for various reasons, including mockery), but without a marking mask. This festive mockery and licensed foolery have been most fully documented in the South and in the Caribbean.[3] And Cain lurked there. Indeed, the presence of Cain's spirit in the material may well have been a decisive attractor for rebellious white youths. They raised Cain's contrariness to flag their own recalcitrance. They made his resistance their theme.

Mary Kingsley, the nineteenth-century English Africanist, reports an African Cain story that has just the right anomalous kernel to support its tenacious disturbance of the traditional European Cain:

> The story which you will often be told to account for the blackness and whiteness of men by Africans who have not been in direct touch with European, but who have been in touch with Mohammedan, tradition— which in the main has the same Semitic source—is that when Cain killed Abel, he was horrified at himself, and terrified of God; and so he carried the body away from beside the altar where it lay, and carried it about for years trying to hide it, but not knowing how, growing white the while with the horror and the fear; until one day he saw a crow scratching a hole in the desert sand, and it struck him that if he made a hole in the sand and put the body in, he could hide it from God, so he did; but all his children were white, and from Cain came the white races, while Abel's children are black, as all men were before the first murder.[4]

Blackface performance melded this African Cain story with the European Cain.

Early-nineteenth-century minstrels unearthed the African body that a crow's scratching steps taught the weary Cain to bury. Blackface performances paraded that body across a gamut of stages high and low, on both sides of the Atlantic. Blacking up and alluding to Cain, replaying the etiology of fraternal strife, minstrelsy constituted a secular ritual that made arbitrary preference of one group over another its central topic.[5] The crow taught the horrified Cain to bury his burden. Atlantic performers danced out that African crow's steps, too, reinforcing the connection between Cain and crow. Both Cain and the crow have African lineaments along with their others.

After his forced migration across the Atlantic, this African crow merges in the coastal southeast of the United States with the Black Vulture, a legendary figure in both African and African-American tales. Particularly along the seaboard of the southeastern states, a vernacular name for the Black Vulture has been the Jim Crow.[6]

Besides serving as a model for blackface performance, Cain's African etiology has other purposes. It inverts the prejudices of the European Cain, for instance, making whiteness the cost of the crime. In the African story Cain hides his crime from God, but not from himself, not from his conscience. The crow teaches him a dance that relieves his conscience. But he cannot remove the mark of whiteness from himself or his generations. That minstrelsy grasps this African story as its kernel is of real importance. Its folk etiology was widely enough disseminated along the southeast coast that it was overheard by early white observers.

Here is the story as it emerged in the shadow of the Blue Ridge mountains. The version below was "told between the years 1820 and 1829" by the black preacher Charles Gentry and recorded thirty years later by a white man, Harden Taliaferro, who in his youth had heard Gentry tell it:

> Beloved Breddrin, de white folks ar clean out of it when dey 'firm dat de fust man was a white man. I'm not a-gwine to hab any sich doctering. De fact is, Adam, Cain, Abel, Seth, was all ob 'um black as jet. Now you 'quire how de white man cum. Why, dis a-way. Cain he kill his brudder Abel wid a great big club—he walkin'-stick—and God he cum to Cain, and say, "Cain! where is dy brudder Abel?" Cain he pout out de lip, and say, "I don't know; what ye axin' me fur? I ain't my brudder Abel's keeper." De Lord he gits in airnest, and stomps on de ground, and say, "Cain! you Cain! whar is dy brudder Abel? I say, Cain! whar is dy brudder?" Cain he turn white as bleach cambric in de face, and de whole race ob Cain dey

bin white ebber since. De mark de Lord put on de face of Cain was a white mark. He druv him inter de land ob Nod, and all de white folks hab cum from de land ob Nod, jis' as you've hearn.[7]

This version of Cain is obviously kin to Mary Kingsley's West African variant, but it comes down to us already nested in dialect conventions imposed on black speech. Taliaferro heard the story when he was a boy living under Fisher's Peak in northwest North Carolina. He wrote it down after he had grown, moved to the city, and, I presume, heard the story again on the minstrel stage in a version like some I will recount shortly. Between hearing and recording this story, Taliaferro's memory was overlaid with dis rhythms and dat enunciations and pouting puns. His story, then, is a good instance of the work that blackface did. It absorbed and conveyed elements such as those in Taliaferro's remarkable western Atlantic folk instance of the African Cain. The persistence of this Cain shows the resilience of a people's identity bobbing up like a cork within the overwhelming wave of racism and blame. But the costs, too, are high. They include finding all this out by wading through the belittling stereotypes that threaten to drown all this material.

After the Civil War, nearly all the commercial blackface troupes consisted of black performers in blackface. Perhaps that's why this African-American folk Cain is at last *then* recorded stuttering its way to the surface in New York City:

We am all wicked sinners hea below—it's a fack, my brederen' and I tell you how it cum. You see
    Adam was de fust man,
    Ebe was de tudder,
    Cane was de wicked man
    'Kase he kill his brudder.
Adam and Eve were bofe brack men, and so was Cane and Abel. Now I s'pose it seems to strike yer understanding how de fust white man cum. Why, I let you know. Den you see when Cane kill his brudder de massa cum and say, "Cane, whar's your brudder Abel?" Cane say, "I don't know, massa." But the nigger node all de time. Massa now git mad and cum agin; speak mighty sharp dis time. "Cane, whar's your brudder Abel, yu nigger?" *Cane now git frightened and he turn white; and dis de way de fust white man cum upon dis earth!* And if it had not bee for dat dar nigger Cane we'd nebber been trubbled wid de white trash 'pon de face ob dis yer circumlar globe.

This is not an anomalous reference to Cain, but standard, if fuller than most. One of Dan Emmett's regular personae, Brudder Stebin Guess, confirmed this *African*-American Cain when he preached: "Adam was de firs man an Ebe was de tudder; dey was boaf brack men, an so was Cain an Abel."[8]

This verse as I have quoted it in these two instances appears throughout the songsters of the nineteenth century. Here is another reading of Cain by Emmett's Brother Stebin, discussing "In Adams Fall, We Built 'tone Wall; But Ebber Since We Built 'tone Fence." Adam and Ebe have been driven out of Eden, Stebin announces, and "hab to dig dar own tayters by de sweat ob dar brow": "in de short ob de long, dey 'footed it' to de lann ob Cainaan whar dey got Cain, but he was a bad chile, and he mudder wallop him wid a cane stoalk ebry day: an he was de fusst niggar dat got cane bottomed, he warr nuttin but a half priced niggar, and when he fadder tole him *'go hoe in de garden'* he sass back an say: *'nix a weedin,'*—he den run off wid a sarkus." How often Emmett was caned as a boy we will never know, but after the U.S. Army discharged him for enlisting under age, Emmett did run off with a series of circuses. Emmett told his own story through Cain's.[9]

So it was that blackface performance transmitted these African Cains overlaid onto the European Cain. When American fiction started nabbing imagery and strategies from minstrelsy, beginning no later than the 1850s, the samplings display widely diverging estimates of Cain's tractability. Harriet Beecher Stowe cross-dresses Cain as the initially recalcitrant Topsy. Topsy's mistress describes her as " 'raising Cain' generally." One of the dreamiest conclusions of this novel, however, is that Topsy might be redeemed by little Eva's loving touch and Ophelia's concern. Stowe's assessment, therefore, is that Cain's power can be house-broken. At the other end of the spectrum, Herman Melville's estimation of Cain's recalcitrance starts high and climbs still higher between *Moby-Dick* and *The Confidence Man*. When a storm breaks out on the *Pequod* in the dramatized "Midnight, Forecastle" chapter of *Moby-Dick*, the men calling Pip to play his tambourine for their breakdowns, a Spanish sailor takes umbrage at Daggoo's black pride and snarls, "He wants to bully, ah!—the old grudge makes me touchy." This old grudge is the fraternal strife between Cain and Abel. The other sailors form a ring around this row between the Spaniard and Daggoo. The Old Manx Sailor speaks: "Ready formed. There! the ringed horizon. In that ring Cain struck Abel."[10]

The ring is the horizon: within it this dance and this strife are naturalized.

This ring is also the semicircle that the minstrel show re-created, and that the audience completed as they all contemplated Cain: within *this* ring such strife is constructed. Melville's Cain, both natural and staged, neither disappears nor diminishes during the novel. But he is not yet central, either. No material entity in *Moby-Dick,* not Ahab, not the whale or the *Pequod,* is central alone; everything is centrifugal except the teller's struggle to knead it all together.

By mid-decade, in "Benito Cereno," as I discussed in Chapter 2, Melville has centered the issues of fraternal strife that minstrelsy had been keeping open. He is also, as in the shaving scene and the generally ciphered action, sharing strategies and codes with minstrel performances. By the time Melville publishes *The Confidence Man,* in 1857, his central character has become an outright minstrel Cain, openly daring to fulfill such remarks as the despised minstrel might only hint. Melville's forthright declarations were one part courage and another part formal momentum.[11] Having already lost his audience in the centrifugal turmoil of *Moby-Dick,* Melville was now free to develop the signs which the still-popular minstrel show had to keep under wraps. The many versions of the confidence man within that novel all deal in masked doubleness, enact tumbling inversions in their every conversation, wear elaborate motley minstrel costumes. This shape-shifting main character, appearing sometimes as black (Black Guinea), other times in varying white hues, is, like Stowe's Topsy, directly associated with Cain. As in so many minstrel skits, type confronts type. In mid-novel, a coon-skinned frontiersman, a solitary man named Pitch, asks the Cosmopolitan confidence man, wearing an "Indian belt" and smoking a calumet pipe, whether he is imitating an "African pantomime." Retorts tumble over ripostes, until Pitch is asking, "How came your fellow-creature, Cain, after the first murder, to go and build the first city? And why is it that the modern Cain dreads nothing so much as solitary confinement?"[12] These remarks rouse Melville's awareness of the Cain that minstrelsy transmitted—a Cain disciplined to inoculate the world with trouble. Cain was the Cosmopolitan's, the trickster figure's, and the minstrel audience's "fellow-creature." That audience went to the theatre, Melville knew, as he must have hoped his own smaller public would come to his novel, to see Cain raised. Cain was authority's antibody.

The professional career of the black blues singer Ida Cox began as Topsy in a blackface show in 1903, matured in the shadow of Ma Rainey and Bessie Smith, and reached one of its peaks when she organized and headlined a minstrel tour in 1929 called "Raisin' Cain."[13] I adapt this book's title from her revue. In my way, too, I aim to adapt her spirit of having fun while acknowledging the contaminated cross purposes of the lore cycle that is our mutual problem.

Through the devolutions of minstrelsy, medicine shows, and Hollywood's blackface movies during Ida Cox's time, and after, Cain continued to affect such modernist meldings of African-American culture as Jean Toomer's *Cane* (1923) and Zora Neale Hurston's folktales of the black foreman John (in *Mules and Men*, 1935), and continued even into such contemporary songs as Elvis Costello's early "Blame It on Cain" (1977). In Wesley Brown's remarkable 1994 novel, *Darktown Strutters*—which reprises the whole palimpsested history of minstrelsy's evermore bitter inversions—black Jim Crow kills his white owner with the master's own "raised cane."[14]

These allusions spread underground like rhizomes. They raised and lowered Cain for reasons we shall want to distinguish, although certainly no one can keep them discrete. These Cains crossed and recrossed the fictional borders of race at least as relentlessly as they pretended or intended to police those borders. They gouged out racial border lines even as they sapped them. They produced borders as sieves. Their effects were as tangled as the publics they expressed.

> Dey hab had no blows yet,
> And I hope dey nebber will,
> For its berry cruel in bredren,
> One anoders blood to spill.
> —T. D. Rice, "The Original Jim Crow"

Minstrelsy's accumulated references to Cain began perhaps with these lines in the earliest Jim Crow lyrics. Minstrels claimed Cain, not Othello, as the performer who made "the *first black face turn*."[15] To claim Cain as one's earliest ancestor is to claim a performative pretext rather than a purported race as one's first resource. It is to claim a legend more than a genre. Minstrels certainly performed variants on *Othello*—Maurice Dowling, T. D. Rice, Charles White, and many others did an *Otello* burlesque in blackface. Each time they blacked up, however, the mask itself made broad reference to the mark of Cain. The performers thus proposed, and I am trying to lift back to the surface, a genealogy much more troubling than has usually been acknowledged for popular culture.

Who was this Cain whom minstrels mustered as their founder?

Cain was the first angry young man. As the earliest agent to take significant action after the banishment from Eden, Cain became talismanic to those young workers suddenly driven from the country to cities to inaugurate the industrial era.

Cain was the first person born of human sexuality. In his own throes of passion, Cain was first in the line of men who have killed their brothers. Cain pioneered fraternal strife and its consequences.

Cain was a farmer who founded cities. Cain nurtured roots, but he was uprooted. Cain's pain, and the conflict of his banishment and license, were the first fugitive truths. His licensed vagabondage, and the paradox by which he took it on, are keys to understanding Cain the way blackface performers and their early audiences did. Their Cain founded the very cities to whose complexity these youths were contributing. Like them, Cain was transient not sedentary within the city. Like theirs, Cain's energy was more than unsettled. It was unseatable.

I pause in this string of dire complaints to notice that Cain comes on the minstrel stage clothed in humor. A good reason to study cultural transmission through blackface performance is just this mixture of modes. The small fraction of (popular) culture with staying power pumps up into a cycle with momentum by way of a strong web of internal tensions. Its various parts pull in different directions—toward violent anger, toward farce, toward delicate myth, against pretentious eloquence. Gradually a web of internal tensions evolves that can absorb and counterbalance these pressures. Then it can roll on its own. The competing elements of humor and dire complaint moderate each other's edge. Consequently, they both sneak in more deeply past the audience's defenses. Early blackface actors invoke fratricide but sidestep the audience's repulsion by framing it as a joke old as Genesis.

Cain had been rooted. After he slew Abel, Cain was routed into cities. The city is the place into which strangers come to exchange material goods and transfer immaterial values. Founding cities, working in cities, Cain embodied the micromotions, the work, of these changes. Cain's story trades roots for routes. It exemplifies the plentiful petty swaps of journeymen and truck farmers working the markets at urban margins. By God cut off from his parents, Adam and Eve, whom the Genesis Cain never mentions; by his own hand cut off from Abel, who obsesses him; focusing intensely on the arbitrary but moderate discipline of absolute authority—Cain's relationship to power and authority is talismanic for the conditions of wage laborers in nineteenth-century Atlantic cities.

There is in Cain's story, then, the primary doubleness that his infamous act meant to annihilate. In slaying Abel, Cain struck a reflex blow against preferential differentiation. He struck against the shadow of doubling. This not-quite-sameness is what excluded groups often fixate on; they magnify the otherness of competing marginal groups in order to make the characteristics of their own group seem more includable. In striking against this principle, however, Cain did not resolve the issues. Rather, he became their sign. He wanders forever betokening doubleness: the cursed man who is protected; the brother-killer who evokes brotherhood; a once-rooted man of agriculture now hoboing through cities; a divided self whose experience broadcasts the need for brotherly love.

Cain became the figure of inevitable inversion. He is a figure oscillating between contraries. In this resolute oscillation, the actions of blackface dance along the thresholds of several movements that emerge along with it. Blackface overlaps but does not relax into the boundaries of romanticism, Chartism, socialism, nationalism, abolitionism, and racial essentialism. The linkage of Cain and blackface, in fact, stubbornly bedevils these contemporary concepts. I can illustrate Cain's disturbances if I compare early blackface performances with a corollary strain in Romanticism.

In the period of minstrelsy's gestation, a main location of romantic attention to Cain was in Lord Byron's updating of Medieval mystery plays as *Cain: A Mystery* (1821). "One of the most stunning cultural facts of the modern world," Ricardo Quinones argues, is that in the early nineteenth century Abel becomes conventionalized and Cain daring: "It has the effect of removing a stable moral center and guide from the endeavors of the theme . . . Through [Cain's] thoughts and responses, the author will struggle to assert . . . a new moral and ethical code."[16] But since the blackface Cain melded into the African Cain and identified with the biblical Cain, rather than holding him in disdain, the minstrels' Cain is mostly outside the received traditions Byron worked. The blackface Cain moves parallel to them, sometimes fudging their borders. Byron devised sympathy for a proud Cain, but minstrels empathized with a furtive figure. No, the popular blackface performers did not follow Byron. Instead, their blackface Cain was buttressed by a cogent, bastard reading of the Genesis passages. I can show this blackface Cain diverging from the Romantic Cain by contrasting the way the two traditions received their distinctive mark.

Byron's Cain has a noble self-sufficiency that is quite different from the more politically alarmed and cynical Cain who figures blackface. When the Angel moves to mark Cain in Byron's play, the murderer dismissively waves him off, wondering "who are they / Shall slay me?" Byron's Angel insists that marking Cain is necessary to provide "Exemption from such deeds as thou hast done." Rather than be disciplined, Byron's Romantic Cain cries out, still, "No, let me die!" But there is no escaping the Angel's discipline, to which Cain responds: "It burns / My brow, but nought to that which is within it. / Is there more? let me meet it as I may."[17]

The blackface Cain contrasts with this brazen arrogance of the Romantic Cain. In the blackface reading it is the minstrel's Cain, himself, who solicits the mark ("it shall come to pass that everyone that findeth me shall slay me"). He will need all the help he can get, Cain complains. Following the Bible in this interpretation, Cain is frankly afraid, not at all brazen. He will need God's license if he is to wander, bearing witness to the crime against brotherhood.

The mask is the sign of discipline that licenses scandalous actions in blackface performance. In the vernacular variants of the legend, Cain solicited his protective seal and negotiated with authority for his wandering life. He accepted his punishment, said the blackface performer and historian Edward Le Roy Rice in 1911: "Cain was punished, as he should have been," and "his complexion was changed from Caucasian to Ethiopian."[18] Here, Edward Rice's Cain is no longer the African Cain who appeared in Dan Emmett's sketches. Sixty years later, Edward Rice's Cain has reverted to the European Cain. But the primary point about Rice's remark is that he emphasized a Cain who adapted a performance space within punishment. All the Cains evoked in blackface wheel about in a nightmare space of punishment *and* protection. Cain is the first oscillator turning among these poles: uncertain of race, uncertain of class, uncertain of approval, never sure if his protracted life is not a punishment.

Practicing minstrels relied on the detail of a self-solicited seal because they themselves pressed to tell dangerous stories. The intended rupture of their culture's basic assumptions—the Cain they hoped to raise—needed unusual licensing tropes. The tar they smeared on their faces, like God marking Cain, was one assertion of their license. Others were the motley extremes of dandy and fieldhand, and the abstracted argot they constructed—clear stage conventions all. Minstrels were quite aware they were defining liminal territory for the enacting of cultural obsessions. They licensed themselves to inoculate their publics. Thus to our puns on a rooted/ routed Cain we add a further dimension: the canny evocation of Cain's seal enabled performers to rout public complacencies.

Invoking Cain raises Cain. The use of Cain's story to license one's performance is itself further marking. Retailing its retelling, making Cain's mask a masque, intensifies cultural awareness to the order of a grand wink. This pattern of invoking Cain's rich story amounts to a cultural convention performed within a commercial pattern. Performers and audiences agreed to use Cain to signal their mutual awareness of an aura of larger, charmed meaning to their participation.

Invoking Cain became a gateway to a fable of identity shared among a community that was working the border between folk and popular lores. You were on one side or the other of the border. Some people got it. Some people just didn't get it. But some people were in process; they were *getting it*; the fables of their emerging community were dawning on them. Much of the positive charge of existing in this zone must have come, as it still does, from playing with this dawning. It was a way of creating knowing identity under the nose of those who would dampen that knowledge, control it, and deny its independence.

In this reading, the vernacular performers who were transmuting folk gestures into a popular culture fit for its era were anticipating by a century and a half the sorts of social analysis that now seem persuasive to many of the fields contributing to cultural studies. In their blackface masking, early minstrel performers were showing to themselves and to their heterogeneous audiences the processes of social control that were gripping them. They were making dramatic the corporeal inscriptions, the discipline and surveillance, the hegemony and habitus which Antonio Gramsci, Michel Foucault, and Pierre Bourdieu have since made proverbial. In the space of the songs and plays that raised Cain, the background assumptions and codes became apparent and plastic. In the space of the performances that raised Cain, players and publics found room to manipulate their basic assumptions.

Minstrels performed this service quite in the teeth of the forces they dramatized, however, and without the hundred and fifty years of hindsight backing up our more current and more celebrated theorists. To the blackface performers and their audience, the blanket of control did not yet seem so total as our recent theorists have claimed it began to be during the early nineteenth century. To the performers of the 1830s and 1840s social control was serious, but so were their tides of wayward motion, their hardy manner of squeezing past suppression. In their time, what the minstrels acted out was discipline, yes, but also its undercutting. Cain's blackface drama was a liminal process that displayed both community authority and a strong argument with that authority. Cain negotiated a nomadic space for himself in which he reminded audiences of strife. Within authority's domain he kept space for himself, so he might enact authority's antibody.

Speaking generally, not about Cain and in a quite different vein, Michel Foucault has subsequently analyzed this process as "discipline." He shows a diverse meting of control in the seventeenth and eighteenth centuries. From centered examples of punishment, classically on the scaffold and after the fact of a crime, society moved to small and spread-out doses of containment, latched daily, before the transgression might occur. This wider latching of the public scene into the private space was a necessary accompaniment, Foucault has argued, to the political and economic changes which built massive cities and industrialism. Rather than singling out individual transgressors after they had crossed authority, discipline and its partner practice, surveillance, began trying to anticipate the threat of mixed and moving populations. The aim was continually to observe them, segment them, and clamp them down before they could rise out of control. Anticipatory discipline preempted transgression before it might be *thought*. Foucault's principles of discipline and surveillance extend and fill in Antonio Gramsci's concept of hegemony, the capacity of one group to impose its will on other groups in such a way that the other groups think that will is their own.

Hegemony, discipline, surveillance: this externally imposed trinity is increasingly replacing any presumed internal factors in recent explanations of what glues modern cultures together. To those who would govern them, as well as to those resisters who encourage people to follow their separate ways, it is clear that modern cultures are composed of unwieldy, ill-fitting, and irascibly antagonistic fragments. Moreover, these parts are increasingly finding media to broadcast them and their values. Anyone who stands on the curb along Shaftsbury Avenue on a Saturday night or walks Times Square in the dark must wonder why the bricks have remained rectilinear. How did the social fabric find its warp and woof in any first place? No society could conceivably afford to police its riffraff into orderly crowd movements if the riffraff chose not to cooperate. How is it people do not rampage amok? Postwar social theory increasingly answers such musings by arguing that crowds are composed of isolated, atomized persons. Each atom is violated by externally imposed principles that support control rather than individual or small-group agency. This violation is a *discipline,* inscribed on minds. It replaced the older socialization to familial or tribal or village values that Clifford Geertz has given the happy name of "local knowledge." And it replaced the spectacular *punishment,* by which monarchic power broke and scarred bodies singled out for their crimes. Public lessons at the scaffold were no longer necessary if institutions could separate, survey, and thereby inculcate order.

Despite the cartoon simplicity of the transformation, especially when one shortens its description into a few paragraphs as I have here, for the sake of the discussion let's accept the movement from spectacular punishment to discipline as one that is generally agreed to be important. Let's suspend discomfort at the reduction of complex cultural conditions into a binary rupture. Let's forgive Foucault his generalization of a modern principle from his tiny sample of mostly French examples. Let's defer recognition that discipline was practiced earlier than he says and that gross state punishment has survived Foucault's dividing line. Those are all real issues, but they do not, in my view, blunt his fundamental point—that the weight shifted from punishment to discipline when people moved toward apparent democracies in megapolitan cities. Furthermore, it is instructive to realize that although the Cain story had been lying fallow as an example of a disciplinary judgment that preceded spectacular punishment, its dramatic potential was not invoked until after the Atlantic world flowed over Foucault's watershed.

This general move in disciplinary power activated the distinctive blackface interpretation of the Cain story. When blackface actors referred to Cain and embodied his roaming, they were exploring their disciplinary confinements. The best of them were slipping through the bars of their cages, and rattling them as they passed.

I want to pose questions implicit in the idea of raising Cain that naggingly remain beneath, and stay after, what Foucault specifies as the "power of normalization" and disciplinary "formation of knowledge in modern society."[19] In noticing that blackface actors both relay and resist discipline, I am asking: What raises Cain and how does it do so? What *organizes* this effervescent routing of disciplinary order? Why is *raising* an ongoing action?

In framing such questions I do not dwell on the anarchic, addictive escapes into ecstasy continually possible—even arguably encouraged—in welfare states. I want to ask, instead: What keeps modern society from separating into two unfocused camps, one of panoptic order, the other of incandescent burnout?

The short answer is that there must be a principle of proportion that makes each local culture find its own distinctive balance, precariously, on a characteristic threshold among the pressures pulling it apart. This always contested zone makes each culture distinctive in its complex blend of discipline and innovation maintained over time. The long answer is that this proportion is created and sustained in a culture's lore cycle.

Peter Linebaugh's study of relations between crime and capitalism in the eighteenth century, *The London Hanged,* pointed the way to this question. He wrote that the era may have been "an age of 'the great confinement' " but, if so, its "counterpoint of excarceration was played out in escapes, flights, desertions, migrations, and refusals."[20] I am arguing that the nineteenth-century blackface Cain became a totem for this "counterpoint of excarceration." Cain is a figure whom nineteenth-century actors of mobility invoke as someone who preceded spectacular punishment and whose spirit continues to inspire resistant action in an increasingly carceral society.

> . . . it remains the responsibility of each reader always to strive for an inside perspective, whatever the source.
>
> —Richard Price, *Maroon Societies*

> Not quite the Same, not quite the Other, she stands in that undetermined threshold place where she constantly drifts in and out. Undercutting the inside/outside opposition, her intervention is necessarily that of both a deceptive insider and deceptive outsider. She is this Inappropriate Other/Same who moves about with always at least two/four gestures: that of affirming "I am like you" while persisting in her difference; and that of reminding "I am different" while unsettling every definition of otherness arrived at.
>
> —Trinh T. Minh-ha, *When the Moon Waxes Red*

Trinh Minh-ha writes these days from the angles of performer and informant, object and subject, Vietnamese inhabiting the United States, and more. Crossing her third and first persons, Trinh insists on the multiplicity of her selves in an "undetermined threshold place."[21] I believe her positions are not so much unusual as expressed extremely. She writes as if she is coming from further outside and drifting further inside the sameness of her audience than other writers admit. And she pursues the implications of these interchanges with particular persistence. But the precondition of her connection with her publics is that we have also been to those nexuses. She makes audiences notice their multiple affiliations.

The "undetermined threshold place" that Trinh Minh-ha describes is in fact the place of art high and low since modernity began acknowledging its ethnic complexities. It is not an accident that this problematic place, which high art has more repressed than not, is also more or less the urban transference spot that blackface performance pushed into view. It had early instances at Catherine Market in 1820, in the 1830s when Jim Crow started jumping in the United States and when the 1832 reform bill in England pushed its initial wedge between property-owning and laboring classes. The scandal of modernity, still not widely acknowledged through the 1950s, perhaps a more conscious problem today, is the very problem of thresholds where multiple selves intersect. That threshold, that problem, is what blackface took as its topic.

It was a scandal because people felt the need to find, impose, and police a unitary self, one self more real or authentic than the others. In such a grab-bag, of course, what achieved definition as real and authentic was what was most powerful, or served powerful interests. Some parts of one's self might be defined as more useful—say one's property-owning self, or one's whiteness. It would apparently make sense to focus one's identity there, and the now conventional take on blackface performance is that it helped white working Americans distinguish themselves from their threatening connections to a Black Other. But the more these performers and their publics tried to peel away and resolve conflicting tensions to speak a commanding view, the more their work built up its contradictions and slipperiness.

One sees a shadow of that need for a unitary self even in the remark by Richard Price quoted above, from his important study of Maroon resistance and otherness within dominating American societies.[22] He warns that it is the obligation of the researcher (from a dominating culture) to strive for an inside view of the (subordinated) culture. But what is inside? What is outside? To raise Cain as the blackface stage busily did is to pose this problem. To raise Cain is to lever into view and play with that "undetermined threshold place" where inside and outside overlap, where combinatory gestures, patches, and puns teem together.

Blackface performance is a paradigmatic instance of the disdained and fugitive figure popping up on the dominating culture's center stage. It is a theatre of interpenetration, sponsored by the dominating culture, in which both the fugitive and the dominant culture agree to understand the motley figure is impossible to seat or resolve. Blackface fascination shows a miscegenated culture becoming aware of itself. It makes theatre out of mingling selves trying to understand their inversions.

Minstrelsy acted out this overlap a century and a half before any theory mavens acknowledged identity imbrications. Minstrels in rags danced out these principles in realms disdained even then as culture too popular, too vulgar, for polite people to pay it mind. One senses just how taboo the minstrel show was by recalling that one of the most radically freethinking American women of the nineteenth century, Margaret Fuller, who forthrightly had a child out of wedlock, declared that she had never gone to a minstrel show, but fondly cited her knowledge of Jim Crow from watching it performed in the street.[23]

The Cain theme in blackface performance goes hand in hand with the theme of excarceration. More generally, Cain affiliates with a theme of breaking bondage. Despite a common misunderstanding, the blackface characters of the minstrel stage were not plantation *slaves*. Some of them had supposedly been slaves, but their condition on stage was invariably free. This cannot be overstressed: these stage characters were free. Sometimes their freedom was of the runaway variety, a condition still perilous and reversible, and more so after the Fugitive Slave Act of 1850. Dan Emmett:

> I'll sail de world clar roun an roun,
> All by de railroad under groun.

Until the Fugitive Slave Act made the runaway slave contraband even in the free states, minstrels routinely explained their presence in a feckless troupe as "Joe ob Tennessee" sang in Christy's Minstrels:

> My massa one day try to whip
> Dis nigger, who gib him de slip . . .
> I den made up my mind to go,
> Trough all de States my jenus show
> To sing and dance the banjo glee
> Dat's made by Joe ob Tennessee.

This is one sort of standard lyric for the early period of minstrelsy. It exposed plantation cruelty and assumed that flight is a fact to declare outright.

After even such liberal jurists as Lemuel Shaw, in Massachusetts, started returning runaways southward, however, minstrels had to find further authorization than their feet for their represented freedom.[24]

Stephen Foster and many others solved this problem quite explicitly by having the blackface singers of their songs declare:

> Old Massa sent me roaming . . .
> I's going to roam the wide world
> In lands I've never hoed.[25]

The nonsense of this excuse is too patent to rouse anger. It is simply a ruse to be able to continue the convention that these "black" performers could freely roam from town to town without some sheriff serving papers on them and returning them to the plantation.

Sometimes their freedom was a ground for boisterous contest, much in the vein of the ring-tail'd roarers and flatboat men, whose lore they were absorbing and supplanting. Sometimes they were assigned freedom, and pushed out into it by Ol' Missus, as if into a swamp. Their freedom, like their journey through it, was neither singular nor formulaic. Their differing pictures of vagabondage corroborate the paradoxes in the Cain they evoke. And vice versa: the paradoxes of Cain corroborate the complicated costs of their own freedom.

The varying blackface delineations of roaming and breaking bonds also confirm the conditions of the traveling players who impersonate them. Cain and the runaway slave become favorite themes of the nineteenth-century traveling player in Atlantic communities not only because their figures dance out the experience of Atlantic audiences but also because these figures stand exactly for the conditions of the players themselves. The disdained position of the player, relative to the constraining propriety of pulpit and lectern, established a special case analogous to Cain.

Whether or not they represented blacks, actors were themselves marginal and partially educated. They were spoken against in many churches and classrooms. In England and especially in the States, most players traveled a circuit that extended from the Atlantic to all the frontiers. It could appear that they were disciplined to vagabondage, traveling from house to house to stage their plays. They weren't called "Strolling Players" for nothing. They were nomads telling anti-sedentary stories to audiences who were also quite mobile, but probably less so than the peripatetic players. Like Cain, the players were an extreme version of their audiences. This wandering instability takes us to the formal instability of minstrelsy itself.

There was a plausible logic in the unusual popularity of the minstrel stage. I do not believe that the most popular form of entertainment in the nineteenth century achieved its initial success primarily by displaying the superiority of young white men in their several cultures. Rather, I believe minstrelsy amounted to a secular ritual that proved useful to its practitioners in explaining themselves to themselves.

If one is willing to say, first, that all these people were chiefly fomenting racism and, second, that the form they favored made codes of its simplicity, then the extant commentary on the form of minstrelsy is satisfactory. But if one is convinced, as I am, that publics attend to forms over a long time for more satisfyingly unschematic reasons, then there is more complexity in blackface minstrelsy than its commentators have allowed it.

The basic problem with which current commentators must contend is that with the exception of Constance Rourke, whose account remains refreshing despite the way she sidesteps the issue of racism, the tradition of minstrel criticism has reduced a vastly popular and multiply meaningful form to one-dimensional simplicity. In the terms that Clifford Geertz borrowed from Gilbert Ryle, our task is to restore what has come down the years to us as a twitch to the meaningful wink it had built up by 1832 (when T. D. Rice brought it all back home to New York City), 1843 (when Emmett's group and the Christys consolidated the minstrel show), and 1848 (when Chanfrau reincorporated dancing for eels). The main thing to recover is the minstrels', and their generating audiences', own perspective. As I have considered these problems, I have repeatedly turned for inspiration to the cartoon shown in Figure 3.1.

This is a contemporaneous cartoon of a rudimentary show in a distinctly pre-prime-time variant. The low ceiling and narrow hall illustrate the constrained position of this audience. Their view is valuable because it contradicts so much of the written commentary. This torn and crumbling cartoon pictures the show from the audience's own perspective—not that of journalists. We see the boys clearly compressed and vulnerable, young and on their own, pumping up their own fantasies within lowering space. As opposed to the middle-class articles in *Putnam's* and the *Atlantic Monthly*, it shows minstrelsy's gestating public trying to understand itself in its own terms rather than in the terms which the enormous forces of church, state, and industry were attempting to impose.

3.1   Newspaper cartoon of boys at a cellar minstrel performance

Since we cannot see through their eyes, I want to look along the angle of these boys, over their shoulders, at what it is *in blackface* that provokes and sustains conflictual interpretations. The form itself builds in disagreement. To North America's earliest urban youth culture, burnt cork provided protective camouflage. It ensured they would be two-faced. With their masks they could hide in plain view what was politically aggressive toward authority. They could fob off on "Ethiopian" agents their own anger and need to break out of their assigned lot. With their masks, minstrels signaled to congenial publics their mutual identification with valuable attributes perceived to be black. Conversely, when performing before hostile publics, the masked minstrels could disavow their barbs by appearing to belittle their subject. Curiously, this diagnostic attribute of the minstrel mask as doubling cover is what minstrel theory has not faced. The mask is not simply an "eye-catching novelty," in Robert Toll's phrase, but the axle around which the multiplicity in minstrelsy turns.[26] And turns.

> "No confidence in dis poor ole darkie, den?" . . .
> "Fact is, I begin to feel a little qualmish about the darkie, myself. Something queer about this darkie, depend upon it."
>
> —Herman Melville, *The Confidence Man*

Wittgenstein's doodle of the duck-rabbit conundrum toward the end of his *Philosophical Investigations* (Figure 3.2) shows the abstracted form of many

3.2   Duck Rabbit, as Wittgenstein illustrated *Philosophical Investigations*

issues that are much more emotionally charged in the interpretation of race and gender masquerade. Wittgenstein's duck-rabbit is like a white performer in blackface: Is he white, is he black? Is he yaller? Is it a duck, is it a rabbit? Is it a duckrab? Something is queer about this duck-rabbit, depend upon it. Although it is like the blackface performer, the doodle allows us to separate common issues from the emotional and political commitments that have overwhelmed Jim Crow.[27]

Once you get the hang of it, you can see that the doodle has both a duck and a rabbit aspect. Now that you see them both, when I ask what you see, you say, "I'm seeing both a duck and a rabbit." By which you might mean, "Now I'm seeing it as a duck; now as a rabbit." Or, you might mean, as I do when I really concentrate, "Now they are oscillating so that I see them both, abstractly together." Thus begins the vertigo that Melville's character feels when he looks at the shape-changing Black Guinea in *The Confidence Man*. In the duck-rabbit you come to see the duck and the rabbit as aspects of the same shared totem. What's more, once you see them as combined, it seems wrong to say, "I'm noticing the duck"—because you know the rabbit aspect is lurking there, coded, awaiting notice. You have lost confidence in the singularity of the image. The way I read minstrelsy and Melville, both are about these multiple affiliations.

These notions of aspect-dawning and aspect-lurking are the means of aesthetic reception, high and low. Aspect-dawning is the leading edge of complexity. Aspect-dawning comes at the point before analysis, before receivers have translated thrilling perception into extended meaning. Sensing that the duck is also a rabbit, and vice versa, is an aspect-dawning moment.

Aspect-lurking is the truck of meaning. It carries the meaning even when no one perceives it, even where no one wants it. Aspect-lurking ensures that meaning becomes part of gestures that performers learn by rote, even if they do not develop the meaning. Thus even when the duck-rabbit is only seen as a duck, the rabbit remains in it, lurking, trucked along with the duck. It can be unpacked by some other viewer on whom the rabbit's aspect will dawn. Its aspect can be forced, as a conjurer forces a card or a gardener a blossom, should a performer want to bring it out, or a receiver find it. Otherwise, it lurks.

Wittgenstein says one aspect dawns from the other. Yes, it does seem that way. In a grotesquerie hardly foreign to minstrelsy, the rabbit emerges from the duck, and, vice versa, the duck dawns from the rabbit. But the dawning of aspects is neither inherent to nor controlled by the image. The duck-rabbit doodle itself enables but does not enforce our seeing its several aspects. Instead, the wider context, which includes but is larger than the image, induces and inhibits the way we see dawning aspects.

If I show you the duck-rabbit in a context of other doodles that you see as ducks, you are much less likely to see the rabbit aspect. Or, if you build up an associative history of seeing the duck-rabbit as a duck, it then becomes increasingly more difficult for the rabbit's presence to dawn on you. But the rabbit remains packed in the codes, trucked along, awaiting notice. A culturally inhibited aspect, once it is performed and coded, can lurk a long time even though perceivers of the image may be blind to it. When that blindness is relieved, congenial publics and performers can find it and force it out much later. In extreme versions of this flipflop, one orthodoxy effaces another: a duck-rabbit that was seen as a duck can become a duck-rabbit that is seen as a rabbit. The hard part is to see the oscillating inversions, rabbit to duck and back, duck to rabbit. Most difficult is keeping track of all the presences in their moving ratios through time.

As a cultural historian, I want to map the dawning of aspects—in this case, within blackface images. But this is not the way casual inhabitants of a culture experience images. They grow accustomed to seeing such loaded images in one way or another. When repressed or disdained aspects start to peek through, when they are forced by performers or cultural conflicts, they are often described as grotesque. The frequent use of "grotesque" to describe first black folk performance, then white and black actors in blackface, is significant. The commonplace that black and blackface performance is grotesque unconsciously locates it in the term's etymological domain. "Grotesque" literally refers to the underground art and gestures developed in the grottoes below Imperial Rome. These grottoes were early petri dishes in which transgressive culture might gestate. Resistant subcultures are grotesque virtually by definition.

Handing out pieces of scarlet ribbon to her husband's slaves on his early-nineteenth-century coastal Georgia plantation, the afternoon before the ball where she first saw "Jim Crow—the veritable James" danced out in all its "ineffable black conception," Fanny Kemble gave us one of the most telling phrases for sympathetic white reception of plantation dance. She called it "the grotesque mask which life wears on one of its mysterious faces." And she recognized her connection to this mysterious, partial face: "a savage propensity for that same color in all its modifications being a tendency of my own." She was following in the footsteps of Nicholas Cresswell, who had described southern slave dancing as "grotesque" when he saw it half a century before, in 1774. Pauline Hopkins had her polite black characters use the same terminology for uninhibited members of their set who start "cutting grotesque juba figures" at a party in her novel *Contending Forces* (1900). Sampson Raphaelson had first been attracted to Al Jolson in a minstrel take-off of Robinson Crusoe, when the actor was playing "This grotesque figure in blackface." And the broadest collection of plays from the minstrel stage is entitled *This Grotesque Essence.*[28]

Using "grotesque" in this way may not suggest disapproval or disgust at the gestures of black folk performance cycling through commercial phases. Maybe it points to a perceived misshapenness when the suppressed double rises within the one. These counter-aspects seem grotesque when one sees them dawning from customary features.

To call this material grotesque in this way is to relate it to the thematic content of the Cain story. There is a lot in Mikhail Bakhtin's analysis of carnival that is too easily applied to minstrel performance, but he put this correctly: "The mask is related to transition, metamorphoses, the violation of natural boundaries, to mockery and familiar nicknames . . . It reveals the essence of the grotesque."[29] Cain's murderous action is not alone what makes people watch him. Also important is the way he carries his double within him, and the way Abel dawns on us as we see Cain. The mask reinforces this effect.

On one hand, the minstrel mask was like the duck-rabbit. It enabled viewers to see and performers to show in one figure the connections between working whites and disdained blacks. It compacted together the showing and seeing of sameness along with difference. They appeared to dawn from and on each other. That is to say, the blackface mask allowed young white callows to see themselves in the hounded image of the free/escaped black continually on the lam. The blackface performer enacted an identification of whites with blacks. But the performance also allowed working youths, using that same metaphor, simultaneously to engage and to understand the belittling of blacks. Performers could represent, and publics understand, blacks as childlike or stupid. And they might construct their own whiteness as the polar opposite of what they were rehearsing as blackness. Thus, while the minstrel mask encouraged identification, it also encouraged racialist differentiation. While both could go on simultaneously, they might also go on separately, as in these instances when publics saw only one of the mask's aspects.[30]

On the other hand, the minstrel mask was always more complex than the duck-rabbit, which, in the spirit of Wittgenstein, I pursue merely as a laboratory example, a clean and well-lighted doodle. One of the ways the blackface mask was more complex than any lab experiment was that it existed in time; it pulled a genealogical freight train behind it. This past inhered in the images of the present even if they were not always seen there, and they became part of the future.

Before U.S. whites started inscribing, painting, and staging black talk, song, and dance at the end of the eighteenth century, slaves had long been performing public put-ons of whites. The cakewalk is probably the most familiar example. The John Canoe revelries of Jamaica and coastal North Carolina are a second example. A third is the needling songs that punctuated cornhuskings. Together, these and their sibling gestures amount to a highly formal and elaborately conventional form of resistance. William Piersen richly describes many instances of this resistance as being "too civilized to be understood by Western categorization." These were not revolutionary actions, to be sure. They were recalcitrant. They operated within a pattern of absolute authority that was fortified by the ruling ethnographic allegory. This allegory draped the life of working people, of every hue, during the nineteenth century.[31]

The way they worked under that blanket—within it without being *of* it—was impressive, and their achievement was large. These recalcitrant patterns found free space for their audiences. They kept alive a critique of the dominant culture, and they used its discipline as license, as had the legendary Cain. Like those who danced for eels along the New York wharves, these performance patterns folded African form into the midst of Euro-derived festivity. This interleaving arranged and nurtured a space of display within the traffic of the dominating community. It also made the strategies of camouflaged black recalcitrance accessible to disaffected white publics—like those gathering in U.S. cities in the 1830s. Thus, the earliest white imitations were of performance gestures that included preexisting black imitations of whites or, at the very least, of African-American cultural combinations. That's why a dizzying series of inversions works through the simplest minstrel re-presentation.

One of the most remarkable locations of these turnings within the minstrel lore cycle is chapter 20 of *Uncle Tom's Cabin*, named after the character Topsy. In her preface Stowe said she wanted "to awaken sympathy and feeling for the African race, as they exist among us." During her novel's serial publication, readers had already begun to argue that she was racist.

Others argued No—as if she might be one but not the other, racist or not. This argument did not end in the nineteenth century. It continues still, parallel to the dispute about whether blackface performance, to which Stowe's fiction was joined, was or was not racist—as if it, too, could be one and not the other. Although clarifying these positions has its importance, it is also diversionary. It distracts from the impassioned way Stowe's writing, as part of blackface performance, executed the cultural work of seeming to change a thing into a man, and back again, in tidal circulation.[32]

Instead of wondering about Stowe's racism I want to notice the tides. Cultural work never produces a clean before-and-after situation of replaced categories, as in "man" for "thing." Rather, it gives a ratio in which categories slide over and among each other, obscuring and peeking through their counterparts. Arguing about racism in cultural works, or in culture's workers, can easily replace studying the process of cultural transmission. What's being transmitted is hardly any one thing. Culture transmits codes that are complex. People decode them differently.

Is Stowe racist? Doubtless. But how does she—at the same time—manage to arouse so many liberatory feelings in *Uncle Tom's Cabin*? To ask that is to ask, How does the process of cultural work produce liberatory change even through racism, and in spite of it? I nudge the question to this variant because simply isolating and exhibiting Stowe's "romantic racialism," apart from her intended dismantling of slavery, can only disrupt and falsify the olio that her novel serves us. I do not want the question of racism to be an end in itself. To see that Stowe's images of blacks are sentimentally racialist is true but not whole. The racialist parts elicit counterparts that ghost around them, cohere with them, and have continued to dawn, and set, as they travel through time together. They cohere in a cycling ratio.

When St. Clare introduces Topsy to his cousin, Miss Ophelia, who will be her teacher and overseer, he locates her in a blackface genealogy. St. Clare calls Topsy "a funny specimen in the Jim Crow line" (p. 207). Furthermore, he whistles her into a formulaic dance much the way the novel's very first scene had Shelby, the Kentucky slave master, whistle Liza's son Harry into "wild, grotesque songs" and comic imitations (p. 3). Topsy spins out her dance

in a wild, fantastic sort of time . . . producing in her throat all those odd guttural sounds which distinguish the native music of her race; and finally, turning a summerset or two, and giving a prolonged closing note, as odd and unearthly as that of a steam-whistle, she came suddenly down on the carpet, and stood with her hands folded, and a most sanctimonious expression of meekness and solemnity over her face, only broken by the cunning glances which she shot askance from the corners of her eyes. (p. 207)

Topsy's steam-whistle imitation is one indication of her indebtedness to the minstrel stage, for it was a chestnut there, as we saw in Chapter 2. Another indication is her "wild," syncopated time. A third is her body-warping, which Stowe might have lifted from any of the grapevine-twisted figures spelling out the titles on minstrel-show posters. Any of these signs would have pointed contemporary readers to Topsy as a wench figure from the minstrel show. What clinches them all together is Topsy's askance glances. These looks going awry flag her recalcitrance even when Stowe sanctimoniously downs her on the carpet. Especially then, Topsy is hiding behind an elaborately rehearsed mask.

These clincher clues are no less important for being obvious. They exemplify the excess symbolism by which all performers indicate their self-consciousness. They do not so much mark simple reversal, transposing one thing for another, as show a *peeking through* of coexisting, alternative levels of reference. Topsy's askance glances demonstrate a combining rather than a replacement. But their obviousness has not been admitted by most writers about Stowe, who generally claim that Topsy was bestowed on the minstrel show, so to speak, rather than lifted from it. Thus, part of the difficulty in analyzing such passages is that both Stowe and the popular culture she is recycling here are usually thought to be so simplistic that no one will vouch that Topsy, the various Virginia Minstrels before her, and the black folk performers before *them* have ever vexed us with conflicted messages. Once one admits popular performances include such conflicts, indeed that their purpose is to embody conflict and to endow it with hyperbolic excess, then the performances seem more important. To admit meaning in this surplus is to admit that Topsy's dance deploys neither racism nor its absence alone but both in a ratio that extends from one end of the spectrum to the other, spinning in a mixed ground that has as its originary Cain's "first black face turn."

I insist that this turning ratio is present in the earliest isolable instances of a form. I challenge any perspective that denies complexity to minstrelsy and its nineteenth-century literary heirs from Stowe to Delany but bestows it on those performers who come variously late in the cycle—Bert Williams, Louis Armstrong, Ishmael Reed. In truth, as early as one looks, one finds intercultural borrowing, combining, and adaptation. The folk drawing of black performers dancing for eels at Catherine Market in 1820 is already mannered, thus already evidences accumulated meaning. There is no identifiable point in a lore cycle when meaning is not already rich.

By the time blackface performance has come around to such mature-cycle mannerisms as Topsy's askance glances, or Louis Armstrong's rolling eyes, or Bert Williams' portrayal of Martin, constant reiteration has marked out these gestures.[33] They then seem beyond stereotypes. They become embarrassing, they become surreal, and as such they have exceptional usefulness. This transference from kinetic to active meaning is not a matter of greater or lesser art. It is not a question of more or less cultural resistance, but of visibility. Some gestures become more evident because they occur in tandem with other changes happening in culture, changes that confirm meaning in rolling eyes, or askance glances, say, as signs of another part of the self peeking through and contradicting the apparently dominating part.

One way to see this peeking out of another self is as the dawning of an unsuspected aspect. Another way is as what George Marcus has called our "crossed selves" emerging. Marcus speculates as an anthropologist about the shift away from a nineteenth-century vestment in a coherent, unified self. In the late twentieth century, Marcus says, people typically believe normality includes a "radically nomadic," crossed and contradictory sense of self.[34] Topsy came chiefly from the minstrel show, which was a main producer and conduit in Atlantic communities for the problem of conflicted selves. Topsy is a prime example of the nomadic, crossed self. In responses to Topsy, both inside the novel and beyond it, Stowe's readers see an embarrassment about Topsy's incorrigible mutation starting to become both more visible and more irrepressible. Therefore, Topsy yields a good view of the conflicted load the popular stage conveyed even to those who did not experience it directly, as Harriet Beecher Stowe probably did not.

Topsy is coming into conflict with white domestic order in the household, and with the world that blacks were making alongside or beneath that order, too. Eva's death later in the novel tames Topsy, who becomes a Christianized and orderly part of Ophelia's northern household. Indeed, in an over-the-top final trump card, Stowe even sends Topsy to Africa as a missionary, where her "multiform" restlessness can be "employed, in a safer and wholesome manner . . . teaching the children of her own country"

(p. 377). Likewise, even George Harris, who had been charismatic for his creative disguise in escape, his gun-toting determination, even he is similarly tamed. At the end George, too, is to become a missionary: "As a Christian patriot, as a teacher of Christianity," he writes in a final letter, "I go to *my* country" (p. 376).

Nevertheless, it is not these aspects of the earlier, resisting, now housebroken characters who have stayed alive in American vernacular lore. Despite Stowe's novel and all the Tom plays which tried to break them nightly on their racks, it was the resistant George and the recalcitrant Topsy that readers remembered. It was the minstrel—the unreliable, the spontaneous, the unseated—Topsy that survived to be quoted and evoked as an insouciant shrug: "I spect I grow'd" (p. 210). And much more memorable than the Christian patriot was the George Harris of the slave narratives, the man who would talk his way through Kentucky disguised as a Spanish gentleman or shoot bounty hunters to protect his family. George closed his letter pleading, "do not divorce me from your confidence." Tamed characters do have our confidence, but not our memory. They are not legendary.

Take the famous scene of Topsy rehearsing her effects when Ophelia has busied herself elsewhere, leaving only readers "overlooking" her. In this scene we readers have become her overseers; we permit, even stimulate by our viewing, what Miss Ophelia outlaws.[35] In such a case,

> Topsy would hold a perfect carnival of confusion, for some one or two hours. Instead of making the bed, she would amuse herself with pulling off the pillowcases, butting her woolly head among the pillows, till it would sometimes be grotesquely ornamented with feathers sticking out in various directions; she would climb the posts, and hang head downward from the tops; flourish the sheets and spreads all over the apartment; dress the bolster up in Miss Ophelia's night-clothes, and enact various performances with that,—singing and whistling, and making grimaces at herself in the looking-glass; in short, as Miss Ophelia phrased it, "raising Cain" generally. (p. 216)

That Stowe has Miss Ophelia connect Topsy to Cain is not incidental. Miss Feely and Topsy are figures of opposing orders. They come into the novel, and the subsequent plays, as already developed stereotypes, already oppositional figures by implication. Characters like Ophelia were prefigured from the outset of blackface performance as foils to charismatic insouciance. For instance, Pompey Duckellegs, the runaway slave turned preacher in Thomas Dartmouth Rice's *Bone Squash Diavolo,* had tried to tame Bone Squash, as had the "Yankee Debil" in the same play. And the minstrel show, as elaborated later in the century, had set up this Ophelia-Topsy opposition explicitly in the struggle between the Interlocutor, with his long-tail'd blue coat and proper enunciation, and Tambo and Bones, the shiftless endmen, Topsy's male exemplars.

Unless it would be a somersault, Topsy cannot be said to have a characteristic stance. Topsy is anti-stance. She tumbles in topsy-turvy motion, and Ophelia's purpose in the novel is to *seat* Topsy. She fails as wholly as the middlemen in the minstrel show failed to seat the endmen. But the interlocutors failed by design. One point of the show was to laugh at the inability of long-tail'd masters to control the force of working-class self activity. Only in the novel's economy can Eva's death redeem Topsy. Like everyone else, in and out of the novel, Ophelia is helpless against Topsy's secular, vernacular force. It takes a saint to solve Topsy. It takes a lore cycle to keep her turning.

Stowe's shorthand creation of Topsy's rich characteristics in this scene depended on the way blackface theatre had already written them over and over in longhand as winks. Topsy's acting out of a "carnival of confusion"; the way Topsy would "hang head downward from the tops" of her mistress's bed "grotesquely ornamented with feathers"; and Topsy dressing up Ophelia's bolsters in order to perform antics that dress her mistress down—all these would have been understood by Stowe's contemporary public as allusions to the constructed blackface figure. Stowe's publics would have seen Topsy as a terminally cute variant on the dangerous lessons of Cain. They would have understood her intention of taming that figure, and they would have understood, also, that taming it was a dream, for Cain/Topsy was by legendary definition uncontainable. Topsy, as one who raised Cain, was a vagabond self, crossed, vexed, nomadic.

Seventy-five years later, the blues belter Ida Cox put together her traveling revue as a minstrel show touring black theatres across the Southeast and westward through Texas at the end of the 1920s. She was a mature woman, at the height of her powers. One measure of her independent confidence is that she could name the revue after this scene in Topsy's legend. The name of Cox's show was "Raisin' Cain." Cox had come by the name early on. She had begun her professional career twenty-six years earlier, at age fourteen, in 1903, working in blackface as Topsy in White and Clark's Black & Tan Minstrels.[36] Self-employed star of her own troupe now, and singing anthems of frank, feminist strength, Ida Cox betokened her power by referring to Topsy's resurgent wiles.

Now let's take Topsy's resurgence as an opening to a nagging question. Specific publics are keen to raise Cain, but is it possible to contain Cain? Ophelia and Stowe, her creator, are not alone in imagining that topsy-turviness can be housebroken. Many cultural historians share their fancy, with varying intentions. Some lament, some applaud the containment of recalcitrance. The blackface lore cycle, however, gives evidence that the whole plot of containing Cain is, itself, a fantasy.

The fantasy is widespread and recurrent. A regular plot in the histories of Atlantic encounter, for instance, has been the discovery of quirky rebellion: locally terrifying, perhaps, but disconnected from any real base, easily snuffed and eradicated. Storylines consistently emphasize how authorities plucked blooming challenges to dominant power before any dangerous seeds could disperse. Rarely has anyone wondered how the seeds matured in the first place. For gods and rebellion, the handiest explanation is always immaculate conception.

These plots determine how we remember the past. Cultural history has developed strong narratives for explaining how dominance became dominance, but it neglects stories of revival and dispersion. Characteristically, the plots of modern Atlantic history involve the challenges that dark people cause colonizing powers. These Others may be Caribbean natives or western Zuñi medicine men; they may be witches or Caliban; they may be African slaves, African-American runaways, or freemen; they may be blackface actors—but their presences typically teach two summary morals in the tales of cultural history. First, encountering their pesky challenges shows the Prosperos who they are, western scientists their methods, civilization its rules. Second, challenges are transmuted to conquests in these tales' long line of irreversible events. Not only history, but also its plots, have belonged to the victors. These plots keep victors out of touch with the real life of the vanquished—and happily give the beaten room to breathe.

Let's imagine these two morals from the angle of the challengers. On the first point, the duration of encounter not only teaches the victors who they are, it also teaches the vanquished. But teaches what? Does it convince the vanquished that they or their practices are insignificant? In some cases, it has done so—but that is more often what the victors think than what the beaten believe. Underdogs know when they have been whipped, of course, but obedience and submission are no surer consequences than a capacity to nurse wounds and to cope. Underdogs learn fugitiveness. They learn the lessons of Cain.

Preserving their identity behind a mask, disciplined people learn to carry on past defeat. They still exist within the frame. Stowe says in her preface: "They exist among us." They may be partially assimilated, but their memory of themselves has also been determined by their encounter. If we could diagram the kind of learning that sticks after these cultural engagements, it would not be like a gate, open or shut, turvy or tame. It would be more like a roundabout in time—a traffic circus with irregular incomings, outgoings, and positional flux. Cultural encounters bequeath their messages down generations as ghosting codes that fade, pulse, peek through erasure, and sometimes recover.

These covert codes bear on our second summary moral, the supposedly irreversible victories in the march of history. Since fugitives often remain unacculturated even as they and their society pretend they are assimilated, their physical presence and their residual codes continually excite the old grudges. Excite: sometimes in actuality, more often in symbolic action, in displaced dramas, songs, dances, and farces, enjoined whenever two or three are gathered together. These rehearsals seize what vengeance is possible and smile at the rest. In Kenneth Burke's insight, they are "strategies for the encompassing of situations." They discover a rapprochement with events that played first beyond the performers' control.[37] These new secular rites are the places where seeds of old crossings ripen, and may yet bloom.

Stowe thinks it's progress when Topsy abandons her disorderly recalcitrance, her memorable feature, replacing it with the dominant culture's orderly virtues that readers seldom associate with her. In Stowe's vision, this replacement is the way the past becomes the future. Although her logic is dreamy even for a novel, it is in fact a characteristic modern logic. The same loopy confidence in even and steady progress appears over and over in some of our most progressive cultural history, which believes that what Miss Feely calls shiftlessness, with all its weird social practices, has been whitewashed from the pages of civilization. At risk here is what sort of presence disorderly ritual is allowed—not in general culture, where it is surely recurrent, but in the representations of cultural history, where the typical confidence is about its repression.

The scourged scene of modern life, the very definition of modernity as that which has flushed away irrational, disorderly behavior, is a gate-keeping critical shibboleth. A long list might be made of the chronicles of modernization that depend on this plot, and here's a start: Freud's Id replacement program, Marx's dialectic, Norbert Elias's civilizing process, Foucault's totalizing "power of normalization," and the biographies of countless Western boffins marching together toward laboratory control. Neither least nor last in this list would be Stephen Greenblatt's assurance in his powerful essay "Filthy Rites" that from "the early Renaissance onward, such paradoxical doubleness" as the fascination with feces in European Carnival and the "powerful medicine" of Zuñi coprophagous rites in North America "is more and more widely repudiated, and then repressed, so that by the nineteenth century, it is recoverable only in ethnographic descriptions of savage rituals."[38]

But wait: blackface performance deeply contradicts this trust that modern behavior has scourged the medicine of paradoxical doubleness. Just as much as it counters the spectrum of modern politics, Cain's resurgence also tars the dominant plots of modern cultural history. Whether it was a savage or a secular ritual, blacking up erupted everywhere in the Atlantic, throughout the nineteenth century and well beyond. A century later, when the National Association for the Advancement of Colored People levied legal actions against the last minstrel shows, chiefly in the Northeast, during the mid-1950s, that also was not the end of minstrelsy, but once again forced a change in its mode, this time retiring the blackface mask. In the 1950s TV's vaudeville and amateur hours and the yawps on 45-rpm records snatched and carried forward the baton that MTV is still pumping at the front of the race. Ever since the 1950s rock and its successors have been bootlegging filthy rites into livingrooms and earphones, cars and consciousness. So it is only because History scorns these matters that anyone can possibly decide that civilization has scrubbed filthy rites. Their powerful medicine is now spread so widely that commentators breathe it like air they cannot see. Cultural history passes over the meaning of popular rites no more gracefully than people step over the homeless on their way into the museum.

Cultural histories of the Atlantic encounter now generally picture the minstrel show as a ritual of acculturation in which whites ridiculed blacks, thus minimizing discrepancies among white ethnic groups by exaggerating marks of blackness. "Blackface literally stepped in as a popular entertainment craze," David Roediger correctly notices, "at the very moment that genuinely Black performers and celebrations were driven out."[39] But to what end did blackface step in? Certainly not to eradicate complex black rites and draw boundaries of sense and sensibility—not that primarily. Underlying what I am calling the consensus view is its drastic devaluation of popular ritual ("entertainment craze," indeed). The northern folk celebrations of Pinkster and urban market dances, the southern cornshuckings and John Canoe were important but little-known local secrets until blackface performers started trucking abstracted combinations of them to the Atlantic populace. Blackface not only stepped in, it primarily brought in and broadcasted blackness.

While blackface has certainly demeaned blacks, therefore, it has also done much more. Its enduring function has been to transmit a toughened version of blackness that more powerful sectors had enslaved and thrown out. Any open reading of minstrel texts shows that they establish at least as much connection among slaves and hirelings, and against employers, as they document rifts between workers or solidarity among white workers and their employers. This mutuality among many middle-class youths and lower-class workers across race is the dimension slighted by current accounts of popular rites.

The supposedly defeated cultural attributes anathema to civilization survive their seeming containment. Sure, we have erased the scatological humor of the minstrel show, scrubbed away Zuñi coprophagy, and knocked Amos 'n' Andy off the air. To what avail? In their stead we have Lenny Bruce and George Carlin, Red Foxx and Eddie Murphy; we have John Waters movies of actors eating—and audiences scratch-'n'-sniffing—dog scat; we have In Living Color and gangsta rap. What some dominant group deems filth is not banished beyond the boundaries of civilization, "recoverable only in ethnographic descriptions of savage rituals." Rather, it remains diffuse in our own fascinations, determining us all the more by being fugitive.

Blackface performance does emerge at the early-nineteenth-century moment when chroniclers say Western civilization had finally wiped clean its double rites of waste. However, minstrelsy was no replacement. Rather, it has prolonged and stretched out the effects people gained earlier in skimmington rides, tarring and feathering, and other profound rites of baptism in wastes and disorder. The sister activity of the male minstrel show is the chorus line with its feathers, its makeup, its highkicking, lowbending flashes of forbidden zones. These disturbing and sometimes genuinely filthy forms thrive, persistent in one mode or another. Instead of disappearing and losing his function, Cain hides now in plain sight and sneaky petes his hybrid lesson into popular commerciality.

In the early nineteenth century, entrepreneurial capital begins to underwrite the older folk transgressions, paying folk motifs to uproot and reroute. Traveling gestures are now able to mediate even more fluently between the groups and genders, regions and classes of Atlantic life. They are cultural pests. Like the fire ant and the well-adapted weed, these rites proliferate fastest in disturbed sites at times when authority tries to eradicate them. Hostile attention makes them thrive.

Policing is always the cultural pest's best friend. That's why the "landless blood of Cain," as in Robert Lowell's poem "Children of Light," will always be "burning, burning the unburied grain" of conflict. One of the most enduring responsibilities of culture, canonical and popular, is to flame again and again an era's most painful transgressions. At least since Genesis, turning up this heat is what meaningful culture has been marked out and licensed to do. Policing this vitality only forces it to find other ways, other arenas, in which to wheel about, turn about, and dance out its troubles. "Blame it on Cain," Elvis Costello began pleading as recently as 1977, singing about his need to break out "before I do someone in": "Don't blame it on me. / It's nobody's fault. / But we need somebody to burn."[40]

4

Finding Jim Crow

Let us go down. We enter a cellar, where we see a few males and females, black, yellow, and white, seated or swaggering about the room . . . It is certainly the last place in New-York.

—William Bobo, *Glimpses of New-York City*

Depending on when one intercepts the strange career of Jim Crow, one flushes birds of different feathers. I am of course not trying to scare up the crow that C. Vann Woodward studied. He found a codified body of laws, culminating in the segregated 1950s, and defined Jim Crow as "the most elaborate and formal expression of sovereign white opinion upon the subject" of racism.[1] Rather, I will watch the cultural image of Jim Crow take initial flight. I want to find this callow crow before it became law, while it remained fledgling and distinctly anti-sovereign. This crow's early flight is bold but hardly commanding. Middle classes diverted its energy to sustain their own sovereignty. Thus I speak here ultimately of two fugitive entities.

First, just as Chapter 1 explored a pre-terrain for minstrelsy, so is there a pre-career for Jim Crow, which I will disclose here. It is a folk process and an early popularization, across race, of gestures gathering a critical momentum. This early gathering of gestures and lyrics into an iconic blackness pushed across the codes that Woodward studied. Indeed, Jim Crow as T. D. Rice conceived him moved toward cross-racial affiliation. Poor people's neighborhoods where races mingled were not even anomalous during the early years of the nineteenth century. They were common. Intimate integration was the way lower classes lived in New York City's Sev-

enth Ward, as in dock areas of most North American ports. These conditions fostered this earliest *integrative* Jim Crow culture. The pre-career of
Jim Crow is opposite to the received, segregative meaning the term has
today.

This opposition takes me to the second fugitive intention of these pages.
What began in a folk and popular combination became, as it gathered
momentum, a location of trouble. Polite external forces struggled to maintain sovereignty over it. (They codified this sovereignty in elaborate laws,
but instead of eradicating the Cain in its spirit, as they intended, they
dispersed Cain's traces.) In this chapter I will show more completely why
Jim Crow seemed to require policing. I will tell how Jim Crow became the
figurehead of a nascent, Atlantic lumpenproletariat. This story is neither an
account of victory nor a narrative of defeat. The twentieth-century tendrils
of the story are still spreading, both in life and in cultural reckonings.

For early aspects of the story, I return to "Daddy" Rice and the way he
knotted together the Jim Crow figure from: (1) a widespread folk pattern
of gesture, dominantly black, prepared for public scrutiny and competition
in urban markets and provincial festivities; (2) a dance called "Knock Jim
Crow," which has black children still turning and clapping and kicking in
the North Florida Panhandle, on Georgia's Sea Islands, even inland in
Gary, Indiana; (3) farcical themes and stage conventions imposed by the
rigidly controlled history of the English theatre, divided into patent and
illegitimate stages; (4) resentments and class formations that were creating
strangely clumped antagonists: burghers and socialists, say, combining to
scorn an independently fearsome ragged cohort.

Jim Crow tokened a new underclass alliance. It was above all else separate. It proceeded by its own lights—flambeaux ignited, often enough, in
theatrical spaces which were only sometimes proper stages. That separate-
ness was what frightened upright middle-class types whose politics on
other matters might range from left to right. That was why these relative
elites united to scorn it. That was why ragged publics united behind Jim
Crow to prop him up. Jim Crow wheeled about within a larger circle of
scorn. Push came to shove, not at all gradually, over Jim Crow as a cultural
token.

The story I propose here veers awry from the usual account of the origins
of Jim Crow. That usual story, reiterated from the earliest middle-class articles on working-class performance right up through the latest scholarly

accounts of minstrelsy, has it that Rice nicked "Jump Jim Crow" from a real man, usually specified as a crippled black hostler named Jim Crow. A corollary story, equally dubious, specifies a source in an individual named Cuff, who it is supposed wrestled luggage along the Pittsburgh levee.[2]

These stories are false in fact and spirit. There was no such hostler, no such baggage man. What's more, the way these stories tell it is simply not the way cultural gestures come into being. These apocryphal tales indicate, instead, how distant our stories are from the way people produce culture and how starved they are for legitimating detail. These stories might be analyzed to say something about polite guilt. But to pretend these stories were actual is to hide everything about the rude impositions that blackface performance first scored. The legends hide whence blackface derived and how blackface tried to gird itself against its antagonists. The conventional stories tell nothing about the early meanings blackface had within its early public. These internal meanings were initially so surprising and powerfully enabling among the budding underclass that well-placed antagonists felt challenged to wrap and pickle them like so many mummies.

These repackaged stories about the crippled hostler and Cuff divert attention from the sparks that flew when working whites adopted black lore. Not Edwin Forrest, not George Washington Dixon, not Rice himself, not Dan Emmett—not the men who blacked up—but the actors whose plays blackface had supplanted were the ones who evidently started the phony legends. They were the actors still barnstorming North American boondocks with melodramas and pratfalls about the squirearchy in the English Home Counties. Newspaper men and the *Atlantic Monthly* picked up and embellished their stories.

Why did such stories gather momentum? Perhaps simply because this sort of demeaning and racist sugar fed the sweet teeth of magazine publics. The legends divert the integrative protocols that blackface performance reinforced among its publics. But it would be a mistake to make too much of this diversion. Even the transparent exciting of exploitation and racism in the later career of Jim Crow did not successfully stamp out the urge white youths expressed to adopt black cultural signs. (Witness Bix Beiderbecke, Mezz Mezzrow, Benny Goodman, Jerry Lee Lewis, Keith Richards, and House of Pain, to name just a few who have continued in this vein.) And what has been overwritten may not in fact be gone. It may yet be lurking.

Every goodbye ain't gone. All sickness ain't death. And every big
man ain't strong.
    —Whisper to Jim Crow in Wesley Brown's *Darktown*
        Strutters

In the push come to shove of social history, the legends of the hostler Jim
and the levee luggage man Cuff are reflex maneuvers. They react to blackface actions that preceded them. The challenges young workers posed just
by rallying round and championing Jim Crow dances were what pushed
those burghers to shoving back. The burghers told countering stories of a
pitiful hostler poorly paid for his marvelous steps. They told, too, of the
strong but gullible Cuff, outwitted and begging for his clothes. They told
these condescending stories to contain blackface performance and to root
it in racism. Jealous of blackface popularity, they told stories to belittle and
wedge apart its affiliations.

Rice's early plays were aware of this containment, and they demonstrate
it. Rice showed his audiences how they were being boxed. *Bone Squash
Diavolo* trapped young Bone in a deal with a Yankee Devil. *The Virginia
Mummy* wrapped up Rice's character and stuck him in a coffin masquer-
ading as a sarcophagus. *The Black God of Love* imprisoned him in a large
cabbage. *Flight to America* packed him around in a large sedan. *Oh! Hush!*
closeted him in a flour cupboard. Then, in each case, Rice played out
exciting ways for his own, and his public's, extrication. Bursting bondage
was the crux of each play, and their whole mutual point.

The break was the moment that knotted together the white and black
working youths in the audience. Make no mistake: there *were* black publics
for early white performers in blackface.[3] All these scorned people came
together around Jim Crow and against the forces that had tied them down
and apart. When Rice as Ginger Blue, or as Cupid the "Black-amour,"
stepped out of the coffin or the cabbage, imaginative whites in his audience
were able to link their own condition to the runaway black who was the
center of their attention. As Rice burst each confinement, the metaphor
gave audiences both their condition and an image of their deconditioning.

Anyone who reads the manuscripts of these plays in enough variety to
see the mutual direction in their core stories knows that the middle-class
legends imposed on the plays, purporting to tell about the origins of minstrelsy, are far wide of the spirit and modes of blackface performance's first
decades. The middle-class accounts in newspapers and magazines instead

exactly access the clampdown spirit which the plays tried to burst. I want to disclose those stunning early links within blackface that provoked belittling foundational legends.

The texts of Rice's Jim Crow plays clearly integrated English farce traditions with black folk dance and gesture, with backtalk licensed in African tradition and carried over into slave slowdowns, Jack's ridicule of ol' Massa, and more. Adaptation was not a one-way street occurring, for example, only when Africans adjusted to European religion and power in the Americas. It was not confined to associating West African religions with Catholic icons and coming up with Voodoo. Sometimes, as in blackface performance, whites adapted to black charisma. To make sense of *these* affiliations one must find or recover the texts and songs as their gestating publics performed them. That means one must avoid, or read very skeptically, the versions that journalists patronizingly reconstructed (and that scholarship has validated). After locating these early blackface connections, one must read them sympathetically. This is hardly to say it is necessary to approve of them as Ethiopian delineations, to use their own term. But beginning in disgust or anger does not aid understanding of their cultural transmission further down the road.

Rice found the elements for a blackface figure in a wide range of sources which were already actively cycling for years before his youth in Catherine Market. He fitted those black sources into his apprentice experience in broad English comedy and melodrama. He recast the lumpen allure of these plays' seamen and highwaymen into the adventures of busted black bondage on his side of the Atlantic. His transference, however, retained intact many of the corniest British puns and conundrums. For instance, as Long Billy Black, a punning English bootblack in Richard Brinsley Peake's *The Hundred Pound Note*—a staple in Rice's early stage career before he started jumping Jim Crow—Rice asks, "Sir, why am I like a West Indian blackamoor?—Do you give it up? Because I am going with a driver." (He exits with a postboy driver.) A second example that shows up *mutatis mutandi* throughout Rice's career: "I say, Mr. O'Shocknessy, if you was married, what would you be? Do you give it up? You would be a united Irishman." William Leman Rede wrote essentially the same joke into *Flight to America,* his 1837 blackface vehicle for Rice: one character warns another to be careful he doesn't talk himself into another marriage in America like the one he is fleeing in England. The man at risk replies that he will be safe there because "All the ladies in New York are in the united state already."[4]

When he started blacking up, Rice copied old jokes but he did not copy old conventions. He rejected the British black stage talk that had also carried over to U.S. theatres. Then he set about refiguring a new black vernacular. In the process he absorbed and shaped what he could of the emerging North American conventions for representing black acts—speech, steps, and songs. He had ample opportunity to continue observing interracial interaction on the North American circuit—just as he had observed interracial life in the Seventh Ward during his youth—when the groups he traveled with pioneered inland American theatre in Louisville, Cincinnati, Mobile, Pensacola, and other out-of-the-way places, along with the major target theatres in New York, Albany, Boston, Philadelphia, Washington, Charleston, and New Orleans. He tapped into and goosed along a hybrid blend that still lives by its confounding connections in performance lodes today.

In this chapter I want to consolidate a pattern of origination for what became blackface performance. It was invented neither out of some individual's sudden psychic whim (Rice thinking, Ah, I will steal Jim Crow's dance and take it to the bank) nor from spontaneous combustion (youths from Mobile to New York all at once wheeling about and doing jis' so). Rice and his audience found the seeds of blackface in transactions of fascination among Africans and Europeans circulating in the Atlantic, sharing gestures within unequal and exploitative political situations that were continually changing. These gestures became as involved as their longevity proves they were by carrying and continually re-embedding traces in their performance. They display that most fundamental lesson of lore: use it or lose it.[5]

Thomas Rice was not the Irish or Catholic immigrant that many writers have assumed. He married in London in the Church of England (on Smith Square, Westminster, 18 June 1837), and his funeral service was in the (Protestant) St. Thomas Church, corner of Houston and Broadway, New York City, on 21 September 1860.[6] All the evidence is that his family and upbringing were poor, Protestant, and English-American. He was born in New York's Seventh Ward, just blocks from the docks. The most likely candidate for his father is John Rice, a ship's rigger, whom Longworth's Directory lists on 60 Catherine Street at the time of Rice's birth, 20 May 1808. As I showed in Chapter 1, this neighborhood was an inverted rainbow culture of saloons and brothels, groceries and commerce, bustle and performance that William Sidney Mount and his uncle Micah Hawkins drew on in the 1820s to funnel vernacular material into North America's first opera and some of its most telling early graphics.

After his schooling, Rice apprenticed as a ship's carver, probably with a man named Dodge.[7] But Rice's urge was for more plastic representation than wood allowed. He would dance out a much more jittery, nimble, and lumpen icon. Its gestural figuration would cross and recross the Atlantic more lastingly than the carvings breasting sailing ships. Already as a young man, Rice was moving rapidly into the theatre. During this apprenticeship he practiced all the extant options in comedy, copying and remaking them as he passed.

While a youngster, Rice worked in at least one small theatre—on Cherry Street, probably a saloon with a raised platform in a cleared corner. Even scuffing peanut shells and sawdust under that low ceiling, however, those Cherry Street players had ambition—the piece was *William Tell,* a staple European celebration of nationalism. Another notice had him appearing early in George Colman's operetta *Inkle and Yarico.* Both these early locations remind us what the repertoire was for American actors in the first third of the nineteenth century. High and low, American theatres were then doing conventional English melodramas. Indeed, even after he became famous for jumping Jim Crow and after he had started writing his own farces, Rice was still occasionally performing *William Tell.*[8]

I can find no record of Rice performing in Colman's *Inkle and Yarico,* however, after his leap into blackface. That's because Rice's performance of his Jim Crow character moved representation of black gesture well beyond its figuring in English stage conventions. Rice's innovations provided much more nuance than a vaguely abolitionist vehicle like *Inkle and Yarico* could convey. Rice stepped inside the romantic racialism of *Inkle and Yarico.* His tight-focus specificities and the peculiarities of his stage business simply obliterated Colman's distantly drawn generalizations. Rice's up-close mimetics substituted colonial observations for imperial clichés. His Jim Crow figure installed the black character of burst bondage as the leading role, raising him from a servant in secondary or tertiary sidelight. Jim Crow took occupation of whatever spaces he jumped. He was the new center of attention.

Indeed, the theatres from the Park and Bowery to the saloon stages along Water and Cherry Streets, and up to the Five Points, were all changed after Rice brought his blackface home to New York in 1832, quite the rage. This early success of proto-minstrelsy brought whites in blackface onto the stage of proper theatres. Contrary to the disinformation that blacks were excluded from American stages, in fact, black and "yellow" performers, along with those whites in blackface, were on view every night in the Five Points dives, just as they all mingled in these low audiences. The generalization about the exclusion of blacks from the American theatre is another instance of historical attention limited to polite reality.

The classic minstrel show, as the Virginia Minstrels and the Christy Minstrels presented it a decade later, did exclude blacks from its stage, in obedient emulation of the elite theatres. But its classic formulas also carried forth cultural precipitates from the Five Points and Catherine Market nexus. Just as important, they reminded everyone at the slightly uptown theatres of what was available in the Seventh Ward, at Five Points in New York City, along Lombard Street in Philadelphia, and at comparable mixed locations in cities from the Great Lakes to the Gulf of Mexico. Insofar as these white minstrel companies embodied that precipitate from Catherine Slip, they provided a frisson of danger and supposed authenticity that gave edge to the sentimental corn in the proper shows. They were embodying the urban margin quite as much as they were evoking the plantation. They were excluding blacks from the fancier stages only, but even there they were also reminding audiences of black existence so troubling that it must be counterfeited. This exclusion and reminding did at least two things. They pointed to, propped up, and affirmed the appearance of blacks in saloon and other low stages. And they imported a diluted version of blackness even into the masculine half of the middle class.

Dabbling in the dilute led at least some people to the full solution. William Bobo was a scandalized visitor from South Carolina to New York City, at the beginning of the 1850s, who went looking for the real thing. Writing about the city's underbelly, Bobo warns his readers that no written description can capture the life that the minstrel show was shadowing—though, of course, he tries his best to record it:

> But now it is time for Pete Williams's ball to open. Let us go down. We enter a cellar, where we see a few males and females, black, yellow, and white, seated or swaggering about the room; as many males smoking segars and swearing off some story of the day. Upon a sort of platform sit two or three negroes representing the orchestra, and opposite is the bar, behind which stands a negro, or Pete (who is a negro) himself, dealing out whisky, tobacco, beer, and segars, at three cents a glass, or a penny apiece. The music commences, and out sally two or three cotillions of this piebald party, and away they whirl in a most disgusting and revolting

manner. The negroes seem to attract the most attention. What a commentary upon the authorities of the city.[9]

Bobo is programmatically unenthusiastic about the Chatham and Five Points scene, but we can read his comments with a correcting lens. His dismay shows that black performance modes took over the area, that performers were as integrated as the ward, and that degradation or misrepresentation of blacks was hardly the salient purpose of the mode.

In this passage and especially the next I will quote from Bobo's screed, it was clearly not just black but also black*face* performance that upset him. Authenticity was not the issue with this observer (who hailed from a state where blacks were in the majority). Rather, blackface was to Bobo and his contemporaries a heightening of effect that all concerned took to be mimetic. These theatres had whites cohabiting stages with actual black performers and performance—just as whites were living with blacks in the streets and local bedrooms. From Pete Williams's cellar to the large houses like the National (formerly Chatham Theatre, then Chatham Chapel, now returned to its native rites) and the Franklin Museum, the whole scene was black performance that this slumming South Carolinian made no attempt to call inauthentic. Pete Williams's raised shingle, or platform, was continuing, if heightening, what Bobo (along with Melville and others) called a "piebald party" that was already ongoing in New York's nexus of Catherine's Market up past the Five Points and along the lower Bowery.

What disgusted Bobo was how far some whites had fallen into this piebald charisma. What's more, Bobo observed early the way other immigrant groups would be important in carrying this attractiveness to the wider culture. He reported they were already showing prominently in the mix: "The National theatre . . . is patronized by the 'two shilling' fraternity, the b'hoys and the g'hals, and Jewesses and Jews of Chatham-street. Just above is the Franklin Museum, as it is called, but nothing more than a place where a set of men and women play, and sing a few negro songs in a sickly manner, and a few disgusting women pretend to expose themselves as model artists. It is certainly the last place in New-York."[10]

The last shall be first: how that transformation was produced is the plot of this chapter. It is a twisted knot, this plot we are figuring out, not a direct line. The intermingling of peoples and their cultures in the Seventh Ward did not directly translate into the intermingled blackface performance by which members of an alternative culture chiefly came to know themselves and signal who they were thereafter. Instead, New York actors and their urban publics first told their stories as transplanted English dramas, as Jacksonian parables, as coonskin tales, as plantation exotica—anything but the story of the North Atlantic's metropolitan poor.

Only gradually were the mingling poor able to discover their mutuality in the elements of these heterogeneous stories. Blackface performance was the abstract configuration that allowed all these scorned modes to coexist. In one actor's turning, an elementary story of burst bondage portrayed as comedy, various spurned peoples and their narratives came together under the blackface sign. Rice brought their stories to them refreshed, with disparate elements all melded together, all tumbled on top of one another. His congenial publics called his representation true, or true enough, and recognized it, now that it was retold in blackface, as their own story. They applauded him. They themselves danced the blackface gestures Rice conveyed to them. They sang along—rehearsing, inscribing—until their own intimate version of identification became for its while the most popular form in the Atlantic world. As I showed in Chapter 3, traces of this popularity still penetrate into current consciousness, though their shunned status often makes them feel raw and weird. The contemporary heir to blackface history who perhaps most consciously registers this unseen weight is Bob Dylan. His insistent recording during the 1990s of extraordinary old songs from that muddy terrain between folk and pop—"Delia," "Stack A Lee"—show how the weight presses on contemporary repertories, but lurks mostly unacknowledged by either those who perform or those who listen:

> Mighty Mockingbird, he still has such a heavy load.
> Beneath his bound'ries, . . .
> Who's gonna throw that minstrel boy a coin?[11]

Rice's earliest successes in blackface were in the American South, in the slave states, and in the lower Ohio Valley, where he was touring as a very young actor with Noah Ludlow's troupe. Indeed, Ludlow provides some of the earliest information about Rice, including some interpretable tips about his talent. In August 1828 Rice was a stock player in New York City, at the Lafayette Theatre. That summer at the Lafayette, George Washington Dixon, who always billed himself as a "buffo singer and comedian," was performing several popular songs in blackface, including "Coal Black Rose." This song would be the core of more than one of Rice's subsequent blackface sketches.

Without a doubt, Dixon's act made Rice rethink the folk performances he had absorbed as a boy in Catherine Market and elsewhere in his Seventh Ward neighborhoods. That is, Rice hardly needed to wait until Ludlow's troupe landed in Mobile, much less wait until Cincinnati, Pittsburgh, or Louisville, to see black dance. He had observed many practiced dancers combining black folk gestures and emerging theatrical counterfeits of those gestures well before he left home.[12]

For instance, Dixon was already specializing in the figure of the dandy-dressing poseur, a heavily mannered type that cartoons and tales were shading in during the early 1820s. This cartoon figure was an Anglo-American aggression against local youths who were starting to pattern themselves on the Parisian flâneur. This figure that Dixon was bringing back to the stage seemed to be a blackface variant on such cartoons as David Claypoole Johnston's caricature of the Dancing-Master and his spruce black servant negotiating the mud and pigs at the corner of Nassau Street and Maiden Lane (see Figure 4.1). The Johnston-Hawkins collaboration was in fact the polite part of a much ruder undercurrent of woodcuts and lithographs, broadsheet poems and songs that were vigorously censoring unusual behavior. This graphic enforcement especially abused those youths of either sex who would bridge black and white culture. One favorite target was Phillis Wheatley, and the general resentment was toward people changing their presumed places.

I emphasize two aspects in this relationship of the theatre to the street woodcuts and lithos. First, to look at these graphic images is to open up a realm of origination for enduring Atlantic stock figures. The theatre was an early creator of Negro stereotypes. But it was itself responding in part to prior images from a kind of reverse colportage, a negative hagiography, in which elite Americans tried to prune their multiculturalism just as it was budding rebarbative among poorer citizens and slaves. The enforcing images were attempts to nip off early postcolonial radicals. It's not just that the street images in question were lapidary stabilizations, carved in wood or etched in stone. More important is that in the sharp contests of their day graphic propagandists rapidly chose sides. Almost immediately these caricaturists moved to extreme positions—racist derogation vs. liberatory abolitionism.[13] In one corner, wooden images of approved mob violence against thick-lipped black poseurs; in the other, abolitionist images of kneeling slaves asking "Am I Not a Man and a Brother?" and slaves packed like sardines in slave ships during the middle passage. These contending

4.1 David Claypoole Johnston's drawing for Micah Hawkins's *Myneheur Von Herrick Heimelman, the Dancing-Master: or The Confluence of Nassau-Street and Maiden-Lane, As it was Whilom* (1824)

images provided stepping stones for early-nineteenth-century citizens trying to ford the stream of race. That's the way things stood when the curtain rose on George Washington Dixon in blackface singing "Coal Black Rose" and "Long-Tail'd Blue" at the end of the 1820s. T. D. Rice was turning twenty and watching in the wings.

The second point to make about these contending images is that although the graphics do indeed open up an originary realm for what would occur in the theatre, the street graphics did not efficiently reproduce their sentiments in the theatre sketches they helped generate. Theatrical realities ensured that actors treated their material differently from the way cartoonists and political agitators used their graphics. When Dixon and Rice took the stage, they stood at the bottom of a Niagaran fall of extreme stereotypes washing over them and their audiences. One way to look at Dixon's and then Rice's task, the task of early blackface performance, is to see it breasting this wash of types. Wading through what remains of this torrent of images, including the scabrous and anonymous Bobalition broadsides, one sees that Rice and (even) Dixon richened and deepened by continual performance what was given them.

The wooden directness of the cartoons was one background against which the later players worked their indirection. The woodcut stereotypes punctuate both the songsters affiliated with early blackface and the throwaway advertising handouts that begin to appear at theatres and stores during this era. What's more, the publics in the popular theatres were not a stable audience but a mixed lot. Some theatregoers surely inclined toward the aggression legitimated in Bobalition broadsides and parodies of Phillis Wheatley's letters.[14] Others, however, sought in blackface something like the opposite of these broadside stereotypes; these others sought confirmation for their sense of black allure. Others, perhaps most, divided along these lines within themselves. These more-conflicted publics would have been natural audiences for the theatres.

Carving or setting a graphic image once and for all is one thing; but embodying it night after night, acting it out often to repeat ticketholders, is quite another. This repetitiousness of theatrical presentation demanded variance and improvisation. And this necessary variation obtains even before one factors in unstable casts and the various venues of frontier performances in brothels, hotels, saloons, and makeshift halls. For these reasons, analyses that admit ambiguity and outright conflict in blackface images are preferable to those which read minstrelsy as merely fixing stereotypes.

Theatrical improvisation, night after night, necessarily put variation into inherited graphic types. In the theatre, types existed on different levels simultaneously and reinforced contrary audience needs. These unstable theatrical types are therefore more different from than like the graphic street images to which they seem to refer. In fact, the apparent stereotypes of rowdy and dandy, which eventuated in Bones and the Interlocutor, are not rigidities that lock in behavior. Rather, they are *fields* which encourage querying of behavior. Within limits, they generate relational positions that sneak up on and undercut expectations.

> He sits upon my stomach like a nightmare.
> —Lawyer Capias about his clerk Wormwood in John
> Buckstone's *The Lottery Ticket and the Lawyer's Clerk*

Decidedly the least of New York's four proper theatres at the end of the 1820s was the Lafayette. It may therefore not be surprising to find ambitious T. D. Rice, twenty years old that autumn of 1828, leaving the Lafayette to George Washington Dixon and joining Noah Ludlow's company at the Chatham Theatre. But the Chatham was no large step up, and Rice was joining Ludlow's company only as fill-in actor and assistant to the property man. Why, then, would this young actor, just achieving parts that put his name in the paper, have shifted theatres and companies? The answer has to be that he knew Ludlow was going to leave the city on one of his pioneering loops creating frontier theatre, journeys Ludlow had been taking since 1815, when he began as an advance man for Sam Drake out of Albany. Ludlow closed out his term at the Chatham, hired more actors, and sailed around Florida's peninsula for a season in Mobile, preparing once again to breach the land through its underbelly, like a mawworm. It is entirely fitting for this anecdote and for the future of this actor, whose will would declare him simply a "comedian," that the name of the ship conveying these players toward the American omphalos was the "St. John, Jr." Like the Magi in Eliot's poem, they journeyed at "just the worst time of the year," arriving in Mobile three weeks later, in late December 1828.[15]

Of Ludlow's leading actors, several turned out duds. These failures created opportunities for Rice, who was working his way into Ludlow's repertoire and shaping it to his own keen energies. "Mr. Rice soon began to display," Ludlow recollected, "in a rudimental way, that peculiar talent that afterwards, being more fully developed, became the source of considerable wealth to him." Ludlow remembered the "first effort . . . that attracted my attention particularly was [Rice's] performance of *Wormwood*, in Mr. Buckstone's farce of the 'Lottery Ticket.' " And, in a remark of a sort peppering all the early commentary on Rice's hustle, Ludlow recalled that the young actor "possessed the only book of [the play] convenient to be had, and at his request I cast him for that character."[16]

Reversals upon reversals, surprises turning inside out, sprout as plentifully in the plot of *The Lottery Ticket* as in any popular farce; its story is too tangled to untie here. Worth emphasizing, however, is that Rice *wanted* the part of Wormwood, for Wormwood is both a novel figure in the story of this farce and, most important, a role of ambiguous attraction. No character anything like Wormwood appeared in the play's clear precursor, Henry Fielding's *The Lottery* (1795). Fielding's farce occurs in a village, its conflict arising between squirearchy and servants. Buckstone's variant occurs in a town, its conflict arising between professionals and servants. Fielding's *The Lottery* bequeaths to Buckstone's *The Lottery Ticket* its reliance on greedy chicanery, the same pretense that arises upon winning the lottery, and the same failed attempts to marry in order to capitalize on the ticket. Both plays have the obligatory dance at the end, and moralizing.

But Buckstone's nineteenth-century play introduces an additional character, "the lawyer's clerk," perverse Wormwood, who not only sets the conflicts going but also continually disrupts the happy plot resolutions, Malvolio-like, even as the curtain is falling. Fielding's play had still a natural morality to which the confused squirearchy could return, at last. In the play that Rice brought into the Ohio River valley in the early nineteenth century, on the contrary, a new role reflects new characters in the riparian towns. This new role neither fitted into extant social categories nor would let them settle down happily apart—not in the society, not in the play.

Wormwood is a hunchbacked town observer. He is an outsider never involved in the shenanigans of sexual attraction or conventional power. His bent back excludes him from the usual payoffs, social position or attractive marriage. He does not go happily; he is not resigned; he lives and acts on his resentments. His fascination for Rice, and for the public Rice was organizing, lay in Wormwood's power to eat away at pretense. Wormwood bites the social stomach from within.

An early-nineteenth-century anthologist glossed Wormwood's part: "There are some dispositions so intensely perverse, as to derive happiness from the miseries of their fellow-men. They . . . chuckle over vexations, and . . . mar the bliss of others, that they themselves may make merry! Of such a crooked disposition is Mr. Wormwood, the hero of The Lottery Ticket."[17] This remark declasses Wormwood's recalcitrance into ethical terms. It combines a disdain for his ethics with his hump-back disfigurement: "crooked." And it chooses not to notice that the "others" Wormwood vexes are his employer, who disdains the clerk's class, and the attractive servant girls, who shun his hump. This anthologist is still understanding *The Lottery Ticket and the Lawyer's Clerk* within a normative framework that admits no irresolvable conflicts. But Rice saw Wormwood's possibilities differently. In Wormwood, Rice saw a systematic perverseness which he seized as his own signature property throughout his career, in blackface and out. Wormwood fouls up the lives of the lawyers and staymakers, employers and pretenders. Wormwood sits on their stomachs, says his boss, "like a nightmare."

Rice saw a recalcitrance in Wormwood onto which bitterness in working audiences might latch. This exciting the anger in audiences, legitimating and organizing what they were feeling, is what turned Wormwood's villainy into—what? The anthologist calls him a "hero." But it is not anything positively heroic, which is too affirmative, nor anti-heroic, which would be to map postmodernism back onto the frontier. Say, then, this figure is something that crosses hero and anti-hero, something sliding and turning, something attractively and comically troubling. Rice's wanting such parts— later writing them himself, and hiring others to write them for him— illustrates a cogency on which his sort of theatre was able to pounce.

New character types were emerging that cause problems of interpretation until one sees that they do not fit in the inherited stories. New publics needed new stories to display and confirm themselves. Thus, new parts emerged to render and explain the emerging publics that eat the maw and bedevil the consciousness of extant forms. Stage one showed characters whose place no longer fitted into the existing stories (*The Lottery Ticket*). Stage two was entr'actes that existed in limbo, dancing without context of their own or stories to extend their implications ("Jump Jim Crow"). Stage three was the figuring out of narratives that gave these new characters and gestures some contextual gristle and gravity (*Bone Squash Diavolo, Otello,* and Chanfrau and Baker's *A Glance at New York*).[18]

What was this recalcitrance that Wormwood represented? These new publics might make themselves merry by discomfiting the middle class. Wormwood is a positive figure for *calicots* frequenting theatres in the early century. Within Rice's schema, Wormwood is not so much a deracinated as a not-yet-racinated English grotesque. He prefigures the American bones of contention on which Rice would gnaw the whole rest of his career, from Jim Crow to Bone Squash to Otello.

Rice had learned from this spirit when, a little later that year, he started playing the Jim Crow character. His personation of Jim Crow was a standoff embrace. Jim Crow had qualities both likable and not. He was victim and boor, at once raggy and ragging, crippled and crippling. His contradictions were similar to those Rice chose to impersonate in Wormwood. Neither Wormwood nor Jim Crow was one-dimensional. Both busily upset the scenes they occupied rather than calming or resolving either their surroundings or themselves. A feel for the way Jim Crow chafed and pricked every way at once is in any cluster of his verses:

XVII
I met a Philadelphia niggar
Dress'd up quite nice & clean
But de way he 'bused de Yorkers
I thought was berry mean.

XVIII
So I knocked down dis Sambo
And shut up his light,
For I'm jist about as sassy,
As if I was half white.

XIX
But he soon jumped up again,
An 'gan for me to feel,
Says I go away you niggar,
Or I'll skin you like an eel.

XX
I'm so glad dat I'm a niggar,
An dont you wish you was too
For den you'd gain popularity
By jumping Jim Crow.

XXI
Now my brodder niggars,
I do not think it right,
Dat you should laugh at dem
Who happen to be white.

XXII
Kase it dar misfortune,
And dey'd spend ebery dollar,
If dey only could be
Gentlemen ob colour.[19]

    Neither Wormwood nor Jim Crow was frozen like the pietistic tokens of blacks, printed on silk or cast in medal, that Arthur and Lewis Tappan were selling on Pearl Street in New York City. Rice's dramatic use was unlike the Tappans' use of blackness. Abolitionists and businessmen were ultimately interested in stroking the symbolic categories of blacks into productive patterns. But what Rice inaugurated for young people poorly employed and flocking to his song and dance was an interest in black figures going in opposite directions. Rice enacted a figure that was continually raising Cain with categories dear to the merchantry.

    Already, early in his career, Rice's power of mimicry became an issue. What made Rice's Wormwood "commendable" to his manager Ludlow, for instance, was none of this burrs-beneath-the-saddle business. Rather, Ludlow liked that Rice so exactly imitated the original U.S. performance of the part by James Roberts at the Bowery Theatre. No one spoke of Rice, in his own time, as a great originator. Instead, his contemporaries saw him as a mimic, a translator of perceived reality. His comedy hauled features from one domain to another.

    words . . . of our origins
In ghostlier demarcations, keener sounds
    —Wallace Stevens, "Idea of Order at Key West"

Noah Ludlow thought that the upstart Tom Rice "had more talent than genius."[20] What did that mean? To list geniuses Ludlow might have proposed is to list blooms now virtually extinct: Edwin Forrest, Charles Kemble, Junius Booth, tragedians all. Even a comedian like Charles Mathews, with his astounding polymonologues, left scarcer footprints along Atlantic coasts than Rice. What Rice set rolling, furthermore, has compounded between his era and ours from comedy into cultural flashpoints, obstinately and continually troubling. Let's wonder, therefore, at Ludlow's "talent," applied so confidently.

To what end was Rice's talent? I cull here three contemporary comments about his performance as mimesis, for accurate is what Rice's performance most seemed to his fellows, rather than innovative or inventive, which were qualities of genius. This accuracy is just what seems most incredible today. The following remarks display expectations about what seemed real in the theatre in the early nineteenth century. Ludlow, first, certainly knew what he meant, and he wrote exactly: "That talent consisted in [Rice's] great fidelity in imitating the broad and prominent peculiarities of other persons, as was evident in his close delineations of the corn-field negro, drawn from real life." Second, a London reviewer in 1836, after Rice established his contagion there: "We will not say that we like Mr. Rice's performance, but there cannot be a doubt of its extraordinary reality. The shuffling gait, the strange whistle, and the more strange laugh, could never have been invented by Mr. Rice." Next, Frank Wemyss, the important theatre manager in Philadelphia and Pittsburgh, who knew Rice early, before his New York successes, and stayed close to him late:

> This gentleman . . . improved the opportunity his popularity afforded, by collecting all the really beautiful airs which the negro sings while performing his daily labour, and writing himself the "libretto" . . . With this capital, Mr. Rice crossed the Atlantic, and turned the heads of the chimney sweeps and apprentice boys of London, who wheeled about and turned about and jumped Jim Crow, from morning until night, to the annoyance of their masters, but the great delight of the cockneys. That his financial affairs have been improved by the trip there is little doubt, but his popularity in his native country has been lost, by his endeavour to ingraft the English dandy with the American negro.
>
> In London where a black man is scarcely seen, it might be remarkably "*funny*," but the broad caricature of the American negro was the attraction of Jim Crow at home, who, when converted into an English gentleman, was a most insipid creature. As an actor, Mr. Rice's reputation depends upon his black face; and how he contrives to keep it white, might be

matter of grave debate, begrimmed as it has been for the last ten years, at least three hours in each of the twenty-four.[21]

These remarks help display significant aspects of what actors and publics took to be "real," what "invented," and what interrelations they had in the early Atlantic theatre, early nineteenth century. Ludlow and Wemyss were knowledgeable pros who knew Rice well, the one managing his apprentice performances for months, the other hiring and corresponding with the maturing actor down the years. Although Ludlow never thought to yield center stage to the figures Rice would ensconce there, Ludlow's barnstorming attempts to apply his English repertoire to frontier particulars gave him a canny eye for the behavior Rice was imitating. Thus, when Ludlow awarded Rice's gestures "great fidelity," his judgment had weight. What seemed true enough in Rice's day, however, now seems false.

Ludlow's phrase "prominent peculiarities" points out the core of what Rice was doing. Just as the young actor in New York City had scripts from London earlier than others, so out in the field he seized on dance steps, dialect, and "airs" before others realized they could sell them. What evidently distinguished Thomas Rice from his blacked-up precursors Andrew Jackson "Dummy" Allen, Edwin Forrest, and George Washington Dixon was his "close delineations" of speech and gesture. He did not repeat the stereotyped *stage* dialect for blacks. Instead, he collected "airs which the negro sings." Likewise, he garnered the other gestural practices, angular dance and jittery movement, recalcitrance and lip. He thoroughly imagined and noticed particularities that were already givens in the gestural vocabularies of peoples under scrutiny—English town clerk or black American fieldhand.

Then he produced them. Or, depending on how much one wishes to say they were given to him or he stole them, perhaps Rice *reproduced* them, as hallmarks. The givens might have been broad when Rice noticed them, but it was his close delineation that made them prominent. His copying was such that his own era could see it as "talent." Most critics in our own era have seen this copying as theft. But some others might own that Rice was translating gestural practice more precisely. Wallace Stevens named this abstract accuracy, in "Idea of Order at Key West," when his characters heard surf as "words . . . of our origins / In ghostlier demarcations, keener sounds." Rice's delineations, both marking and bridging, transmitted details of movement and sound to publics who were at least as eager as Stevens's speaker to figure out their origins.

The spin Rice put on these keener demarcations might count as inaugural. Anyway one wishes to put it, Rice's mimetic talent assembled new codes of representation. He compacted closer approximations of the gestural vocabularies among clerks and workers, white and black. These he mingled in the figure of blackface fun, knees bent and turning, always bent, always turning. That's how T. D. Rice took occupation first of frontier then of metropolitan stages.

Rice treated gestures in such a way that, to his audiences, he seemed to be retaining them exactly in their context. "Drawn from real life," Ludlow said. His moves "could never have been invented by Mr. Rice," the English reviewer said. But this actor in motley also generalized gestures so that other groups in other contexts could identify with them. The "chimney sweeps and apprentice boys of London," Wemyss said, "wheeled about and turned about and jumped Jim Crow . . . to the annoyance of their masters."

Unless Rice's execution had been extraordinary, it would not have merited Ludlow's comment, enriched Rice, nor excited the spate of current reconsiderations more than a century and a half later. He must have recomposed the types for his congenial audience, as of old—so that the gestures retained their town or field contexts. But he also showed the gestures anew, surprising and funny. In the process, he must have been tickling the conventions of reality: finding the line that George Carlin notes between totem and taboo, crossing and smudging it: "The obligation of the comedian is to find where the line is drawn, deliberately cross it, and make the audience glad you took them with you."[22]

           play, you must,
       A tune beyond us, yet ourselves.
               —Wallace Stevens, "The Man with the Blue Guitar"

What we know as *real* floats above the multiple presences of objects. The real is what holds together for the viewer the supposed natures of the object. The real bears no close comparison with individual versions of the object, in themselves, of course, or with objects' senses of themselves, their own supposed natures. In Rice's *The Virginia Mummy,* his character Ginger

Blue is not a real black servant in a frontier hotel, and was not to be taken as any real black servant by the white working publics to whom Rice played. Certainly he would not have been understood as black by any black public, or black member of a minstrel public, either. What did people see when they watched Rice perform? Everyone but the most remote yokels saw Jim Crow, Ginger Blue, Bone Squash, and Wormwood, for that matter—all Rice's delineations—as tokens. They brought together what his public thought of themselves with taboo behavior they imagined incorporating. They amalgamated the many presences, both living and fancied. In that way, Rice's song and dance of blackness played what Wallace Stevens's modern understanding has called "a tune beyond us, yet ourselves" ("The Man with the Blue Guitar"). Stevens understood the necessity of this transforming push that retains contingency while enabling others to identify with us, and we with them.

"Remote yokels": the wonderful coinage "yokel," which came into usage in 1812, not long before Rice's dance, refers to the chuckle sound of the English green woodpecker, specifically, and all woodpeckers, generally. The green woodpecker inhabits disturbed spaces between the country and the city, also urban park areas, also greenbelts. Bobolinks, chuckleheaded woodpeckers, gamecocks, crows, turkeys, buzzards, geese, chicks, street sparrows: metaphorical social (dis)placements were and remain frequently avian. *Yokel* is one of many avian demarcations.

One of the impulses to jump Jim Crow during this early transition from an agrarian toward an industrial order was to play along the dividing lines between the two positions, smudging, maintaining, and installing them. The greenest audience members did not recognize this procedure. Some of the deepest Kentuckians, reported the minstrel trouper Sam Sanford, mistook white minstrels in blackface for actual black people. "Many, many people really thought us black," Sanford wrote, "and would wait after the performance to see the 'Niggers' come out, some asking 'say' do them chaps sleep in Hall, them Nigger chaps." One night an owner of a rooming house where Sanford's troupe was lodging went to the hall where he had overheard them say they were going that night. All returning after their performance, by separate routes, the players asked for beer and Welsh Rarebit. The landlord brought it, "saying I thought you would have been to the Hall to night I looked around but did not see you. We were there [Sanford said,] and if you was you could not help but see us—what part of the hall did you set [in, asked the landlord]? Why on the stage, of course [replied the players], where else would we set: I don't understand you [replied the rube], I saw no one but the Negros."[23]

This naiveté poses an apparent problem for anyone claiming, as I do, that the blackface mask was a legible sign of complex overlap. If his audience only perceived black actuality in his act, can what Rice pushed along in his early jumps and songs, later in his plays, have been a conscious enactment of democratic recalcitrance? Can it have helped form *lumpen* agency?

The short answer is yes. Not everyone understood Rice's jumps and skits as self-aware hybrids. Nor did anyone focus on blackface codes as hybrids all the time. Maybe they never consciously articulated it that way. But, as babies learn the meaning of words and fledglings learn to flock together, so do a lore group's novitiates learn to read signs that join them one to another. This coming to recognize the protocols of congeniality is what Clifford Geertz, following Gilbert Ryle, calls the ability to distinguish a significant wink from an inadvertent twitch.[24] It is every group's glue. The thicker a person's understanding is at such seams, the more secure is the person's membership. This helps explain why crowds flocked to Rice's performances. While he danced along those divisive seams, he thickened his congenial public's understanding of who they were.

The blackface mask was a bait hiding many hooks. It lurked to catch its publics sometime during a slow reflective process that had its effects well past the performance itself. In the theatre, occasionally, but more likely later, recollected in tranquillity, while clerks and workers were getting and spending in the market, or treating in the saloon, they might remember more multifarious dimensions in the performance than they recognized in the theatre. What took place in the Chatham and Bowery gave publics their place later.

What if they never saw the doubleness at all, never understood that the purported blacks on the stage were not conventions or signs? Then there would have been no hooks, no bait, nothing but impoverished reality— for them. For these innocents, as for the middle-class and religious policers of minstrelsy, there would have been nothing but the disdained popular culture that literature, high culture in general, and earnest religion are all said to transcend.

So it's worth talking about when the audience just doesn't get it. This is the *yokel effect,* when a cultural performance produces outsiders. Such boondocks sensibilities, along with comparable misconstruals along urban

class lines, were both awry from the daily experience of blackface performers and, simultaneously, one of their proudest achievements. Sanford and
others report audience mistakings of the theatrical "real" as being both
ridiculous and, also, proof of their accurate portrayals. The fun of both the
portrayal and the perception—on both sides of the apron—must have
revolved around this getting it, this moving from yokel to member, woodpecker to crow, green to black.

Sanford's landlord so misinterpreted the codes of representation that his
gaffe tokened insiders' lore about how dumb those yokels in the audience
can be. Thus, audience members sometimes made mistakes about what
they saw, but it would merely compound their mistake to understand this
anomaly as typical, as the response which blackface conventions generally
elicited. The whole point of the anecdote, and of similar stories told by
other performers and viewers, is that in fact most publics did sufficiently
read the performers' multiple invocations. Their correct reading is precisely
what organized them into a public, and what blazoned them as such to
others.

Just as it was remarkable when naive audience members mistook Iago's
scheming for real evil—angry faces across the apron threatening to wring
his "infernal neck"[25]—or stormed the stage of melodrama to unwax the
mustaches of melodrama's velvet-caped villains, so too was it exceptional
in early blackface performance when rubes misread the rapidly imbricating
codes. The mistakes were not limited to whites, of course. Nor to early
moments in the (blackface) lore cycle. The lore cycle is new to the young,
always.

When she was eighty-five years old and learning to read, Mrs. Ruthie
Taylor, a black woman who was born in 1905 and grew up working in the
virtual slavery of the turpentine camps in the Florida Panhandle, recalled
for her teacher not only the Silas Green Minstrel Show coming to Tallahassee in the 1960s but also the minstrel parades drumming and dancing
through the hamlet of Woodville when she was a little girl. "I would become
scared and cry if a minstrel show was coming to town," Mrs. Taylor remembered. "I would see a wagon with men dancing and singing in front
of it advertising the show. The accents were so perfect that I could never
tell what race the men were under the black face. The shows revolved
around making fun of the boss man." Her parents, she remembered,
spanked her for running up to one of the black-faced men and telling him,
"You're no Mr. Sambo."[26]

Unrealized blackface codes befuddle Kentucky adults and set up a Florida child's spanking. These recurring moments some three generations apart point at the kernel of what blackface performance communicates. In every correctly received blackface performance there must be a duck-rabbit acknowledgment. You are a yokel if you see only part of the experience. The mask, the doubling, all the performance protocols ensure the overlapping of several identities held together as one. During this identity moment the form makes both its most fundamental and its most fulfilling claim, suddenly, together. Every member of the public, you, me, Ruthie Taylor, Sanford's host, we all either get it or we don't.

Getting it allows recipients to describe the richness, the webs of connections, that the identity moment conveys. When they correctly read the protocols they recognize that the blacked-up performers both are and are not like what they seem. Straying away from that combined understanding might mean mistaking the white man's codes for blackness, per se, as happened to Sanford's white host. Alternatively, straying away from the understanding of combination means failing to see the black actor's codes as codes, not seeing the Sambo aura beyond the black actor, as happened to the spanked black youngster in Woodville. Failing to see that there were connotations beyond the dance and the songs was a misreading also common to reviewers and commentators trained in other traditions. Such reviewers were able to respond to other works of art, but not yet to these. All these misreadings have been produced by the doubling terms of the mask; all these misreaders have been chuckleheads, all in their ways.

> They not only carried on their race-mixing and sex-switching among themselves, but the one they called Jim Crow sang a song that told . . . how they were going to mongrelize the whole country with their foul and filthy ways.
>
> —Vigilantes describing a Jim Crow dance in Wesley Brown's *Darktown Strutters*

One of the most engaging meditations on blackface performance as an enterprise troubling all the communities connected to it is not a play or a film, not a critical analysis either commercial or academic, but a novel called *Darktown Strutters* (1994) by Wesley Brown. Brown takes large liberties with the legends surrounding both T. D. Rice and the postulated figure of Jim Crow. The latter becomes literal in the novel, a speaking agent, a dancing genealogy. The novel writes him out as a crippled figure, husband

and father, proud and anxious, who refuses to stay passive when whites copy his dance. Instead, he teaches the dance also to an adopted son, Jim Too. This ensures the steps will be transmitted in black as well as white performance. It also ensures that this new Jim Crow, who is the novel's main character, will be a stereotype fleshed out. But Brown's Tom Rice is also more than stereotypical. Brown builds him into a frontier trouper more like Sanford or Ludlow than like the metropolitan star who was the actual Rice. Quite conscious that his samplings from black culture obligate him to return some of what he has taken, and quite comfortable within this obligation, the Tom Rice in *Darktown Strutters* hires Crow's son, Jim Too, while he is still a slave, to be a featured dancer in his minstrel show touring the West and the South.

None of this is historical. But it is paradoxically much closer to the real spirit of early blackface than the ways written history has mistakenly told these stories. Not until very late in his career, in fact, when he had lost his voice and his dancing grace, did Rice travel as a *minstrel* performer, and then in Tom shows, not in the formal semicircle with ragged gags and vaudeville tunes that made up the form as the Christy and Virginia Minstrels put it on—and as Brown recreates it in *Darktown Strutters*. Until illness broke him down, the actual Rice toured as a star actor in his narrative plays, and performed as song-and-dance man during entr'actes. There was almost certainly no factual Jim Crow, father or son. Nevertheless, *Darktown Strutters* is idiosyncratic, provoking, and certainly mold-breaking in the present climate of scorn for all things blackface.

Brown shows a thoughtful black dancer, in Jim Too, coming to understand the risk and menace and charisma in blacking up—no matter what color is beneath the mask. Brown also shows Jim Too realizing the use of the mask in the formation of identity. At the novel's climactic moment, but only then, Jim Crow himself willingly blacks up. While I abbreviate this story and its effects in the next few pages, I mean to suggest that, by showing his character's growing awareness, Brown indicates how lore cycles gradually generate, appreciate, and enforce their own protocols.

Brown estimates minstrelsy as a national tag-team wrestling match, intermittently fatal and often violent, over "who's who," with everyone except Jim Crow donning blackface for different reasons. This account is close to my own take on the issues. So, too, is Jim's novel-long struggle with the meaning of the mask. Even as he gradually comes to appreciate and trust Rice, even after understanding that Rice's intention was to "put shows together that played both ends of the talk about slavery and freedom against something funny in the middle"—still Crow refuses to black up.[27] Even after Rice has been shot to death by an angry white spectator during a performance along the Kentucky border, even when Jim is dancing a eulogy on his employer's coffin at his burial service in New York's Five Points, Jim dances as himself—unmasked. And of course everyone but the racists, who are trying to enforce their own rigid interpretation of the protocols, appreciates Jim Crow's intentions. For who among us opposes people being seen as they are?

According to Brown, however, Jim's refusal to mask is a mistake. His earnest projection of an authentic self simplifies who he is. When audiences see him unmasked, they do not see all of him. He sees himself as untainted by whiteness and not marked by the filthy rites he passes through. He wants to perform as truth a self that is not a performer, a self that is pure. This emerges in one of Brown's riskiest scenes, indeed a scene risky in *any* novel, and one which leads to an ultimate meaning in blackface performance.

I will move toward it crabwise.

I'm standing outside my door, talking to Huey, a friend and builder come to estimate some damage. We are looking at my fence after a tropical storm has dropped a massive pine tree on it, on my car, on my garden. Huey asks what I'm writing about. I tell him, Minstrel Shows. Huey pauses a second, studies the snakeskin points on his boots, glances at me, peers at the fallen pine, says, Well, I have some ex-wives who could write that book.

Huey's punchline became routine while I was preparing this book. Its pun on minstrel and menstrual show points at an implicit meaning of the tarred face in minstrelsy, the gooey blackening in tarring and feathering, the smearing that runs through related popular rites from rough noise (charivari, shivaree, riding skimmington), even to the feathered chorines high-kicking in Las Vegas, New York, Paris. It shows us why Jim Crow blacked up, finally, toward the end of *Darktown Strutters*. And crabbing through these connections bolsters the claims I will make about the apparently harmless assertions that the actual T. D. Rice and other early blackface performers released when they started jumping Jim Crow in the first third of the nineteenth century.

Wesley Brown's character Jim Crow in *Darktown Strutters* survives the death of Tom Rice, sits out the Civil War performing in Five Points dives, but returns to the road after the war with the Featherstone Traveling Theatre. Brown is basing this second troupe on the quite different sorts of black minstrel shows that cropped up during and following Reconstruction. He takes liberties with some of their famous performers, just as he has earlier with antebellum Rice. The Featherstone troupe is integrated, run by two black women, and still rouses racists in its audiences, who now want the troupe to exclude the whites in their cast. Brown is silently laughing at the absurdities of racist tides that first disallowed blacks into racial representation, now disallow whites. Through it all, Brown's Jim Crow refuses to wear the mask. What brings him to reverse himself? What makes him don the mask, and to what effect?

One character, Jubilee, whom Brown bases on the actor Billy Kersands, proposes a two-sided metamask. "First we white-face one side of our faces and black-face the other side," Jubilee explains (p. 174).[28] Jim refuses this mask just as he earlier refused masking when he worked for Rice. This refusal has stabilized his life, he tells his lover, for it was the one thing about which he could always feel clearly. In a key conversation near the novel's climax, told in Brown's oracular style, this woman scoffs at Jim's naive belief that he "never had no part in it." She tells him, "It don't matter that you never blacked up. You made a name for yourself from it, same as those who used it" (p. 184). You smell, too, she tells him, It's what makes you alive and worth bothering with.

Now trembling and holding the cloth she has used to clean her blackened face, Jim tells her about the time rednecks attacked him for having performed without blacking up: "They wiped this all over my face and tried to cut a shit-eatin grin up to here . . . they left me a face I can't wipe off!" (p. 184). But all this is preparatory to her remarkable response, which plumbs one core meaning for the blackface mask:

> She reached out and took the stained cloth from him and wiped the palm of her hand with it . . . Then she lifted her nightgown, put her hand between her legs and showed him the blood . . . [She] wiped her hand over her face . . . [She] put her fingers up to his mouth. Jim's eyes were like blisters about to burst when [she] moved close to him and rubbed the scarred side of his face with the hand that was black and bloody. The water broke in his eyes and she held him while his whole body shook without let-up. (pp. 184–185)

This blood knowledge is a vernacular mark of Cain that Jim has been resisting. It brings him to a fuller sense of himself, just in time for the novel's climax.

Jim brings on the climax by deciding to use blackface for what he assumes is a performance viewed only by the rest of the integrated company. Moved by Jim's joining them, the company are all inspired to swap clothes, bending gender, merging race. Vigilantes secretly watch this performance, however, from a distance. They report to the inflamed white community that those minstrels "were going to mongrelize the whole country with their foul and filthy ways" (p. 202). A mob sets fire to the wagons of the Featherstone travelers in a final conflagration. The mob destroys the troupe, but Jim survives as a token of spasmodic, uncatchable improvisation. Like weed seed scattering, Jim Crow moves on. Thus it is that blackface performance can sometimes deliver blood knowledge to its ripest participants. Thus it has its effects which can be devastating, subtle, lasting, and underground.

Darktown Strutters links the commercial phenomenon of blackface performance with clowning and trickster traditions in Africa as well as in early North America.[29] Wesley Brown shows that the most powerful aspect of minstrel performance was neither its inevitable quotient of demeaning attributes nor its opposing urge to authenticity, both trying to approach an exclusive essence, but instead its radical portion of contamination, literal overlap, and identification with this muddier process.

This earlier tradition of the clown as transgressor and trickster lurks behind minstrels and can lend them menstrual signification. The tar, the pitch, the grease of the mask sustains and triggers this trickster dimension. Brown's remarkable scene in *Darktown Strutters* is an especially clear instance of this. Both the vigilantes, who carve "a shit-eatin grin" on his young face, and his mature lover, who smears her menstrual blood and burnt-cork stain over that scar onto the face of his prime years, are in their competing ways enforcing his trickster license.[30] It is no wonder, of course, when some performers and parts of their publics resent this enforcement. But if we recognize the mask as a fundamental sign of radical trickster license persisting to very near our own time, perhaps we can understand better the reasons for these stubborn transgressions.

The clown in anthropological ritual in both African and native North American cultures does not just release the tension attendant upon ritual, but much more. Clowns have crossed into taboo territory or experience in order to convey a medicine that is derived from dealing with the taboo—usually symbolized by menstrual blood, but sometimes, also, by feces and urine mixed with female pubic hair. Sometimes the blood is symbolized by brown water, other times and in other cultures by mud smeared on the body or face. Burnt-cork blackface is clearly relevant here, and Jim Crow's lover in *Darktown Strutters* makes it explicit. Clowns bring medicine from forbidden experience into acceptable arenas, so that timid but longing fans will not need to go where clowns have gone. Wesley Brown has given us a novel that shows the shaman in Jim Crow. He shows blackface performance that recovers an etymological sense of *minstrel* ritual, referring back to the transitive verb to *minister.* Jim Crow ministers to his publics when he dances. He ministers to his publics most comprehensively, most radically, most effectively—when he dances smeared in his form's accumulated symbolization.[31]

Blackface performance is a ritual that inoculates its congenial publics in motley experience. It takes on the burden of the trickster to carry out its own peculiar mission of talking back to power in the industrializing Atlantic. Bearing this in mind we are ready to crab back. Now we are like a hermit crab bearing the protection of another critter, even though it is comically ill-fitting, toward the legendary persona of Jim Crow and his re-creation by the real man T. D. Rice. When we left him, Rice was twenty years old, in Mobile, playing Wormwood in *The Lottery.* He was seeking roles that disturbed society's established positions. He was playing them without resolution. He was displaying their irresolvability.

> I wish de bobalition folks, would only set me free,
> I'd go to work I swan, an write my doleful history,
> But if in bondage sooty, I my hours must prolong,
> I hope de buckra peoples pleased to hear my song.
> Singing sweep O! lo, sweep O! lo, sweep O! lo.
>
> —T. D. Rice, as Jim Crow, singing "Hard Hearted Was My Master"

As I return to the young white actor T. D. Rice slogging around the frontier looking for his main chance, I am expected to recount a pair of standard stories. I am supposed to tell how he stole the Jim Crow dance and song from a crippled black man named Jim Crow. I am supposed to tell how he nicked further behavior and rags from a levee layabout named Cuff. But what if—as I believe—these scenes never existed? What if the emulation was cumulative, incremental, began early and continued late? What if the model for the Jim Crow figure was no single man, at all, but a black folk pattern glimpsed here and absorbed there? And if I believe those obligatory retellings about Jim Crow and Cuff defame the way common people of every hue fit themselves to their dominant culture, what is my responsibility then?

I should displace those stories.

No single man authored Jim Crow; no single stable hand made up or taught the song. Instead there was a widespread African-American folk dance impersonating—delineating—crows, based in agricultural ritual and, some say, "magical in nature." In the 1970s Bessie Jones described learning the Jim Crow song as a child on the Georgia Sea Islands early in the twentieth century: "When I was a little girl, I thought Jim Crow might have been a bird, because it was 'going down to the new ground,' and they always shoot them birds out of the corn. 'New ground' is ground where the trees have been cut off, but it's never been planted in. So that was what I understood at the time, that was my idea. But we don't know what the old folks meant, we sure don't."[32]

There were lyrics to the song as Bessie Jones learned it, and I quote them below. However, the lyrics are only a fraction of the whole event. Clapping and slapping, double-timing and patting Juba, kicking and high-stepping, the staging and the lyrics were all part of dancing "Jim Crow." In 1830 in New Orleans, the white performer George Nichols learned "Jim Crow" from a black street performer named Picayune Butler. Children and adults sang these lyrics in Georgia, early in the twentieth century. Black children still do this dance, to my knowledge, at least in Tallahassee, Florida. The folklorist Jerrilyn McGregory sang and danced this song in the 1950s up along the Great Lakes waterways transmission route, in Gary, Indiana—also the home of Michael Jackson and his siblings. This song and dance lives. It may be as lively, and circling as separately, today as when the young T. D. Rice saw it performed, I believe probably first at Catherine Slip, but maybe not until he sailed south along the Atlantic coastal barrier islands with Noah Ludlow in December 1828.[33]

Here are the folk lyrics:

> Where you going buzzard?
> Where you going, crow?
> I'm going down to new ground
> To knock Jim Crow.
> Up to my kneecap,
> Down to my toe,
> And every time I jump up,

> I knock Jim Crow.
> (Speed increases)
> I knock,
> I knock Jim Crow.
> I knock,
> I knock Jim Crow.
> I knock, I knock,
> I knock Jim Crow
> (repeat ad lib).[34]

This is undoubtedly the song that Rice gradually adapted. Many of the earliest printed versions of the song as Rice sang it have a verse like this one, printed in 1832:

> I neeld to de buzzard
> An I bou'd to de Crow
> an eb'ry time I reel'd
> Why I jump't Jim Crow.[35]

There is no good term for these events. They are more than one thing, more than a song, more than a dance, not really a play or sacrament, much more than a reflex. Whatever we call them, however, such jumps took on particular force in the western Atlantic. The clustered gestures delineating common animals and birds that are in "Jump Jim Crow" became organizing points for a new identity. This was true at first for Africans in the Atlantic. Then it became true for others who imitated their culture.

It was around just such stories that the people who arrived here separately as Ibo women, Yoruba children, and Hausa men became Africans together. Members of every tribe sold across the middle passage to North America, Sterling Stuckey has argued, lost their specific tribal ethnicities in the crucible of slavery. Their owners denied those particular ethnic signals, and so did the peoples transported from Africa, because they too could not always decode the signs of other tribes. The result for the slaves, Stuckey shows, was less anomie than nationalist reformation. (Never mind the anomalous use of "nationalist.") On these shores, disparate and unrelated peoples gathered kinship within slavery. They eventually became Africans. They gathered together motifs of roaming and freedom that they might share. They applied specific gestures, tropes, and images to the songs and dances of a continuing blackface lore cycle. They were perforce assembling a new mask of identity, an Africanness, a blackness for a new ground never yet planted. They combined their twitches into enduring new winks.

Some tales which had been specific to single African tribes or regions, like the Ibo "King Buzzard," became widespread among African Americans. "It was also understood by many West Africans," Stuckey writes, "that the eternal wandering of the soul meant that it could not return to its native town in Africa or communicate there with the souls of relatives and others it had known in its lifetime."[36] The buzzard seemed to be a nomad. He was most elaborated in African-American performances, but as "Jump Jim Crow" indicates, traces of what he figured stuck in the cultural adaptations of Germans, Swiss, Irish, English, and others come to North America, as well as the displaced local rustics who migrated to the cities. In other words, for all the migratory publics that were adopting blackface performance as the mortar of their identity, the buzzard and the crow became insignia.

Around 1846, the Virginia Minstrels interposed a skit during their performances of "Lucy Long." Dan Emmett sang:

> Pray turkey buzzard lend to me your wing
> Till I fly over de river to see Miss Sally King.

But it turned out that Miss Sally had "a ticklar gagement," said Frank Brower, joining Emmett near the stage apron, "to go to camp me[e]tin' wid dis child."

Dan Emmett knew where Miss Sally went with Frank: "Hah! You went down to de fish Market to daunce arter eels, mity cureous kind ob camp meetin dat!"

> FRANK: It wasnt eels, it was big cat fish.
> DAN: What chune did you dance?
> CHORUS: Take your time Miss Lucy
> Take your time Miss Lucy Long
> Rock de cradle Lucy
> Take your time my dear.[37]

This interlude illustrates what happens to these folk insignia in the turmoil of pop performance. The Ibo buzzard, having become an African-American buzzard, gives a lift to the Virginia Minstrels. And they lifted the buzzard—not for a ride home across the big water, but for a short ride to a sexual rendezvous. Then they embedded and sexualized this token in a series of risqué double entendres. Eels and catfish swim through the song as sexual parts. Gullah mythology stirs together with Catherine Slip performances brought from Long Island by the likes of Bobolink Bob. While Frank Brower and Dan Emmett sing, all these elements rocking slowly in Miss Lucy Long's cradle are continually clearing a pastiche new ground, neither tribal nor African, neither singly folk nor wholly pop, not only commercial and surely not pure: "take your time my dear." That's one of the ways the buzzard was, what? Extended? Nested? Traduced and diluted, secularized? Enriched.

In just this welter of additional meaning, the crow took on perhaps the most ambiguous set of references, differently for everyone. It is clear that "Jim Crow" has bequeathed an infamously strange career of opposing effects. Indeed, oppositions are kinetic already in the folk lyrics of "Knock Jim Crow," well before social control narrowed them down to segregation codes. When Bessie Jones said, "we don't know what the old folks meant," her companion John Davis replied, "Anyway, they didn't tell nobody."

Before Rice absorbed and reprojected it, the crow's charisma stemmed from his trickiness. The singers in Bessie Jones's Georgia lyrics approach Jim Crow warily. The first thing to realize in these lyrics is how many facets this folk crow has. There's one crow aspect to bow before, whose call is absorbed as the singer takes over its role, and other crow aspects—Jims— to knock down on the new ground. The singers bow before they knock, but they do both, and a lot more knocking than bowing. They speak *to* the crow. Then they sing and dance out his answer. They sing *in* his voice: I'm going down . . . to knock that (other) Jim Crow.

So, Jim Crow was already in his black and pre-pop variants both a sympathetic and a harassed character. He had become tricky trying to scavenge within a framework of surveillance and extreme competitiveness for scarce resources, harried by mockingbirds and owls, farmers and hostile flocks. The song itself imagines new ground as a site for a cutting contest, for testing identity through performance. "Knock Jim Crow" enacts this cutting contest constantly, deliberately, speeding up. The folk crow that emerged after the middle passage to reorganize and abstract behavior for Africans, and that Rice would have watched in such clearings as Catherine Market, knew his conditions even if he was unable or too cagey to specify their meaning. Beset and harried, a denizen of surveillance, the crow foraged new ground, nabbing subsistence for himself among all the others overlapping the territory. The crow was the very figure of surviving in overlapped space.

Thus there is identification along with difference in this song, as in black-face in general, as in most thriving popular gestures. "Jim Crow" occupies, dances on, and sings out the border between one character and another. It is "going down"; it is in transit toward a "new ground." It assumes, absorbs, and projects multivalence. Indeed, this chance to play out the contested multiple meanings in identity, I have argued throughout, is what makes certain sorts of popular culture endure. This multivalence is both elaborated and curtailed in the push and pull of the song's cyclical phases over its history.

This new ground, that is really very old, is what I stand on to displace those impudent stories of Rice stealing his song from a hostler named Jim Crow or a levee hand named Cuff. I propose a process of social osmosis to displace tales of individual pilferage. Sticking to pilferage stories, with their individuals and blame, causes frustrating blockage. Everyone is stuck in a quagmire; everyone stands around staring at the same legends, reflex-ively blaming the other fellow, flipping used data over and over. Every way one uses the stories of expropriation, they lock out from serious discussion the motley connections blackface performers and publics were piecing to-gether. However good it may make us feel, a "rhetoric of blame" will not recover that motley.[38] Rather, it prolongs the exclusion.

That's why I'm not adding my link to this incestuous chain. Instead, next to those legends of theft from Jim and Cuff, I will insert a different tale that I discovered in the archives. (I imagine this found tale careening out of the woods. He's a lean tom, sheen-gone and feather-torn, returning to a pam-pered roost of preening birds hand-fed on domestic corn. Maybe this wild tom, toughened in his prolonged exclusion, can send flapping a couple of those familiar softies.) The tale I will puzzle out is endemic to the culture that Rice's performances organized. It shows how his culture was trying to protect itself from the scorn those better-placed magazine pieces conveyed. But the external stories of Crow and Cuff came to block this internal tale from view during what I take to be a fairly conscious struggle for control of the originary territory.[39]

The stories of pilferage from Crow and Cuff have seemed to win—but perhaps what seems now to be a concluded struggle was merely middle rounds. Maybe the tale here returning has not really lost its place, yet, but has simply been knocked aside by the now-standard stories, which continue to block it, so that it remains forgotten. I found this suppressed story, and a couple of its kin, crumbling in those wildwood research archives—the Schomburg, the British Museum, the Library of Congress.

> I hopes I shall hab de honor ob displeasing you all.
> —*Life of Jim Crow*

Relying on mid-nineteenth-century journalism to define blackface performance has had dire effects. At both ends of the cycle, it has erased motley experience. Writers for the middle-class papers and the monthly magazines did not sufficiently map the perspective and the performance scripts that working rowdies assembled. Instead, journalists put controlling spins on those rogues. Tit for tat, descriptions for scripts, indeed: performers fought their commentators for control of the form, already seeming to lose during the 1840s, losing quite clearly by the 1850s.[40]

By losing, I mean that the links white and black common people attempted were turning inside out into scorn and differentiation. However, this talk of winning and losing can be misleading. Entrepreneurs started directing the venues and plays. Theatre professionals jealous of Rice's sudden success, and middle-class commentators deriving information from actors' stories, stepped in to divert meaning along orthodox vectors. And many of the improvised early skits became formulaic. All this is true. But it is not true that merchant control eliminated what was radical in the early mimicry. Instead, when the merchantry attempted to snuff the links blackface performance made across race and class, they forced it to become subtle and sneaky. They made it continually disperse and recombine in variants not generally understood to be related to blackface roots, like the rock and rap videos of the present. Continually repressed, it has continually returned. These struggles over interracial fascination, against it and for it, leading to transmission, recombination, and the cultural work they do, are the ultimate concerns of this book.

Build the case from clues in its own texts, and blackface performance becomes the body of lore by which ethnically mingled working and scavenging people in cities of the Atlantic diaspora during the 1830s and 1840s negotiated the terms of their coherence. By using its blackface actions, a young working public so organized itself around its own tokens, so tickled into being its own expressive capacity, and so fought against the atomization of its cross-racial base that it mounted a real challenge to merchant hegemony. This underclass independence, much more than its racism or vulgarity, provoked the contempt that clamped down on this emerging motley in its first heyday.

After all, racism and vulgarity were widely shared and surely exceeded in the imaginative actions of other peoples around the Atlantic during the era—if only because these richer people had far greater power to elaborate their inclinations. Exhibit A in such an argument might be the very stories about Rice's theft of Jim Crow's song and Cuff's clothes. The cartooned crudeness of these fantasies wildly exceeds anything Rice, Emmett, the Christys, or even the sociopathic George Washington Dixon projected in any of their actual scripts, stories, or songs. The truth is that these Cuff and Crow legends about blackface are and always were hostile to it: middle-class impositions. They tell us about a world different from Rice's motley connections.

Meanwhile, in the 1830s and 1840s, important early "Ethiopian delineators" were not so much racist as something like its opposite, or something besides. Well before abolitionism in the United States had gathered steam, and about the time it was peaking in England, these white working youths in the west Atlantic were choosing to join with perceived blackness. The reasons and functions of this choice were not simple. But it was this choosing *among themselves* to delineate their cross-racial mutuality, and to organize it into coalignment, that angered the magazine writers and prominent politicians. These motley youths' insistence on identifying with black style was what made the middle class attack Jim Crow excitements. Here was a culture separating from the body of the main culture and finding its own sufficiency.

That the underclass could readily achieve exuberant coherence demonstrated to some that its threat had to be contained. But what first looks like defeat during the chain of cultural history may instead be deflection, may even be an energizing kink. To prepare for this discussion of change played out on the popular Atlantic stage, I have had to uncover the roots of blackface mimesis in African-American performance at market sites, as at Catherine Slip. I have indicated the form's roots in Euro-American folk rites, as in tarring and feathering. I have wanted to indicate the momentum of this separate sufficiency as a lore cycle unto itself. I have slowed down the momentum to look at the decades of the blackface lore cycle's transfer from

folk to popular culture. These were the years of the construction of the
underclass that, as yet, Had No Name—Theodore Parker called them "the
dangerous classes."[41] These are the years when the American Renaissance
fictions were gathering. These were also the years of industrial consolidation on both sides of the North Atlantic. These tangled events all helped
produce one another.

I do not construe blackface performance—Jim Crow—as the eponymous agent responsible for American racism. Minstrelsy certainly accompanied cruel domination, but it did not start that way. Rather, it began in
order to work out, and express, mixed feelings of identification and fascination through a growing grammar of charismatic gestures. Then it gradually molded those gestures into the first comprehensive enactment of
blackness as a disturbing ideal that the United States had. As it evolved,
blackface action encoded racial identification even as it inscribed racial
stereotypes. Good effects accompanied bad. P. T. Barnum, Sam Sanford,
E. P. Christy, Charles White, and other ever more middle-class entrepreneurs gradually realigned the disturbances of this identification, but even
then the multiple aspects of the minstrel mask preserved contradictory
meanings. A late example is pertinent: when asked why not all the actors
donned blackface in *Pitch a Boogie Woogie,* a 1928 movie of black minstrelsy—by and about blacks, for black audiences—one African-American
performer recently remembered, "We put on blackface when we had something really *crazy* to say."[42]

I want to figure out a history of blackface that can account for that eager
spirit of licensed madness. Thus, the alternative story I will puzzle out has
roots crazier than the stories that prevailed in nineteenth-century middle-
class monthly magazines. The tale I uncover here is enthusiastic, positive.
Like the street smarts it brings into prose and organizes, it is self-protective.
It manages this protection by arriving under cover of another's shell. However, the core beneath the shell is recognizably starting to differ from its
cover. It is discernibly becoming a new hybrid voice. Its most prominent
feature is its distinctly tender brio. Before he's even left his introduction,
"To my Feller Citizens de Public," in his earliest prose account of himself,
T. D. Rice as Jim Crow is striking wild:

> I make my infernal sensibilifications yieldify to de "Fox poplar," as I tinks
> dey call de people's breath at de Walnut street Te-atre . . . I am gwaing in
> short time to do like oder great hactors, publish my account ob men and
> manners in dese blessed States, and I trus I shall be inable to do dem as

much justice as dey desarve, on account ob my debilty to use falsifica-
tionority as de foreignificated deatrical ladies do. If I do not howebber
beat some dem up a gum tree, den I trus my dear little Jimmy may fall
off de chimbly top and—pop safe an sound into de arms ob ole moder
Public.[43]

Already here both the dialect and behavioral gestures are in motion. They
skitter between the bluster of the Davy Crockett roarer, with his "infernal
sensibilifications," and the newly created, distinctively tender delineation
of the freed black, with his *b*'s replacing *f*'s, *d*'s replacing *th*'s, with his gum
tree and chimbly and his winking "trus" in "de arms ob ole moder Public."[44]
Rice is voicing Jim Crow almost like the almanacs were already voicing
Crockett and Fink, but the differences, too, are important. The change in
the way Rice registers his figure's claims is evident in this quick sample of
Jim's crowing: "I hopes I shall hab de honor ob displeasing you all, as I can
grin like a wild cat, roar like a bull, and jump jis like de little hop-toad dat
cuts him shines mong de grass in ole Kaintuck" (p. 11). Crockettian brag-
gadocio is here turned down several clicks. The wildcat grinning and bull's
roar are substantially calmed by the hop-toad cutting harmless shines in
the grass.

Jim Crow's real threat is that it is not conventionally recognizable like
Crockett's ramming force. The crow is neither aggressive nor passive, but
devious. The Crockett character is determined to wedge himself off from
every other human. He stands alone. He hates niggers, pukes (Missourians),
hoosiers (Indianans), suckers (Illini), buckeyes (Ohioans), wolverines (Mi-
chiganians), gals, redskins, hates them all equally, hates wild animals, dan-
dies, Europeans of every stamp, hates love: "I got a leetle in love with a
pesky smart gal in our clearing," he says in one of his best stories, "and I
knowed it was not rite . . . So I went out into the forest [to catch] a pes-
tiferous thunder gust. I opened my mouth so that the axletrissity might
run down and hit my heart to cure it of love . . . the litening went clear
through me, and tore my trowsers off as it came out . . . I have never felt
love since." Jim Crow, pretending subsequently to come from the same
Ohio Valley provinces, is quite different from this antisociability. Crow enacts identification with women and others.[45]

Both Crockett and Crow are fascinating instances not only for their cultural force but also for its unpredictable momentum. Cultural forces gain
a trajectory that political instigators cannot control. The robust rhetoric of
Crockett builds barriers between peoples (but ends up fuzzily imperson-

ated by friendly Fess Parker). The cagier rhetoric of Crow, dizzily turning, often turning inside out, was established to build links (but has been warped to symbolize segregation). Crockett's bluster was funny to the politicians and merchants, but Crow's irony was dangerous. Crockett they tolerated. Crow they condemned and made into a pariah. Already, here, Crow's deferential tics reverse into time bomb ticks. Crow's "debilty to use falsificationarity" is a pronunciation blunder, sure, but much more interestingly it is a blunderbuss aimed at Fanny Kemble and Mrs. Trollope, those "foreignificated deatrical ladies" whose recent comments on American couthlessness were local irritants.[46]

There were reasons why the proper portions of the population treated Jim Crow as a pariah. His public set him up that way. Jim Crow's hybrid rhetoric is not only Crockettian and not only tender, it is also the backward talk of a trickster figure. Ritual clowns typically take part in "reverse behavior," Laura Makarius has written. Ritual clowns, like Jim Crow, do the opposite of what is normal. They wear furs in summer, go naked in winter. When General Jackson threw the young Jim Crow a half dollar, the youngster was so excited that he "swallowed de tea cup instead ob de tea" (p. 9). The conventions of the minstrel show express this backward behavior, often during "stump speeches," in the so-called nonsense talk of the performers. Makarius points out that "backward speech . . . is associated with the violation of taboo in order to underline it, bring it out clearly and mark its author as a 'contrary' person, exceptional and *opposed to the other members of society*."[47] This is the spirit in which Jim Crow hoped he would be "displeasing" to all.

The apparent nonsense speech of blackface performers reinforced the way their mask signaled transgression. This overdetermined marking had at least two effects. First, it emphasized the self-awareness and coherence of the working public it was organizing. Second, it therefore further irritated those burghers the working public was organizing to resist. The doubled backtalk, along with the tarry mask and the motley dress, the akimbo nimbleness, the carnivalesque orality—all these became a cohering contrapuntal style.

The style did not jell immediately, however. Jim Crow's persona is both knotted up with gamecock bravado and simultaneously slipping those knots, very evidently in the passage I quoted from the introduction. That is, "roar like a bull" is quintessential Crockett, but jumping "jis like de little hop-toad" is anything but rip-roaring. Like the Crockett character's verve,

Rice's sketches expressed the spirit of a people fighting back. Crockett fought against difference in the natural world (he'll swallow lightning, wrestle bears); Jim Crow countered disdain and exclusion in the social world (he'll break out of confinements and enter parties where he was not invited). Compared to the Crockett stories, however, Rice's sketches are not nearly so defamatory to women and dark people, not as fouled with bathroom humor, nor nearly so violently wounding. Most surprising of all is the relative lack of racism in early blackface delineations. They are nowhere nearly so racist as the Crockett almanacs which the blackface stories and gestures supplant.

All this is manifest to anyone who has compared the Crockett stories with the lyrics to "Jump Jim Crow" and the early blackface scripts (as opposed to the postbellum texts processed by Charles White). Why, then, has Jim Crow acquired its bad rap? If one grants Jim Crow the licensing, backward talk of a trickster, the bad reputation does not comport with the documents, with the texts. The answers must lie elsewhere. The main reason Jim Crow became a disdained entity was that his modus operandi was to keep coming back, to keep causing trouble, picking scabs, jumping and turning and sneaking like a little hop-toad right in your face, polite people. Beyond that, he represented cross-racial affiliation which was repellent to many people in the nineteenth century and seems hopelessly romantic to many people of all hues and persuasions at the end of the twentieth. Another reason for Crow's bad rap is that the early Jim Crow is not the late Jim Crow. Jim Crow went from fond alliance to hateful segregation as the Civil War approached and then as the Nadir replaced Reconstruction.

That Nadir is not the phase of Jim Crow under discussion here. I am engaging a phase during the 1830s when the Crockett almanacs were the touchstone of vitriol, and Jim Crow a softening elixir. The prose passages of *Life of Jim Crow* confirm that audiences saw "Jump Jim Crow" as turning the earliest popular culture in the Atlantic away from the demeaning quality of Crockett toward the brotherly knots of blackface. During this supplanting process, actors were testing stereotypes from other cultural domains, in addition to their own. As they played with those stereotypes, they made them more empathic.

To sum up what I think was happening: when Rice and Dixon took the stage in 1828, there was an inaccurate English stage dialect for blacks; there were more complete rhetorics to represent Yankee skinflints; there were crude graphic prints censoring aberrant behavior; and there were elaborate conventions purporting to put feathers on frontier gamecocks. Dixon, then Rice, entered into this moving ratio. They started consolidating these divers publics, as well as their representational conventions, into an important new hybrid—rebarbative, nimble, self-hyping, and, above all, apparently independent. It's hard for us to see, now, but it was then a scary consolidation. We return to the scare later. Now let's look more closely at early stages of the consolidation.

T. D. Rice yielded specifically to the "Fox poplar" and only trusted the arms of the "moder Public." This confidence limited to common people is quite contrary in fact and spirit to the grand publics later blackface minstrels called upon for protection (even while they were still soliciting Cain as their model). Blackface reliance solely on the demotic lasted only about ten years. By the mid-1840s leading minstrel troupes would be carefully saving clippings to prove that European royalty validated their activity.[48] This shift from separate and antagonistic agency to folding themselves in the Queen's skirts occurred, therefore, in a blink. The way the later minstrel show toadied to royals helps indicate the profits available to actors working pop lodes, and how quickly they learned. Or, barely conceivably, the Virginia Serenaders, the Christy Minstrels, and the rest of that lot were trying to forge even wider class alliances, even unto the throne. That is, these are early instances of familiar problems in and about popular culture. What I do not want to lose track of in these quarrels is the democratic impulse that the young Rice was embodying. I do not want that early impulse to fall forgotten in the heavy grinding of cultural politics.

By the middle of February 1929 Rice had wandered off from the stranded Ludlow troupe, whose theatre burned in Mobile. Always minding his opportunities, Rice filled some larger and more complex parts by joining a veteran actor, Mrs. Hartwig, in the rough cotton-port town of Pensacola, Florida. The two set up a stage in an ambiguous space, the Tivoli Hotel. Rice did three plays: *A Day after the Fair, The Irish Tutor,* and *The Cobbler's Daughter.*[49] We are coming closer and closer here to a phase shift when Rice's stage persona shifted from white to black, when he started creating a new stage life. The momentum is building, but it has not yet pushed past the point of no return. This is a touchy juncture in the cycle, for Rice, as for Atlantic cultural history. Let's stop a minute and look at *A Day after the Fair* for clues to what Rice was feeling just before the shift. What nudged him past that edge?

People of our profession are very apt to change places.
  —Rice as O'Rourke in *The Irish Tutor*

The Lord Chamberlain licensed C. A. Somerset's *A Day after the Fair* on 15 December 1828 for performance in London. It opened there at the Olympic on 5 January 1829. Six weeks later, here was Rice extracting laughs from it in Pensacola. The man was an outpost of turning antennae, greedily seeking data that would capture perhaps just a good chance. But more than most, Rice was impatient with the familiar and sought the new. What he worked up in *A Day after the Fair* was another vehicle for which he was well-suited. The play was a farrago of contrasting conventional and dizzy parts for a small cast. It was prime material for a mimic. Rice alone played six comically diverse types, some stacked on top of each other, at once. Like many other farces, *A Day after the Fair* revolved around reversals of place, class, gender, currency, and fortune.

Rice's primary role, Jerry, is a servant to a Mr. Sterling. The master sends Jerry with bags of money to buy rural Whirligig Hall so he and Jerry can retire there. But impulsive Jerry dawdles three days at the races on the way to the errand. Thus Jerry arrives the day after a London stockbroker, Mr. Zachariah Fidget, has bought Whirligig and already issued terminating notice to Polly and the Hall's other servants. Fidget wants only quiet and rest. Now Fidget's interposition is a problem not only for Mr. Sterling but also for Jerry, who is in love with Polly. Had he only arrived on time, Jerry would have been able to marry Polly, live with her at the estate, and raise their family. Polly and Jerry conspire to expel the stockbroker using noise and bother. They will dress in costumes that the old Squire Whirligig had left in a private theatre behind Whirligig Hall. Jerry and Polly will employ old theatre to drive out the new rich and serve themselves. Rough music will clear their space. Jerry and Polly alternate disruptive roles to drive Fidget crazy. Their roles are punctuated by a rube named Abraham Clod (or, A. Clod), whose slow presence permits Jerry (Rice) and Polly (Mrs. Hartwig) to work their rapid changes.

Jerry dresses as a drunken cobbler who whips Fidget with his leather strap. He cross-dresses as an aptly named ballad singer, Susan Squall. Soon he enters as a novice drummer, Timothy Thumpwell, beating his drum to a "Daddy Mammy" practice rhythm. In the theatre of the rising youth culture, of course, beating one's father and mother is a purpose improved only by drumming the abstracted Fidgets of the world. Meanwhile, Polly has been interspersing Jerry's appearances with changes of her own. Midway in the play she comes on as a theatrical manageress and ballet dancer, Madame Maypole, and mentions to Fidget that her troupe has a dancer named Mademoiselle Dumplino.

> Enter Jerry, r. as Mademoiselle Dumplino—By means of a basket dress, with a little stool mounted on rollers behind, for facilitating motion, he appears to be no more than three and a half feet high . . . The little stool on rollers is fastened round Jerry's waist, and, of course, when he rises, is concealed by his wide petticoats. The effect is exceedingly comic, for, when he stands on his legs, his female garb only extends to his knees, yet there is no indecency in this, as he has stockings, &c. on underneath.[50]

As Dumplino/Jerry, T. D. Rice rises to his full height, well beyond six feet, and punches out A. Clod, who has been drunkenly begging Dumplino to give him a "buss." Next Jerry enters as a madman, Octavius Moonshine, "fantastically dressed with straws, flowers, &c." These capers succeed, naturally. What stockbroker could hold his ground against such a Lear-esque, Bakhtinian shivaree? That coalition ensures happy days for the servant couple, whose dizzying role changes have proved them worthy to marry and occupy Whirligig Hall.

A Day after the Fair shows, then, a compendium of ploys in Rice's progress toward the teetering instability of Jim Crow. The charivari aspects of the play, including rough music and such folklore touchstones as maypole rites that judge the stockbrokers inadequate; its meta-theatrical incorporation of theatre within theatre, performance within performance, identity nested within identity; the interplay between Clod (rube) and Jerry (city) characters; crossed *v*'s and *w*'s exploiting multiple low dialects; and the deft skewering of various class attitudes—these are all strategies Rice would overlay with blackface in his Ethiopian skits. Furthermore, seeing them used like this illustrates that associating these characteristics with a black protagonist is not necessarily demeaning. It's quite likely that Rice, and his audience weaned on plays virtually unknown to us, understood Jim Crow's ploys as endowments of wit, used traditionally by disenfranchised persons of all hues to bang their drums against authoritative pretensions.

Although all the accounts of Rice by historians of American minstrelsy defer to the legends of his stealing his dance and costume in the Ohio Valley, through which Ludlow's troupe toured a year later, it is quite likely, to the contrary, that he was already performing at least prototypical versions of "Jump Jim Crow" at age twenty at the Tivoli in Pensacola. The *Pensacola Gazette* advertised "A Comic Dance by Mr. Rice" on 17 February 1829 (see Figure 4.2).[51]

Assembling Jim Crow, it turns out, was hardly a sudden or whimsical event. Figuring out Jim Crow was a process, a practice, evolving for years over considerable territory. Even to term this practice "assembly" may be too definite. As likely, Rice was stumbling nimbly into gestures and moves that a lot of low people were already practicing. This cohort was not yet able to know itself because the signs that would bind it whole were not yet there. Rice was finding those signs and gradually realizing how to piece them together. He was figuring out Jim Crow in a vernacular mix he was culling at landings and crossroads from Catherine Market, through Pensacola and the Ohio Valley, and on to London and Dublin.

With his impolite infusion, he would be able to stand outside the people and comment on them, show them news of themselves. At the same time, his findings would mark his insider status. He was refiguring for his rowdies a share of their own sensibilities. That is what the staged black voice does for him, and for his audience, as he pushes purported blackness beyond its extant English conventions. He consolidates the low cohort around this figure, including both its white and black constituents, and he does not look for royal approval. In Philadelphia, brags Jim Crow, "I clipsed all de stars dat eber shot dis way from ole England, where I soon spect to go for de parpose ob jumping de gout out ob Johnny Bull's big toe, an handling a few ob de king's pretty golden pictures. Gor bless you, I'd sooner hab a pocket full ob dem jingling tings dan wear de crown ob de original" (*Life of Jim Crow*, p. 15).

This early Jim Crow, then, displays a cohort coming to realize itself. They are outside enough to comment on American mores, as Miss Fanny's journal was, but they are outside from below. Rice will continue this effort at a future date, he says in closing, and "let de publik know how dey do, an gib, like Miss Fanny, my journal ob de manners and customs ob de people, which, like her, I larnt by lookin at dem from de stage or stage-coach window, pretty much as jist de same" (p. 17). Remarkable yoking, this: stage and stagecoach. The watching is mutual. Both ways across the apron, both ways through the window goes the sizing up: people choosing signs of themselves, actors learning how to "let de public know how dey do" their "manners and customs."

4.2   T. D. Rice dancing at the Bowery Theatre, 1833

It is not casual when *The Life of Jim Crow* puns that his blackface actions are "informances" (p. 5). They perform news.[52] They act out a journal of manners for people. These dimensions of information and reporting, foolery and word play, complicate Rice's relationship with his public into what I have been calling a standoff embrace. It is a mistake to miss either the distance or the intimacy he maintains.

Jim Crow's shingle becomes a switchboard on which publics and politics rapidly couple and decouple. Rice's improvised lyrics and shifting scripts, on the one hand, untie the traditional knots to old theatrical expectations of resolution, character, and social boundaries. On the other hand, the new lyrics and rapidly codifying gestures wrap up new commitments to new publics. From static as well as mobile vantages, Crow ogles peekers peeking at him. That's the husk.

The kernel in *The Life of Jim Crow* tells how song and dance were implanted in Crow, not how Rice took them. It is not a story of expropriation. Its story of elfin deposit has European lineaments. But its accents mix regions, ethnicities, and attitudes from around the Atlantic. *The Life of Jim Crow* is "written by himself." Authors use this trope of insistent authenticity in books that their wandering stations had not prepared them to write. Davy Crockett said his 1835 *Tour to the North and Down East* was "Written by Himself." Olaudah Equiano and Frederick Douglass each had "Written by Himself" on their title pages. Mary Prince announced her story "Written by Herself," and so did Harriet Jacobs. However, when Frederick Douglass twice retold his life, self-sponsored by then and fully confident of his power to make books, he signed his name outright. Huckleberry Finn's initial paragraph ("You don't know about me . . ."), Clemens's own posturings as Twain, and his authorial notices about dialects and plots all constitute elaborations of these ruses. In the same vein as Clemens, and much earlier, Rice's claim that Jim Crow's *Life* was written by himself sports with this authenticity and underlines its assemblage from parts. Rice is aware that his own class has even less claim to authorship, and even fewer sponsors, than those nomadic people whose warranted lives his text imitates, teases, and champions. Rice proposes a masked counterfeit in earnest terms. This winking at authentication reminds readers of his doubleness. Oscillating dimensions of selfhood are conscious parts of this tale.

There are two versions of *The Life of Jim Crow*. The first was published in 1835, with no appended songs; the second, which is the one I cite, in 1837, with songs that refer to President Van Buren and to the trips Rice made to London, Dublin, and Paris in 1836. A James M'Minn registered the pamphlet at the District Court of the Eastern District of Pennsylvania in 1835. Announcing on the title page that it was "Published for the Trade," M'Minn confirms what the book's crumbling, ink-blotted appearance suggests: here was the cheapest of books. Think of it as a hop-toad commodity, hacked out at speed to be hawked the same way at streetcorners and theatre entrances, meant for the most casual consumption. No doubt that's why it is so rare, remaining unknown and uncited to this day. In its own time, however, and among those flocking to early blackface performances as the latest thing, it was a *given,* acknowledged and absorbed like air. Its references saturate the subsequent songsters just as its ink bled through its own pages. By any definition, the self that wrote this piece is a composite of time, persons, experiences, and effects. Instability is built into this persona. So is flexibility. Everyone could easily soak up this self, and everyone did.

In this, his first "paper life," as he calls it on his last page, Jim Crow's genealogy is dubious, reiterated intentionally. Before he became famous, he had no father; then, suddenly with his fame, every black man on the plantation and every (white) working butcher in Cincinnati—shades of Catherine Market here—claimed to share his genes. The fatherless and still unnamed author is exceptionally fortunate as infant and youngster, however, to be in league with agents of the supernatural, shown specifically as white and Euro-inflected: an old white woman wielding a mean crutch. When the servants swaddle the newborn babe in a possum skin to present him at the big house, the old woman announces in a voice from above the ceiling: "He will raise to fortune by hopping" (p. 5).

Fancy white folks flee this disembodied voice in terror, concluding that Jim Crow is one son of a witch. A tomcat snatches up and means to eat the dropped baby until the woman's crutch smacks across the tom's back, ending that feline's fantasy: "De ole white woman, (and she war right funny looking) blow'd in my mouth, as she said, to send all melancholy breath out of my ribs, and taking a bottle out ob her bosom she poured some ob de contents down my troat, saying dat was ginsprashun from de fountain ob de nine muses what sing on de Pellicon mountain. Bidding my mudder take good care ob me, she sung something and den went through de floor in a big blaze ob smoke" (pp. 5–6). This white-on-black mouth-to-mouth resuscitation is a novel and sneakily suggestive image for the era. Going through the floor in brimstone blazes, however, was then a conventional departure for the devil on the low stage. Rice was using these blazes at the conclusion of *Bone Squash Diavolo,* which was taking shape during 1835, when Bone escapes the Yankee Devil who has bought his soul. Dan Emmett would also deploy them in *Hard Times,* his 1840s variant on Rice's plot.

Missus frantically calls Massa home from Congress to deal with this horror. Massa intends to burn the baby straight away—until he sees how cute the boy is, and how deeply black. Then Massa simply christens him "Jim Crow." Massa reserves an Adamic power to name. But if the story compliments him in this power, the underlying strategy of cultural break-away ensures that every compliment arrives with a smirk. The motley crew that Rice is organizing focuses its aggression through Jim Crow onto ol' Massa. Massa in these stories is the congressman, the patriarch, the Adam; he represents The Boss, mutually to blacks and whites within the blackface audience.

The crippled crone who appeared at Jim's birth comes back in a clap of thunder at his christening: " 'Keep dis slave,' says de old woman, 'till he be twenty years of age, an by using him well you shall hab eberry kind of good luck, you family all lib and grow rich; ben he be twenty, you mus set him free or all your good luck go to de ole Harry.' Den she make him berry low bow and fly up de chimbly jis like screech owl;—gor bless me tis long while to 'member from I six week ole, but I tink I see massa's face turn blue as him shot out ob de door like a ball out of rail Kaintuck rifle" (p. 7). Thus Massa can pretend to name Jim Crow, when in fact Jim Crow is an African-American folk name for an agricultural trickster who organizes na-tionality among Africans. The story allows Massa his pretense, but embeds it within the crone's easy control. She tells Massa how to treat Crow, or else. This Massa-Congressman pretends to power, but the crone's speech changes his strut to ridiculous scramble.

> De git Fiddles was raisin' cain over in de corner and John was callin'
> for de new set . . .
>
> —Zora Neale Hurston, *Mules and Men*

Making Massa run, as Jim Crow's protector does, is one of the characteristic adjustments black folktales make in the unbalanced power between slaves and owners. When Zora Neale Hurston tells the tales she collected in Flor-ida about the foreman John's struggle with his master, one of their most satisfying conclusions is the scaring of a boss with a hant, a voice, or some sign from on high that sends authority running out the door, shirttails flowing and elbows pumping, either fleeing supernatural wrath or chasing his slave.

Recall Hurston's key tale about John taking over the big house while the slaves believe Massa has gone to Philly-Me-York. There are many variants of this story in collections of African-American tales. Hurston's version has John enthrone himself in Massa's rocking chair on Ol' Missus's conjugal bed. He smokes Massa's cigar. He calls the tunes for partying slaves. Massa and Missus come home, themselves acting tricky by dressing down as white trash, and it begins to look as if Massa has set John up. John banishes Massa and Missus to the kitchen where their sort belong. "De git fiddles was raisin' cain over in de corner," says Hurston. Bingo, as if on cue, here comes Ol' Massa erupting from the kitchen, furiously wiping smudge from his face, yelling he's going to hang John from the nearest persimmon tree.

Massa knows to clamp down on any cain raisin'. He will allow no fiddles to call for a "new set" on his land. But John is ready for Massa. John sends a confederate to climb high up in the tree, hidden in the dark. John kneels, pretending to a final prayer before he swings: "O Lord, here Ah am at de foot of de persimmon tree. If you're gointer destroy Old Massa tonight, with his wife and chillun and everything he got, lemme see it lightnin'." The confederate strikes a match in the treetop. Thinking the match is light- ning, Massa starts shaking, starts begging John to quit his praying. But John prays on, and his friend keeps striking matches: "Ole Massa started to run. He give John his freedom and a heap of land and stock. He run so fast that it took a express train running at the rate of ninety miles an hour and six months to bring him back, and that's how come niggers got their freedom today"[53]

Elbows poke ribs, hands slap knees; elaborate winks follow these verbal stunts. Raising cain has prevailed yet again. Down on the plantation, where power is constitutionally askew, overturning Massa directly or violently is practically unimaginable. Consequently, slaves try to make him sweat and scurry, to unsettle him. It's war by nerves and wit. Stories about the origins of freedom in black culture, as in the white-dominated popular culture that draws on them, both create and parody these marked-off victories. They exist and they do not exist: John won his freedom, or did he? Any "heap of land and stock" given John is unlikely. And why in the world would John dispatch even a milk train to fetch Massa home? The whole fantasy, in both white and black cultures, hovers between hope and despair. It is a crowbar prying open new possibilities and a safety valve letting off pressure.

Rice is participating in this sort of ribbing, bringing it over into the new ground of pop culture. He's not Henry Blake, the exceptional character in Martin Delany's subsequent revolutionary novel; Blake not only conceived but also planned violent overthrow using the cover of festive holidays. There is no evidence that blackface performance ever saw itself as revolutionary in Delany's sense. Nevertheless, Rice is not on the side of the planter. He's detailing a middle ground which both history and cultural history have been occluding and excluding: clamping shut. When Rice was dancing, however, that border ground expanded.

This roominess in time and space, this marking out and apart playing, is recurrently important to the culture which Rice and his publics were launching in the Atlantic. Carnival zest like this is neither black nor white, African nor European, but frequent in both. Not directly revolutionary, not regressive, this zest shimmied at their intersections. Especially was this space important to those mudsill workers who were being squeezed the hardest. It crops up in countless ways in the cultural signs disdained groups seize on to blazon their condition. More than a hundred years after Rice jumped Jim Crow, and more than a century and a half after dancers wheeled about on their shingles at Catherine Market, for instance, Little Richard invoked this charmed space and moment when he sang, in "Good Golly, Miss Molly": "when you rock 'n' roll, I can't hear no mama call." Jim Crow and Miss Molly, more than a century apart, are two tokens of a middle ground continually valuable to modern society's underclasses because in its charmed space they can turn and move. In that roominess, the calls of authority do not reach. In there, no Massa, no mama calls.

After the crone's voice at Jim Crow's christening has sent Massa scurrying, leaving the baby unprotected on the floor, a peddler tries to steal the boy. But the old woman on the crutch swoops down out of the sky and steals him back, depositing her bundle on his mother's stoop. Massa now coddles Crow, teaching him to read and write, and keeping the boy's mother in comfort. Likewise, the old lady on her crutch ensures that Massa also thrives, and his daughters marry well. The mean crutch has charmed the whole plantation.

When he is sixteen Jim Crow wanders away from the plantation so far into the Kentucky woods that he grows powerfully thirsty. Lo, a spring opens up before him. A fairy dressed in gold and green pops out of the spring's center, hands the boy a silver cup, says, Drink deep. He swallows and starts for home, his stomach suddenly aching and twitching: "ben jis as I got over a fence, up come de intents of my tomach into de road:— guy, I to't it war a gone case wid me, but when I look'd down, it war a big roll of music dat I had heaved up. I looked at him, an all at once de tune pat as sugar on de end ob my tongue, ann I rhymed to it from dat dey to dis, for twar nothing more or less den de fashionable air ob your humble sarvant to command. Jim Crow" (p. 8).

Elfin toxins were the cause of it all. Come back across the line from the wild margin ("jis as I got over a fence"), young Jim discovered his "intents" were not his own. Before he had sung one word, Jim Crow was all booked up. Before he had danced one step, he was choreographed. He enjoyed his investiture as slaked thirst, but discovered it as vomit. Thereafter, goes this fiction, he had a free ride. Thereafter, the fiction implies, a tension remained that the vomit betrayed. This fiction figured logorrhea as a roll, a wad, as if Jim's mouth were a cultural valve, like Catherine Slip. Already this early, the charmed space is also clogged. It's an intersection as busy as the culture for which it stands.[54] Scrambling through the charmed space are the protectors, a crone with a crutch or a Euro fairy, Massa, Missus, tomcats, slaves, intoxication. This self-deprecating story by a humble "sarvant" describes his talent as a throwaway gift. But the throwaway gift came in a throw-up scene.

The story broaches the hybridity of the Jim Crow song and dance, but obliquely. Is it oral folklore? Extremely so. Is it composed by hacks and prisoners and actors in the "liderary hemporium" (p. 16)? That too, both at once. Is the voice African American? Sure, as closely as literary delineation had yet been able to come.[55] Is it Euro-American? Sure. Both at once. Is Jim pleased to be in this busy intersection, filching from all these cultures as they go ripping by? It's just the way things are on the street where he lives. Certainly, Jim shows no guilt. Instead he displays ready awareness of the mix he makes, and some of its costs for himself, if not for others. A continual tic in Jim Crow's songs will be an appeal for release from the demands of his audience:

> O! white folks, white folks,
> For nigger nebber feel,

You tink my belly nebber ache
While toeing de big heel. (p. 13)

Between Jim Crow's investiture and his freedom is an interval of childlike oscillation. The youth advises General Jackson with one of his most frequently sung verses of "Jump Jim Crow":

If I war president ob
Dese United State
I'd eat molasses all de day
An swing upon de gate
An wheel about and turn about. (p. 9)

Swinging upon the gate, take one: oscillating between fixed positions, shifting where others are stable, championing irresponsibility and childlike behavior. This libidinal spontaneity hardly ends when Crow moves from the plantation to the world, or from the folk to the pop domain. Rather, he capitalizes on the feature. His unanchored perverseness is what his white audience selects to emulate. Swinging upon the gate, take two: is the gate swinging open or swinging shut? People today looking back on the swinging Jim Crow usually blame him for shutting a gate tight on African-American culture, denigrating it. I am sure, however, that he did not see it that way. Rice and his early public were excited about these songs and dances precisely because they gave access to black culture for new fans like themselves. Their excitement was in moving closer to, not in separating from, perceived black behavior. Swinging upon the gate, take three: an imp of perversity himself, Jim Crow here foreshadows other important imps at gateways. James Clerk Maxwell, for example, soon after the advent of Jim Crow, imagined a sorting demon swinging a gate in the midst of entropy, policing that busiest intersection of all. Maxwell's imagined demon would separate the active from the inert, making renewal and thermal work possible.[56]

When critics have applied Maxwell's demon to cultural work, they have imagined a sorting demon as a force sifting apart the traces of culture as they mingle. The forces of propriety arrayed against the emerging energies of blackface were just such sorting demons as Maxwell imagined. So, inevitably, have been cultural historians as they have tried to untangle the past. Unlike Maxwell's demon, however, and unlike these other forces of propriety, the early Jim Crow scrambles items *together*, rather than categorizing them apart. He figures out a vernacular fantasy. He is an imp of crossing, not of separating. The history of his interpretation has reversed and apparently defeated this function; the imp of links has become, in the stories about him, the monster of segregation.

Meanwhile, back at the plantation, obeying the crone's command, Massa freed Jim at age twenty, and he wandered off to "ole 'Hio." Twenty was the very age at which Rice left New York, lighting out for his own territories, culminating in Cincinnati. Twenty was also how old Rice was when he started performing prototypes of the Jim Crow dance. These are small signs of his identification with Jim Crow. His apparently loose-jointed *Life of Jim Crow* quite consciously fastens the links that his budding black English vernacular promised. His story eagerly overlays its Euro-inflected fables with an even more extraordinary olio of cross-cultural allusions.

These knotted references corroborate and extend his tangled vernaculars. The story goes on to tell of a string of rapid successes. Jim Crow joins a jolly crew of strolling players, follows them to Cincinnati, dances to great acclaim, marries Dinah Rumpfizz Quashdiddle, sells out her cake store because he is so successful, proceeds to the capitol to eat with the kitchen cabinet, performs for Noah Webster, sups with Davy Crockett, is "traduced" to the star, Fanny Kemble, and makes big money from the Congress folks. None of these, however, does he catalogue with as much emphasis as when he "cuts stick" to Philadelphia to see "dat great musicianeer, Frank Johnson" (p. 15).

Frank Johnson was a phenomenon, the nineteenth-century Duke Ellington. He was a black musician, band leader, and composer who lived most of his life in Philadelphia, unless he was doing his summer galas in Saratoga Springs, touring nationally to such unlikely spots as White Sulphur Springs, Virginia, and St. Louis, Missouri, or, in 1837, touring internationally. His popular music, and early examples of what was then perceived to be "distortion," but which would now be recognized as improvisation or jazz, was important for almost a quarter-century, between 1820 and 1844, when he was buried in a massive public funeral in Philadelphia. Frank Johnson was the first great crossover performer in Atlantic life.[57]

Jim Crow calls two men "great" in this first autobiography: General Jackson and Frank Johnson. He hedges on the President: Jackson is too powerful, not playful enough, and the way Rice spins the "kitchen cabinet" reference insinuates that Jackson makes Jim Crow eat in the kitchen. But there's no hedging on Crow's enthusiasm for Frank Johnson. Rice was on to him, too, just as he was on to the latest English farces.

> An I gib'd my opinions dare
> Along wid all de rest.
> —Jim Crow, "Jim Crow's Trip to France"

Rice was by 1835 and 1837 well on his way to consolidating cultural expression for an Atlantic underclass that was discovering itself in his sort of performance. He was making available an independently reformulated oral and printed, informal and commercial culture. He was keeping it swinging, unfixed. When Rice returned triumphantly from Europe, where he had special success in London and Dublin, he sang a song recognizable now as a sort of template for one of the oldest international jokes. A Frenchman, a German (in street argot, a Dutchman), a Yankee, an Englishman, and an Irishman were in a "dillygence / Looks like a chicken coop," he sang, "goin to take a ride." What made it worth crowing about was his own inclusion: "Jim Crow beside." He was in and they heard his voice: "I gib'd my opinions dare / Along wid all de rest." It would be difficult to overplay this integration. Once inside, what did Jim debate? Which country was best. All the other characters liked their own nations for predictable reasons, but Jim Crow has no land and concludes his song cagily:

> I says, look here, white folk,
> De country for me,
> Is de country whar de people
> Hab make poor nigga free.
> Wheel about, &c. (p. 20)

Thus the last verse applauds England, whose Slavery Abolition Act of 1833 had concluded the liberation of slaves in the West Indies. But the phrasing also commends Rice's own state, New York, which had freed its remaining slaves six years before that. However surprising it may be for us today, the antebellum Jim Crow was singing out for freedom on both sides of the Atlantic.

> History is always written from a sedentary point of view, and in the
> name of a unitary State apparatus; or at least a possible one, even
> when written about nomads. What we lack is a Nomadology, the
> opposite of a history.
>
> —Gilles Deleuze and Felix Guattari, "Rhizome"

T. D. Rice opened *Bone Squash Diavolo* in London on Saturday, 9 July 1836,
at the Royal Surrey, just five years after the coining of the word "industrialism" and four years past the first Reform Bill, during the several adjustments of workers' consciousness that were then welling into Chartism. Rice
sang "Jim Crow," played the eponymous chimney sweep in *Bone Squash
Diavolo,* and one might say got the jump on Karl Marx. Certainly the range
of types Rice covered in that play made up the very figure of the lumpenproletariat. That first evening, and every subsequent evening for weeks, the
curtain disclosed a chorus of young white men in blackface rousing political
double entendres:

> We de Niggers dat do de White Washing oh
> We de Niggers dat do de White Washing oh
> On de scaffold we stand
> Wid de brush in our hand
> And de jenus shines out wid de slashing oh.

I focus on this verse not because it is unusual but because the shocks and
density in its intentions are of a piece with so much that has been repressed.
These lines display the strategies of doubleness by which blackface performers simultaneously conveyed and hid both their connections to other
disdained workers and their anger at the employers for whom they whitewashed.[58]

I am arguing here along two lines. First, Rice's performances showed the
lumpenproletariat to itself and did so under the surveillance of the annoyed
middle class. Second, excluding this material from our digested histories
reinforces simplistic stories about the formation of class and ethnicity in
nineteenth-century Atlantic communities. This exclusion makes it impossible to understand the development of such important forms as the slave
narratives, for instance. The earliest slave narratives in English, like Olaudah Equiano's and Mary Prince's, which precede blackface presentation of
runaway charisma, are quite different from Frederick Douglass's and the
hundreds of subsequent stories, often elicited and supported by whites,

that came after blackface performance stoked the Atlantic appetite for stories of escape. Because of the enormous popularity of the Jim Crow character as a free black figure on the lam, as the 1820s became the 1830s,
white actors in blackface were important codeterminants in the molding
of the runaway narratives. Who authorized these narratives is therefore a
wider and subtler issue than wondering about the role of such well-placed
editors and revisers as Lydia Maria Child. The lumpenproletariat had its
many hands and heads in this matter, too. Most important: blackface performance supported expectations that runaways had the wiliness to survive
on their own.

Sixteen years before Marx defined the lumpenproletariat in 1852, here
in 1836 was T. D. Rice coming on in rags. Rice's plays included the gamut
of the lumpenproletariat from bootblack, chimney sweep, and slave right
up through comic intellectuals (*The Irish Tutor*) and clerks (*The Lottery
Ticket*). But no further than the Irish tutor: Rice had his limits, as did the
underclass. Consequently, these plays challenge Marx's conclusion about
the lumpenproletariat that they "cannot represent themselves, they must
be represented."[59]

The opening of *Bone Squash* shows that poor people could indeed represent themselves. They figured themselves out in bitter eloquence and
teeming forms. If we will only re-search for it, we will find the emergence
of a sliding cross-class, cross-ethnic, cross-gender, and transatlantic cohort
in the 1830s. One of the icons that roused its self-knowing was Jim Crow.

Rice had cobbled together from American folk and pop sources three
plays that he took to London: *Bone Squash Diavolo*, *The Virginia Mummy*,
and *Oh! Hush!* English writers composed or adapted seven more plays for
him in 1836 and 1837. Together, these all performed an important class
alliance in London, extending what Rice had begun at home. By midcentury, by the time Marx came around to naming this culture "lumpenproletariat," the alliances Rice was embodying were already under concerted
attack. By the 1850s this lumpen theatre was already turning inside out
into its opposite. What gestures Rice had performed as identification were
warped increasingly into parody. Nevertheless, the plays I have named, in
the versions that Rice first performed in the 1830s, expressed positive white
identification with blacks.[60]

Why was this white identification with blackness the fetish around which
a motley alliance constructed itself? To sign oneself black was unmistakably
to acknowledge and choose alignment with the low, as the sugar and cotton
trade had ruthlessly defined it well before Rice delineated Jim Crow. To

blacken one's face, therefore, was at least in part to profess an oppositional stance. Furthermore, blackface made whiteness a sign, too. Blackface drew a roughly determining social line: on one side, the motley crew that danced defiantly and did the whitewashing for the bosses; on the other side, the range of forces trying to boss and confine Bone Squash. On one side those who planted, harvested, and refined sugar, on the other side those who enjoyed the sugar and its profits. Sugar is one trope for empire, and for the exploitation of labor at the heart of empire. Thus when Jim Crow recalls looking at the roll of music he had just vomited up, age sixteen in the deep Kentucky woods, and says, "I looked at him, an all at once de tune pat as sugar on de end ob my tongue," he quietly acknowledges colonialism had a hand in his making. When Ginger Blue struggles to rise out of his mummy's box, muttering to himself, "Whoo! here I is, pack'd up like a box of sugar," he confirms the connection between empire and enforced labor. Like the more obvious white sugar, Jim Crow and Ginger Blue confirm blackness as a product of colonial practice—not of working-class resentment.[61]

As we have seen, Rice developed the chocked and shocking language that opens his play ("We de Niggers dat do de White Washing oh") during five or six seasons of regularly blacked-up performance before he played in London. Thus, before he sprang them on England, his images of black fettle on the scaffold tested and absorbed pressures from many different audiences, oral and literate, in slave and free states, in metropolitan and frontier theatres. He improvised his lyric, but it was not casual or slack. The lyric was carefully declarative and carefully diffusive. It was punching and hiding. It was both brazen and coy. The self-reference "Niggers" (capitalized in the manuscript) is a prime example, because even in the 1830s its aggression was already inverted as a brand of pride. It had that useful oscillating quality Homi Bhabha has described in colonial stereotypes: it necessarily evoked its opposite.[62]

For white actors in blackface posing as laborers to announce that they were whitewashing was to summon contraries that the rest of the play teased into the open. Instead of covering up seams between groups, this opening maneuver pointed at them and simultaneously crossed over the divisions to join the other side. It signaled a self-consciousness about theatre's spectacle and its ambiguous formative role, rousing and sousing social discontent simultaneously. These players knew where they stood—on the scaffold, a pun. That's where painters and actors worked. That's where the condemned hung. These players affiliated with all three categories. Who hung the scaffold was an issue as much as who hung there. Whitewashing was explicitly cultural work—but to whose advantage its performers might turn it was their consciously ambiguous point.

After Rice, if not following him, writers from Hawthorne to Foucault have confirmed that the scaffold is the turning point in the metaphor of spectacle as site of victim and judge. On the scaffold the displayed can turn surveillant. Evidence such as the verse about the scaffold, as the curtain rose, indicates that Rice's actors knew their relative power. They were not dominant; they were not defeated. They embodied an emergent social formation and their language fitted their ambivalent condition. They were "Niggers" on a scaffold; theirs was a double and difficult position. Yet they would declare their genus, and their genius, by their slashing. Watch out.

Thus *Bone Squash Diavolo* began brazen. It ended involved, coy, and inclusive. The "we" at the beginning of the play expanded by the end to include a wide community of men and women all in blackface, all up on the scaffold of the stage. Everyone remaining on stage in the finale admired Bone as he escaped both the devil and the lovers who pursued him to his predicament. During the course of the play, Bone had tangled himself with the Devil in the person of a Yankee skinflint. He had won away from a dandy rival the pretentious daughter of a nouveau riche preacher. And he was pursued by another former lover. Everyone was after him. Everyone wanted him. They were all calling in his promises. Thus, when Bone floated above them in the final tableau, in a balloon, he was not only a daredevil of the sort then all the rage at both Vauxhall Gardens in London and the Castle Garden in New York, but a figure of protean charisma.

The scene is so over the top that one cannot help suspecting it spoofs the very concept of the transcendent—that hallmark of elevated culture—just as Rice's prose spoofed those "foreignificated ladies" who invoked transcendent values. Bone Squash rose, then, above this magpie nest of connections and references, cheered by his chorus of bootblacks and whitewashing street mates. He remained the lumpen hero, "throwing out his shoes, hat, &c," say the stage directions in later versions of the play.[63] He discarded his flâneur's posture and remained free to heel-and-toe it in the entr'acte. This was both freedom from disastrous commitment and freedom for deepening links with his mates and publics.

Especially in comparison to the sorts of farces then on the stage in England and the United States, *Bone Squash Diavolo* and *The Virginia Mummy* (probably more than *Oh! Hush!*) really mark a new consciousness.[64] These plays that Rice brought overseas with him mixed realism with fanciful elements but did not indulge sentimentality even while, in the instance of *Bone Squash,* including a love interest. They both inhabit a working person's position from the inside. The finale of *Bone Squash Diavolo* is, in particular, a vernacular lodestone that far exceeds the obligatory dance of community concluding so many conventional farces. Even more than the English farces he chose to perform when he was starting out, Rice's blackface farces upset the status quo. After the plays have demonstrated their danger and nonsense, there's no reincorporating the Yankee devil in *Bone Squash Diavolo,* no absolving the mad professor Dr. Galen in *The Virginia Mummy.* In Rice's plays idiots are idiots—often enough, too, they are employers or authorities—and the workers in blackface are dealing with it. This is not revolutionary. But neither is Rice writing or riding out an eternal natural oppression—as he would if he were the conservative he has been made out to be. Rather, he displays the adventuring young squire's irrelevance, the mad scientist's idiocy, and the Yankee devil's just desserts. Most important, he elicits identification with the free-spirited black he installs at the center of concern.

One sees these recognitions most clearly in *The Virginia Mummy,* where Rice plays a provincial black servant, Ginger Blue. Ginger's presence literally moves aside the ostensible heartthrob, Captain Rifle (whom one English playbill termed "a regular detonator"). Along with Rifle, the whole conventional love plot is displaced way offstage. Shoving these expectations aside is the overt drama of the underclass black figure making his way in a hostile world with his wit and his appetite, eating the fine people's surplus proteins, quaffing their brandy, puffing their cigars, gorging on their sugar.

Once he has occupied it, however, Ginger must also defend his ground. After he has gained access to the parlors of the rich, wrapped up as a mummy, other low characters want to cut off his digits to save as souvenirs. Or they stick their fingers in his orifices to check his vitality. Ginger responds by head-butting, biting, and kicking his white molesters in a violent rout that would be either unimaginable or fatal had he not monopolized audience favor. That the audience cheers Ginger Blue's aggressions is less a function of clever lines than of his publics' attachment to what he represents for them.

These escapes, commitments, and displacements drew boundaries for the tip of a thoroughly hybrid form looming ever larger in Atlantic theatre during the early years when industrialism was being thought. This hybrid form has been neither named nor analyzed.[65] Such a lapse can only be due to continuing disdain, because these plays are the first distinctive cultural product of the mixed cohort that industrial metropolises and their imperial plantations were making. Their mixed theatre articulated the overlappings of youth, class, and colonial culture mutating in the Atlantic diaspora. Rice's cohort enacted and instructed the alternate consciousnesses then starting to give lip to power. In commercial form, they were making visible those exuberant, in-your-face actings-out that remain the kernel of popular discourse even into postmodernity. When Rice jumped Jim Crow, he showed the unsettled autonomy of that agency most fearful to the middle-class and to those who would organize the state, noticeably including Karl Marx. They all lowered their big guns at it.

When Marx defined the lumpenproletariat in *The Eighteenth Brumaire of Louis Bonaparte* (1852), he catalogued the links Rice had by then been forging for fifteen or twenty years:

> Alongside decayed *roués* with doubtful means of subsistence and of doubtful origin, alongside ruined and adventurous offshoots of the bourgeoisie, were vagabonds, discharged soldiers, discharged jail-birds, escaped galley slaves, swindlers, mountebanks, *lazzaroni*, pickpockets, tricksters, gamblers, *maquereaux*, brothel-keepers, porters, *literati*, organ-grinders, ragpickers, knife-grinders, tinkers, beggars, in short the whole indefinite, disintegrated mass thrown hither and thither, which the French term *la Bohème*.

Although in his next sentence Marx summed these disparate types as a "kindred element," his catalogue clearly makes every rhetorical move to deny any worthy connections among them. This attitude has underwritten disdain for underclass culture ever since. It is the prototype for our contemporary politics of blaming the victim. It is the locus classicus for blaming fascism on popular culture. Marx's anxious scorn has stuck: despite the equal susceptibility to fascism in well-educated types, like Eliot and Pound, Stein and Le Corbusier, the lumpenproletariat is thought to be that conglomerate most easily led astray by all the manipulating Louis Bonapartes.[66]

Note the ironic conjunctures in Marx's classic definition. Marx enjambs organ-grinders with literati. Wiping the lumpenproletariat with the term *Bohemian*, which is French ethnic coding for Czech Gypsies, Marx reminds us how Europeans long classified dark and nomadic Others at the social bottom. In Marx's representation, because the world of low people has no governing principle of its own, it can only further fall apart. It is the world of *deracination, decay,* and *disconnection.* Two sentences after the passage I quoted, Marx calls this cohort the "scum, offal, refuse of all classes." His language, repeatedly evoking feces, shows that the connection Laura Makarius has found between troublemakers and offal is hardly confined to supposedly primitive cultures, nor to tricksters as *vernacular* intellectuals.

Marx attacked the lumpenproletariat because he worried that a nomadic tendency could prove more compelling than fixedness in organizing mobile metropolitan society.[67] So long as it was accepted that most people wanted the benefits that reliable status provided, then one's relationship to the means of production could be a scientific predictor. However, if "running and dodging the forces of history," like Ralph Ellison's lumpen zoot-suiters in *Invisible Man,* or cynically whitewashing black workers on the lam are the charismatic attractors, then social science is on shakier footing. Marx shored up his science by spurning the social sectors his logic could not contain.

All the disaffected bevy in Marx's catalogue do relate to the economy, of course, but their relations are not single. They are in motion, and that's what Marx emphasizes. He lists their macro motions (discharged vagabonds shooting off hither and thither). He shows them picking, grinding, and porting in micro motion. And he smirks about their sexual movements as maquereaux and brothel-keepers. This churning makes them unpredictable and frightening. But, from the inside, it is also what excites the churners. What Marx disdains, Rice jumps, and his lumpen publics demand encores.

Rice performed ethnographies in which lumpen constituents worked out who they were and what they meant to one another. But his plays also packaged this composite identity for other classes to view. Thus, even as it formed internal bonds, lumpen theatre also served up an icon around which external alliances could cluster to attack. Indeed, mutual hatred of what Rice's performed ethnographies meant brought together very strange bedfellows. Boulevard journalists and the clerics of moral clampdown, for instance, united in their loathing of the lumpenproletariat. They were all drawing lines between acceptable behavior and its opposite. In the following London newspaper notice, one sees how Bone Squash had become a bone of contention:

This week, RICE, the American buffoon, is "Jumping Jim Crow" to the tune of seventy pounds per week, and a free benefit! We saw this "apology for a man," a few evenings since, and notwithstanding our disgust, could not forbear laughing at the fellow's impudence. He is as great odor as ever with the carpenters, bricklayers, snobs, and sweeps of the sixpenny gallery. We rejoice to hear that his days, in this country, are numbered.

Rice's first stay was, indeed, coming to an end. But he would return to London many times, and the lumpen lore he set cycling has proved impossible to stop.[68]

Rice's burlettas are set at the places where lumpen lore is made and transmitted: oyster bars in the Five Points (*Oh! Hush!*), wharves when ships arrive (*Flight to America*), barber shops and streetcorners (*Bone Squash Diavolo*): scaffolds, all. As nexuses themselves, the theatres of New York and London were fit stages to broadcast this lore. The spectacle of spanning the city's spaces and classes was part of the meaning Rice was performing. The Surrey Theatre, where Rice played *Bone Squash,* for instance, was a south London venue in Blackfriars Road. The Surrey was at about ten o'clock on St. George's Circus, a roundabout that connected the City with the West End via Westminster and Blackfriars Bridge. After 1817 and the opening of Waterloo Road and its Bridge, St. George's Circus linked all these domains with the teeming energy of Soho and the Seven Dials. St. George's Circus was London's first designed traffic circle. Like Catherine Market and the Five Points in New York, the location of the Surrey was itself a palimpsest. It was a place for transactions and "informances." In the Roman era St. George's Circus had already been London's prime spot for theatrical spectacle. In 1782 the site that became the Surrey opened as the Royal Circus and Philharmonic Academy, with both a horse ring and a stage. This became the Royal Surrey in 1805.[69]

The Surrey was ostensibly a neighborhood theatre, and its neighbors then were poor workers. But by the mid-1830s its audience also included the up-market elements of Marx's lumpen list. As early as 1827 the Surrey's bills announced that the manager had arranged to sell tickets north of the Thames; he also provided for a coach to deliver customers after the show to south-of-the-river locations as far east as Greenwich. During Rice's 1836 tenure, arrangements were also made to deliver theatregoers home to Islington, north of the central city. And Rice's transgressions proved so popular that for the last two weeks of December he performed nightly at both the Surrey and the Adelphi (on the Strand, north of the river), caravaning between them with his publics in torchlighted tow. In 1837 the two theatre companies merged in a "Grand Union" for a temporary alliance.[70] Rice was playing, therefore, to audiences that had within their heterogeneity the links that Marx described. His playing crossed symbolic boundary lines; his playing enacted exciting affiliations.

This crossing of rivers and oceans, linking together classes and nationalities, ethnicities and genders is what lumpen theatre has been about each time it has broken out—as with jazz in the 1920s, with rock in the 1950s, and with hip hop in the 1980s. As a theatre of emergence it causes emergency for others. Part of the delight that Rice elicited in his lumpen Atlantic audiences is the breaking of confinement, which was at once exciting stagecraft, the physical figure of coming out, the enigma of arrival, and surprising configurations to discomfit the way peoples might relate. In short, Rice's early blackface farces condense and make general the theme of the runaway. His purposeful jumping and wheeling about enact with cunning assertion what the parties of fixed authority fear.

These farces package a politics of fluid identity—it is always forming. In most of the cases I have listed Rice's characters show their awareness of being cooped and cooked up. As Ginger Blue says, "should any ob de faculty hab occasion for a libe mummy again, dey hab only to call on Ginger Blue; when dey'll find him ready dried, smoked, and painted, to sarbe himself up at de shortest notice." He resourcefully outwits the powers that be. And that is a far cry from the pathetic staged blacks of the earlier English melodrama and the later canned minstrel show.[71]

In summary, what is important about the minor theatres and the forms they were spawning is their abstract spaces of consolidation and contest. Players could and did link across the differences the economy was proliferating. What's more, they played with the limits of such spans, with the devil and death, for instance, as in *Bone Squash Diavolo* and *The Virginia Mummy*. The best summary of their mixed audience and the motions of their material is in *The Eighteenth Brumaire,* where Marx caught much of their real experience in his catalogue, in his naming, and in his attitude. But Marx's description was an outside job. Marx had no empathy for the popular lore that is one significant means of cultural production. A century and a half later, partly because of the disdain Marx and others expressed, we can find that lore only in the actual manuscripts, prompt copies, and stray sympathetic remarks in the bourgeois press. Culling them together, we uncover forms so miscegenated that they overwhelm the categorical names bequeathed them. Not operettas, burlettas, nor blackface farce proved sufficient to evoke what one reviewer of Rice's *Black God of Love* threw up his hands and called "ollapodrical extravaganza."[72] Paraphrasing Rice's lyrics, I say their lumpen genus, and genius, shone out with their slashing.

> Dere's music in the horse-shoe, an' in de tin pan—
> Music in dese darkies which you must understand
>   —"Jim Brown's Address to his Sogers," in E. P. Christy's
>   *Plantation Melodies*

Nearly all the issues of this book come to hand when we consider the fate of this slashing and how we might trace it. The formative urges and earliest texts of Jim Crow's inaugural flights, are fore-texts that allow us to understand the cultural reversals of the 1950s. The post–World War II era of rock 'n' roll and the populist core of postmodernism (from bebop and funk jazz to Mailer's essay "The White Negro" to the substitutions for vaudeville found in talk shows and stand-up comedy) are all, at least in part, heirs of blackface performance. Ralph Ellison has explicitly stated that his formulation of the title character for *Invisible Man* "grasped at the range of implication" suggested to him by "a blackface comedian bragging on the stage of Harlem's Apollo Theatre."[73] This widespread grasping after blackface inversions encouraged the disassembly of Jim Crow's codified laws: that hateful Jim Crow of segregation and daily humiliation.

Given the power of these codifications, why did this unraveling happen? Because in the 1950s culturally inverse images of "race" helped prompt the social changes of our time. What had been cooped up in minstrel stereotypes for a hundred years turned inside out and the original energy of cross-racial attraction burst upon the scene. It was manifest in rock 'n' roll, particularly, but also in poetry from Ginsberg to Frank O'Hara, fiction from Ellison to Flannery O'Connor. All these forms revivified the positive cultural codes that the earliest blackface performers had embedded during the Jacksonian era. These 1950s performers, with their reliance on black gestures so fascinating to whites, did not bolt out of a blue sky.

If one believes cultural lightning strikes when atmospheric turbulence has been accumulating for a long time, then it is clear not only that racism deformed blackface but also that its original fraternal affiliations survived the racist packaging the minstrel show gave them. During the era when the racism of the minstrel show was most confining, what happened to the egalitarian urges of the motley rogues? Did their urges go missing?

The democratic urges of the underclass alliance went into undertow. They diffused back into folklore which was independent of the curated texts of middle-class life. The stories of Cain, the dance steps that Rice strutted onto the popular stage, the lyrics and patterns of street talk—all continued to develop offstage as well as on. Like the parallel play of children from different classes, these cultural strands developed unevenly. They were often unaware of one another's moves, but sometimes glimpsed and incorporated this phrase or that cock of the other's shoulder. Thus traditions fed into one another on both sides of the line that marked disdain.

Much work remains if we wish cultural stories to tie up all these uneven strands, but we might begin to follow the threads. The low-dignity strands are traced by historians of vernacular dance; by studies connecting toasts and other black street lyrics to pop, rap, and folk narratives; by a wider recognition that American musical theatre derives from the minstrel show; and by increasing awareness that the most elite culture always relates to a concurrent lore (if only to disdain it).[74]

Not all transmission of these interracial affiliations occurred in vernacular cultures. Some of the most intriguing transmission passed right under the nose of surveillant scorn, right in the minstrel show itself. That is, racist stereotypes in fatlip cartoons also hosted the seeds of change. Here's one example: I have cited songs from *De Susannah, and Thick Lip, Melodist* (1862). It was a ripe and virulent blackface songster that sampled a culture of racial anxiety in the early years of the Civil War. It conveyed racial grotesques—but did it only cement them? Or did it simultaneously undercut them? I think the latter, and I point to Bennie Moten, pianist, big band arranger, and precursor to Count Basie. Moten recorded "Thick Lip Stomp" in Kansas City as late as 1926.[75] A black talent like Moten's could blazon and mock the abhorrent stereotype, the more so the more it hurt. A black talent like Moten's could invert the cartoon, using its own momentum to pick it apart. Much the same spirit of inversion runs through Walker Evans's photographs of grotesque stereotypes—black men wielding razors, scrubwomen in mammy headdresses—in minstrel playbills of the mid-1930s in Alabama.

I have shown that stereotypes are themselves deep structures. As with icebergs, most of what they carry floats dangerously beneath the surface.

And I have shown how inverting stereotypes continued to do cultural work during the century between the Fugitive Slave Act and the Civil Rights Movement. Each individual in a long roster—Al Jolson, Bing Crosby, Fred Astaire, Sophie Tucker, Johnny Otis, Elvis Presley, Jerry Lee Lewis, The Big Bopper (the list could go on and on)—was not balking alone at straight-up stereotypes out of some private softness for African-Americans. Rather, what each expressed had once been the dominant lumpen mode of the original form. But now it was muffled beneath the institutional racism of modern culture. Both the original urge to merge and the countering racism of separation are present in the history. They play off against each other around the figure of Jim Crow: dancing Jim vs. codified Jim. Keeping the tonal proportions merged is the difficult obligation.

The gestures of these white modern performers signaling their identification with blackness were too often feeble. Their feebleness was pathetic, and the general muffling of African-Atlantic mutuality has been tragic. But this pathos is not inherent to the performers or to the segregated white lower classes who were their primary publics. Rather, their pathos displays the dominant cultures' power. It also shows the stubbornness of the gestures that still proliferate through that force. Entrepreneurial clampdown could swallow up and *almost* digest those original lumpen codes of cross-racial allure. But fulfilling that "almost" is where I want to end. That's where I want to take my stand with my kneebone bent, poised to dodge.

Rehearsing these patterns has taught me some of the gestures I admired from the beginning of my research. I pointed to them in this book's first sentence, when I said we all want to dance.[76] Jacqui Malone, following Peter H. Wood, has argued that the chief distinguishing gesture of African-American body retentions in New World dance is the bent knee. I read this as reinforcing the "running and dodging" Ralph Ellison attributes to the youths slinking through the underground toward the end of *Invisible Man.* He, too, was noticing a vernacular anti-stance which is marked out all around the Atlantic, repeatedly attractive, and compelling. This "kneebone bent" is a move nurtured by the same Gullah community on the Georgia Sea Islands that carried "Knock Jim Crow" to us. The cultural bent knee is important because it shows that T. D. Rice was not delineating an individual crippledness, as the conventional story of his supposed theft from a lame hostler has had it all these years. Jim Crow's bent knee was an African-American posture teaching nimble motion. His bent knee fostered coexistence and survival rather than rigid relations and extermination.

Reiterating the cycling patterns of all my chapters, I will dodge back to the skiff-borne moves of Catherine Market and jump forward to the images that cable screens now transmit. We have recently experienced a remarkable pulse of charismatic black dance. The surge of hip hop moves and rap hand italics through the 1980s into the 1990s is another instance of particular charismatic gestures organizing transnational publics just as Rice did in the 1830s when he danced Jim Crow. This recent surge is very much part of the blackface lore cycle.

These hip hop moves pulsing on cable videos derive from black gestures that went Atlantic via blackface conduits: those wide-knee steps and overhead hand signals which contemporary drawings locate at Catherine Market in 1820 (Figures 1.1, 1.2, 1.4, 1.5, and 1.6). Despite or perhaps *through* their apparent simplicity, these gestures conceal their complexity. We see their persistence when we see them peeping like hop-toads through disdaining culture's smothering.

These issues of persistence and recurrent gestation are what I consider here. My fundamental claim is that the Jim Crow cultural codes—as Rice figured them out from black lores—were inaugural codes of a lasting lumpen alliance. Its lore cycle still continues in hip hop dance. That is, the codes of that first postcolonial mingled culture still wheel about, jump, and tap the shingles.

A few videos yield access to these matters. I choose them exactly because they are not revolutionary. (Nor are they counter-revolutionary, nor even conservative.) By hyped standards of anger and street credibility today my examples seem inauthentic—for they are as mainstream as ragged culture can evidently be. However, I look to these wholly digested lumpen images to find what raggedness remains, as earlier I listened to Jolson's reprojections of Bobolink Bob's whistle. Consider the collaboration between Paul McCartney and Michael Jackson, "Say, Say, Say" (1983). Consider also the M. C. Hammer video collection, *Hammer Time,* specifically a sequence in its metavideo, "The Making of 'Please Hammer Don't Hurt 'Em'" (1990). After a long world tour, Hammer returns to Oakland, looking for the house where he was reared.

Rolling their eyes, people wonder what I might possibly find interesting in these scenes. I reply that both are about discovering origins well after the processes of history have apparently muffled them, in the case of "Say, Say, Say," and bulldozed them, in the case of Hammer's past. You can't go home again, I reply to those who roll their eyes, but you can sometimes palm the past, or dance it, into the present—especially if no one is looking.

"Say, Say, Say" is about Paul McCartney shilling potency potions from the bed of his truck. He is Mac in a black-and-tan minstrel and medicine show known as Mac and Jac. More lithe than McCartney, here comes Michael Jackson as Jac: he slinks out of darkness into the light in the video's initial image. As Mac's confederate, Jac plays an outsider visibly tugged into membership after every commotion the show's performances leave in their wake. Playing cat and mouse with the law as they sell patent medicines or perform vaudeville routines in springtime locales set in the California Depression, McCartney and Jackson convey a compactly corrupt history of blackface. It seems blatant pop frippery. Its lyrics are almost wholly askew from its visuals. Everything about it is disjunctive.

The sequences of "Say, Say, Say" will initially dismay anyone concerned with the fate of people's culture.What a loss that the whole cycle of blackface performance should funnel down to these capers in cross-racial attraction played out among stars ashamed to utter its name aloud in public, despite the iterated title. Must they allude to the blackface mask only as a clown's sad lips and painted tears? Must survival in these sequences display itself always as misdirection enabling flight? There is no struggle, always just running and dodging. Nearly everything in the video is backward. Mac's white hand continually helping black Jac on board, for instance, reverses the general process I have shown of blacks providing whites with their sustaining gestures. In a just world, Jackson should be pulling McCartney onto the wagon, not the other way around. But that's just the point this video sneaks into every home's unsuspecting TV. This is not a just world. "Say, Say, Say" displays the plight of the lumpen tradition as it comes down to us, baffled by its embarrassments.

"Say, Say, Say" documents this condition partly intentionally, partly not. Most important, however, the Mac and Jac show is an involved citation of the extended circuitry that carried various blackface styles to every nook and cranny of North America. Larger towns hosted such shows as Ida Cox's "Raisin' Cain" revue and Ma Rainey's mixed show: she sang and Pa Rainey performed comedy routines with a saucer jammed in his mouth. Smaller towns hosted reviews like the one shown in "Say, Say, Say," but grittier. McCartney's setting of his show in the Depression and the size of its cast specifically allude to the photographs of medicine shows that Ben Shahn took for the Farm Security Administration's Photography Unit (Figure 4.3). During this era, Simon Green of New Orleans was the largest black troupe, but countless smaller troupes also criss-crossed the country.[77]

Any video aiming at mass attention and hoping to review this history in under five minutes will be disjunctive. To survive all the pressures it negotiates, "Say, Say, Say" must unsay as much as it declares. Those contradictions are what McCartney and Jackson insert into the slick parameters of their mode. "Getting it" is every bit as much a question here as it was on the streets of Woodville, Florida, well before TV, when young Ruthie Taylor's parents spanked her for running up to one of the Silas Green paraders and blurting, "You're no Sambo." Mac and Jac project their own historical penumbra. They too convey codes, but their codes are one half-century more submerged, one half-century more glossed over by the media revolutions of the electronic era. Mac and Jac document a blackface lore cycle in which the signs are now almost entirely hidden; yet even here, they are still peeping out, still present for those who know the lore cycle's story.

> Ring the bell! School's back in.
> —M. C. Hammer, "U Can't Touch This"

Why these codes are contradictory, submerged, as often slurred as enunciated, is an issue that M. C. Hammer lifted to the surface to teach vividly in a stunning series of videos he released between 1987 and 1991. Hammer tried to take Atlantic vernacular dance to what he obsessively called "the next level." During his half-decade of fame, Hammer's videos vied with Jackson's and surpassed every other dancer's in popularity. The drama of Hammer's short career repeats much of the curve of the blackface lore cycle—the recurring attempt to play out on popular planes the charismatic moves of African-American street dance. He tried to lift those gestures and that styling—abstracted perhaps, but still intact—into the middle class. In pursuing that aim, Hammer more closely embodied early blackface energy at the level of mass culture than anyone who participated in the form since its heyday.

Hammer's choreography depends on three basic steps:

1. The Run Step, in which he and his Posse run in place (Figure 4.4, illustrating a backup dancer running in place against a staged graffiti wall).

4.3   Ben Shahn, Farm Security Administration photograph of medicine show in Huntington, Tennessee, 1930s

4.4 A member of M. C. Hammer's Posse dancing the Run Step in "Hammer Time" (1990)

This is an apparent stylization of Michael Jackson's famous "moonwalk" move, but in fact the earliest minstrel performers were doing these steps as the Virginia Essence, and Cholly Atkins was choreographing it for the Temptations in the 1950s.[78] Running in place—but never arriving—is clearly a process that those performers on the cusp between worlds would emphasize. It grows more and more poignant as the cusp stays there and so do the runners.

2. The Wheel Step, in which Hammer places one foot behind himself and spins on it (approximated in Figure 4.5). This step is impossible to capture in a still shot; but it is so common, and so self-dramatizing in Atlantic vernacular dance, that it hasn't been renamed since "Jump Jim Crow": "wheel about and turn about and do jis so."

3. A knees open, heel-to-toe rock, often accompanied by one or both hands over head (Figure 4.6). This move traces back to "Dancing for Eels *1820 Catharine Market*" (Figure 1.4). Call it the Market Step.

Hammer's breaks are by no means predictable—something that might not be said for his lyrics—but these three moves underpin and punctuate

4.5   M. C. Hammer dancing a turn around Wheel Step, "Hammer Time"

everything else he does. Hammer inflects them as distinctively as pronouncing vowels in a dialect. Michael Jackson does these moves, too. Mick Jagger does the last two of them. Vanilla Ice danced all three. All these dancers dance the same dialect, but they voice it differently. And not even Vanilla Ice, in his most manic Drill Sergeant maneuvers, evoked the dancing-for-eels hustle that Hammer achieved, dizzy in shirtless vests and harem pants.

The consonants in Hammer's choreography are also historical. His pump move is probably the Buck and Wing of cornshuckings and the minstrel stage. He falls back to the horizontal, one hand and both feet on the boards, then springs to the vertical. He jitters side to side, a move featured prominently in "U Can't Touch This." His distinctive windmill step originates in the Buzzard Lope that blackface performers learned from antebellum black dancers in public spaces, North and South. Flashiest of all, Hammer does an extreme hop, both knees up, toes down, shoulders forward, elbows up, hands down. He gives us both kneebones bent.

Hammer's choreography is distinctively "breaks." He is all improvisation patched together with extraordinary energy. Narrative development is not

4.6 M. C. Hammer performing in "Hammer Time" (1990) the same Market Step that his predecessors danced in Atlantic public spaces at least as early as 1820

what Hammer is about. Even his longform videos are spliced breaks that stutter like his dances. No one breaks quite like Hammer, even the thoroughly practiced members of his Posse. And no one breaks exactly the same way twice. But everyone on stage is inflecting vowels and consonants of a distinctive Atlantic dance dialect whose history they parse and teach. They are using, not losing, the charismatic moves that served Bobolink Bob and other market dancers from Catherine Market in New York City to Congo Square in New Orleans.

Why these gestures are so contagious is the mystery that drove me to write this book. Here at the end of the story the mystery is still present, not so much explained away, I hope, as complicated and deepened. These cultural gestures are codes important to black performers as well as white because they find publics for both, with hues overlapping between and beyond. They still pronounce a distinctive style that recovers continuity from erasure run amok. Hammer still dances the moves that the twelve-year-old T. D. Rice saw in 1820 when he fetched fish from Catherine Market stalls. Hammer dances those moves even though, when one goes to Catherine Street now, the Market is long gone and new structures replace the stalls. What conveyed those moves was the blackface lore cycle. It pulses like a syncopated heart in some peoples' Atlantic life.

Two scenes from Hammer's videos wind up the ends of these concerns. They show Hammer recovering a past from the severe dislocations of our time. They show Hammer's moves pulling back into place gestural substitutions for what pop entrepreneurs and modern society have bulldozed.

First scene: "U Can't Touch This," won awards in 1990. It comes at the peak of his popularity and is perhaps his best-assembled video.[79] It is a pop anthem of pride in cultural moves—learnable and teachable but doubtless derived from black Atlantic history. It is a cutting contest staged for cable: "You can't touch this," Hammer boasts and several of his Posse lip-synch, "I'm dope on the floor." Much of the video is performed on platforms, stairs, and a layered stage on which Hammer gets down and jumps up. These shifting layers function like the shingles of Figures 1.1 and 1.2, only made into a moving collage that returns some of the multiple perspectives which a video monitor tends to flatten. Hammer is hustling his street choreography visibly to another level.

At video's end, Hammer lies back, his right hand touching the landing of a rising stair. He chants "Let me outa here," and starts to shimmy up an ascending ramp, off right. Blocking the top of the ramp is a distinctively blonde dancer singular to this video and only glimpsed earlier in it. She bellies toward Hammer, knees and shoulders wide, her gold hair swinging side to side. While the chorus insists "You can't touch this," Hammer and the blonde grind several beats to fade-out. His right hand grips the near banister, closing in on her. His left hand rises anxiously behind his head. His body announces as clearly as if he had sung it, I'm Not Touching This. They can't touch. But they can dance together, both excited. It's one hundred sixty years after Rice jumped Jim Crow. Cross-racial desire and its denial are still mingling in the offspring of blackface performance.

Second scene: Hammer's most ambitious longform video is "Please Hammer Don't Hurt 'Em." It strings several of his hits into a loose portrayal of Hammer returning home to his beloved Oaktown. He visits the church of Reverend Pressure (whom Hammer also cartoons cleverly). He discovers Oaktown is in the grip of drugs and dealers, and decides to purge them. The story is too earnest for words. My intent is not to judge this video's attitude, however, nor the level on which it chooses to teach, but to relate a segment in its accompanying metavideo, "The Making of 'Please Hammer Don't Hurt 'Em.' "[80]

Let's follow Hammer as he conducts associates from the film crew down Oakland's back streets. The crew seek the spot where the star grew up. They want to see where he learned to bust rhymes and dance. The video walks us past neighborhood youngsters rehearsing the very same moves Hammer taught again, in his appearances. Stopping to peer through link fences at scenes along the walk, Hammer grows more and more excited, his voice rising in pitch. He is approaching his origins. When the crew arrives, however, his house will have been erased, the lot scraped and grassed over, no tangible clue to the past.

Hammer's coded dance is all that remains to re-create his upbringing, project it to others, and connect him with the boys and a few girls still breaking down their moves. This tableau teaches what is poignant, possible, and important about cultural gesture. The job of criticism is not to scorn or judge these gestures but to find some way to live up to them, to grasp at their implications, as Ellison said—for they have survived all their judges, as they will us. Cultural history should record and analyze their astounding capacity to maintain meaning down the years against the physical erasure, the constant covering over, and the disdain even of those who chronicle them. They tell a history that does not belong to the apparent winners.

The crew rounds a corner. Suddenly on the site, Hammer is visibly taken aback by his home's complete disappearance. He stutters, crestfallen:

HAMMER: This is, well, it *was*, this is where I was, uh, *reared*, right here.

(Camera pans across a very vacant lot, intensely green. A tall paling fence surrounds random waste strewn across the grass. One obligatory mattress lies abandoned among black plastic garbage bags. Neighboring pastel houses loom over the emptiness. California plain air shines over these matters.)

HAMMER: This empty lot used to be my house.
COMPANION: A lotta memories back in that house?
HAMMER: Oh yeah. I remember running all round here. [He brightens:] I had a dog named Cain.

Notes

Acknowledgments

Index

Notes

1. Dancing for Eels at Catherine Market

1. For this book about cultural cycles, it has helped me to remember that those who early noticed our gestural vocabulary kept their eyes cocked on quite real tides: "The farmers living in New Jersey and the neighboring counties, both on the North and East Rivers brought [their goods] also down in the same manner to the nearest waterside—unloaded into their skiffs; then, with the tide of ebb, easily rowed to the city direct to the various markets on the shores, where they usually disposed of their products in time to return with the flood tide." Thomas F. De Voe, *The Market Book*, vol. 1 (1862; New York: Burt Franklin, 1969), p. 137. Founded on the west side of lower Manhattan around 1771, Bear Market was an early market supplying Manhattan from Jersey's farms. Catherine Market, on the East River, was several along in a series of smaller markets that gradually were superseded as population density moved up, and sometimes back down, the eastern shore of Manhattan from the Battery to Corlear's Hook and as it adjusted to the suppliers across the river in Brooklyn and Williamsburgh.

2. Roger Abrahams, "The Winking Gods of The Marketplace," paper circulated about 1986.

3. De Voe, *The Market Book*. A full-blown reference to bobolinks appears in classic minstrelsy, too. The song, cited in Sam Dennison, *Scandalize My Name: Black Imagery in American Popular Music* (New York: Garland, 1982), p. 81, is "Oh, Mr. Coon": "De white bird an de black bird settin' in de grass, / Preachin' 'malgamation to de bobolinks dat pass; / To carry out de doctrine dey seem little loth, / When along cum de pigeon hawk and leby on 'em both." Even here, well down the pike of blackface becoming racist, the bobolinks are still the birds with which the audience identifies. They are birds that consciously play and stay in the middle, while the pigeon-hawk police lower their hard talons on the propagandists at both extremes.

4. Irving Berlin's family lived briefly on Monroe Street (which had been Bancker in the years Catherine Market was prominent), then at 330 Cherry Street. He performed first as a singing waiter at 12 Pell Street, Five Points, at "Nigger Mike's" saloon, also known as the Pelham owned by Mike Salter.

5. I outline the long cycle of minstrel performance in "Ebery Time I Wheel

About I Jump Jim Crow: Cycles of Minstrel Transgression from Cool White to Vanilla Ice," in *Inside the Blackface Mask,* ed. Anna Bean James V. Hatch, and Brooks McNamara (Middletown, CT: Wesleyan University Press, 1996).

6. Frances Anne Kemble, *Journal of a Residence on a Georgian Plantation in 1838–1839,* ed. John A. Scott (Athens: University of Georgia Press, 1984), p. 131. Dickens wrote about William Henry Lane dancing as Juba at the Five Points in *American Notes* (1842; New York: Oxford University Press, 1987). Robert P. Nevin, "Stephen C. Foster and Negro Minstrelsy," *Atlantic Monthly* 20, no. 121 (1867). Brander Matthews, "The Rise and Fall of Negro Minstrelsy," *Scribner's* 57, no. 6 (1915). Constance Rourke, *American Humor: A Study of the American Character,* ed. W. T. Lhamon Jr. (1931; Tallahassee: Florida State University Press, 1985).

7. Hans Nathan, *Dan Emmett and the Rise of Early Negro Minstrelsy* (Norman: University of Oklahoma Press, 1962). Robert C. Toll, *Blacking Up: The Minstrel Show in Nineteenth-Century America* (New York: Oxford University Press, 1974). Alexander Saxton, in *The Rise and Fall of the White Republic: Class Politics and Mass Culture in Nineteenth-Century America* (London: Verso, 1990), extends pioneering work he did on minstrelsy and Jacksonian democracy in 1975. David R. Roediger, in *The Wages of Whiteness: Race and the Making of the American Working Class* (London, Verso, 1991), shows that antebellum white workers used the minstrel show to distinguish themselves from blacks. Eric Lott's *Love and Theft: Blackface Minstrelsy and the American Working Class* (New York: Oxford University Press, 1993) voices a newly sophisticated understanding of minstrelsy, arguing that even as it showed white attraction toward black culture, the form helped whites control and steal what fascinated them.

8. On New York markets see Howard B. Rock, *Artisans of the New Republic: The Tradesmen of New York City in the Age of Jefferson* (New York: New York University Press, 1984). City Directory cited in Peter Buckley, " 'The Place to Make an Artist Work': Micah Hawkins and William Sidney Mount in New York City," in *Catching the Tune: Music and William Sidney Mount,* ed. Janice Gray Armstrong (Stony Brook, NY: The Museums at Stony Brook, 1984). Probably the first printing of Hawkins's song was in the *Columbian Harmonist* (Albany, 1815). S. Foster Damon found the song reprinted in eleven songsters between 1815 and 1830: "The Negro in Early American Songsters," *Papers of the Bibliographical Society of America* 28 (1934). I have also drawn on Vera Brodsky Lawrence, "Micah Hawkins, the Pied Piper of Catherine Slip," *New York Historical Society Quarterly,* 62, no. 2 (1978); William J. Mahar, "Black English in Early Blackface Minstrelsy: A New Interpretation of the Sources of Minstrel Show Dialect," *American Quarterly* 37 (1985); and "Sable Minstrels and American Opera," *New York Clipper,* 4 April 1857.

9. Roger Abrahams, *Singing the Master: The Emergence of African American Culture in the Plantation South* (New York: Pantheon, 1992). This sense of "shingle" may be an African retention; see A. J. Williams-Myers, "Pinkster Carnival: African-

isms in the Hudson River Valley," *Afro-Americanisms in New York Life and History* (1985). The Europe-oriented OED lists no uses of shingle in the sense of a dance board for performance. The notion of *shingle* as denoting performance capability, as in *hanging out one's shingle*, is a North American colloquialism that postdates minstrelsy.

10. Joe Sweeney joined the Virginia Minstrels in England when Billy Whitlock left, 19 April 1844. Sweeney toured with the quartet through Ireland, then when the troupe broke apart again he teamed up with Pelham for dates in England. Edward Le Roy Rice, *Monarchs of Minstrelsy: From "Daddy" Rice to Date* (New York, 1911).

11. De Voe, *The Market Book*, p. 345.

12. Craig Steven Wilder, "A Covenant with Color: Race and the History of Brooklyn, New York" (Ph.D diss., Columbia University, 1994), and personal communication, July 1996.

13. Shane White, *Somewhat More Independent: The End of Slavery in New York City, 1770–1810* (Athens: University of Georgia Press, 1991), p. 153.

14. Ibid., pp. 153–155.

15. Ibid., p. 186. In fact, the percentage of blacks in the city was about the same as the percentage in the United States as a whole in the second half of the *twentieth* century. It is important to see that white northern performers had at least as much knowledge of blacks in the nineteenth century as white critics do in our own time. Robert Toll's claim in *Blacking Up* (New York: Oxford University Press, 1974), p. 34, that "most Northerners did not know what slaves were like" may be true, but it would be much less true for T. D. Rice living in the Seventh Ward. As I will soon make clear, Rice had more face-to-face contact with African Americans than do most whites today.

16. Rice rendered Desdemona's fond recollection of Otello's courting to the air of "Down Fly Market." Rice's version of *Otello* derives from, but is vastly more imaginative than, Maurice Dowling's 1834 burlesque of Shakespeare. See my *Jump Jim Crow: Plays, Lyrics, and Street Prose of the First Atlantic Popular Culture* (Cambridge, MA: Harvard University Press, forthcoming).

17. *Statement of Facts Relative to the Late Fever Which Appeared in Bancker-Street and Its Vicinity* (New York: Board of Health and Elam Bliss, 1821).

18. Ibid., pp. 15–17, emphases in the original. Given that T. D. Rice was born in this neighborhood, and how little of his provenance is recorded, it may be useful to note that Longworth's New York City Directory gives an Eleanor Rice living at 85 Lombardy Street in 1809 and 1810, Rice's birthdate. Knickerbocker Village now covers this terrain, but in Rice's day Lombardy was a block and a half above Catherine Market, running east off Catherine Street. It seems likely that the intimate interracial relations of 85 Lombardy Street would have been familiar knowledge to the observant boy who became the comedian of crossings.

19. De Voe, *The Market Book*, pp. 95–96. See Thomas J. Davis, *A Rumor of Revolt: The "Great Negro Plot" in Colonial New York* (Amherst: University of Massachusetts Press, 1985), and his edition of Daniel Horsmanden's *The New York Conspiracy* (Boston: Beacon, 1971); Peter Linebaugh and Marcus Rediker, "The Many-Headed Hydra: Sailors, Slaves, and the Atlantic Working Class in the Eighteenth Century," *Journal of Historical Sociology* 3 (1990); and Linebaugh and Rediker, *The Many-Headed Hydra* (Boston: Beacon Press, 1998).

20. Daniel Horsmanden, *The New-York Conspiracy, or a History of the Negro Plot* (New York, 1810), p. 123.

21. Henry Ward Beecher, *Lectures to Young Men, on Various Important Subjects* (Salem, 1846), p. 216.

22. "Dancing for Eels, *1820 Catharine Market*" was part of the Edith Gregor Halpert Folk Art Collection that Terry Dintenfass sold on 14 Nov. 1973 to a buyer who remains anonymous and has not responded to my queries sent via Sotheby Parke Bernet.

23. One of the most celebrated scenes of early minstrelsy was the 57th night of T. D. Rice's jumping Jim Crow at the Bowery. It was celebrated in a large painting by Carl F. Greishaber now hanging in the Museum of the City of New York. Another version of this image was reproduced widely as a lithograph. (The painting and the print are not identical.) Frank Chanfrau claimed he was present for that famous performance, or so states the collector of minstrel memorabilia T. H. Morrell: "Among the many present on that memorable occasion, may be mentioned Mr. F. S. Chanfrau, probably the most versatile actor now on the American stage, and who alone forms a connecting link with the traditional 'Jim Crow,' of plantation memory, no one attempting to compete with him in his wonderful imitations of by-gone as well as living actors, and among which his life-like delineation of Mr. Rice, in his negro character, stands pre-eminent." Joseph N. Ireland, *New York Stage from 1750 to 1860*, Extended and Extra-Illustrated for Augustin Daly by Augustus Toedteberg, vol. 2, pt. 2 (New York, 1867), p. 33, Harvard Theatre Collection. Chanfrau would have been 12 years old when he saw Rice and started incorporating Rice's incorporations.

24. Harvard Theatre Collection, holograph manuscript of *A Glance at New York in 1848*, pp. 16, 29.

25. The Library of Congress has saved Brown's lithograph in its uncontextualized form: Eliphalet M. Brown Jr. and J. Brown after James Brown, *"Dancing for Eels," A Scene from the Play* NEW YORK AS IT IS, *as Played at the Chatham Theatre, New York, 1848*, lithograph, 9[bu14] x 13[bu38] inches. But it exists in the Harvard Theatre Collection in the role for which I assume it was commissioned: as part of a theatre bill advertising the play (as shown in Figure 1.5). On Chanfrau's plays see Richard M. Dorson, "Mose the Far-Famed and World Renowned," *American Literature* 15 (1943). I have been unable to find a copy of *New York as It Is*, but one can deduce much about it from reviews and the elaborate summaries on its

posters. I refer to Benjamin Baker's prompter's holograph MS for *A Glance at New York* in the Harvard Theatre Collection. My remarks on Chanfrau in these paragraphs come from Dorson, Peter George Buckley, "To the Opera House: Culture and Society in New York City, 1820–1860" (Ph.D. diss., State University of New York at Stony Brook, 1984), and clippings in the Chatham and Chanfrau files in the Harvard Theatre Collection. Where dates on posters contradict later newspaper articles or subsequent critics, I have relied on the poster dates.

26. Just how repressed this lumpen theatre was during these early decades is indicated by their occlusion in such a history of the New York theatre as Mary Henderson, *The City and the Theatre: New York Playhouses from Bowling Green to Times Square* (Clifton, NJ: James T. White, 1973). Henderson does not mention the Chatham before 1839—the years I take to be the plinth course of the theatre and of the culture it figured. She discusses the Chatham primarily as Purdy's National, which it became in 1850 when A. H. Purdy bought it. She does correctly note (p. 69) that "the first performance in New York of *Uncle Tom's Cabin* was given on its stage in 1852."

27. George C. D. Odell, *Annals of The New York Stage,* III (New York: Columbia University Press, 1928), p. 356.

28. At the end of one of the many hackneyed legends of how Rice got, copped, or found his Jim Crow dance—this in the New Orleans *Daily Picayune,* 7 May 1841, in a story entitled "The Green Room"—is this useful remark: "when Thomas D. Rice was playing 'William Tell' in Cherry Street, New York, he little dreamed of every [sic] making a fortune by singing *Jim Crow!*" There must have been saloon, amateur, and apprentice theatres that have escaped the chroniclers. There must have been equivalents, in the western Atlantic, of London's Penny Gaffs; Americans had no James Grant to prowl back streets and tell us about our rudest stages at useful length. We only have the author of "The Origins of Jim Crow" in the *Daily Picayune,* telling us that Rice was "a leader of juvenile Thespian amateurs in New York." From that scrap we may very cautiously surmise a similarity to the concurrent theatre pecking order in London. Here is Grant's definition of what I suppose was a loose equivalent, in London, of the Cherry Theatre, on Cherry Street one presumes, off Catherine, in the Seventh Ward: "Penny Theatres, or 'Gaffs,' as they are usually called by their frequenters, are places of juvenile resort in the metropolis which are known only by name to the great mass of the population . . . They exist only . . . in poor and populous neighborhoods. There is not a single one of them to be met with in any respectable part of the town . . . Respectable parents would never allow their children to visit such places. Their great patrons are the children not only of poor parents but of parents who pay no attention to the morals of their offspring." James Grant, *Sketches in London* (London, 1838), p. 161.

29. Theatre bill at the Harvard Theatre Collection, Chatham Folder, 28 Oct. 1829. This was the opening performance.

30. Bertram Wyatt-Brown, *Lewis Tappan and the Evangelical War against Slavery*

(Cleveland: Press of Case Western Reserve University, 1969), p. 72. As I am working on this chapter, I take a break one Sunday morning and thumb through the papers on the dining table, dum-de-dum, what's this? Why, it's Nik Cohn writing about a visit to the Mississippi Delta in the spring of 1994, walking into a blues joint: "After so long in pitch darkness, the room seemed garish as a funfair. Once it had been a Baptist church, but the walls were now lurid with frescoes of Michael Jackson and Oprah Winfrey, and the music was so loud it made the whole building shake." *Sunday Times* (London) 5 Feb. 1995, sec. 4, p. 1. Round and round goes the carousel.

31. *The Diary of Philip Hone: 1828–1851,* 2 vols., ed. Bayard Tuckerman (New York, 1889), entry for 10 July 1834. See Leonard L. Richards, *"Gentlemen of Property and Standing": Anti-Abolition Mobs in Jacksonian America* (New York: Oxford University Press, 1970). Richards shows compellingly that the rioters were not the young workers traditionally blamed but the artisan proletariat struggling to cement their status at the edge of the establishment: "The typical arrestee stood far above the common laborer in the occupational hierarchy. He had a special skill; he had a vocation, rather than a mere job; frequently he was either a shoemaker, a mason, a carpenter, a tailor, a brassfounder, a baker, a blacksmith, or a printer. He had little reason to fear black competition, for precious few Negroes followed any of these vocations" (pp. 151–152).

32. William C. Young, *Famous American Playhouses, 1716–1899* (Chicago: American Library Association, 1973).

33. Samuel S. Sanford, "Personal Reminiscences of Himself Together with the History of Minstrelsy from the Origan [*sic*] 1843 to 1893 with a sketch of all the celebrities of the Past and Present," holograph MS, Harry Ransom Humanities Research Center, University of Texas, p. 10.

34. Howard L. Sacks and Judith Rose Sacks, *Way Up North in Dixie: A Black Family's Claim to the Confederate Anthem* (Washington: Smithsonian Institution Press, 1993).

35. In using the term *nested,* I avoid the alternative associations of "stolen" or "expropriated." Just as there is more than theft going on here, its effect on both black culture and those youths acting as its agents is not singular. It is not only victimization. These nestings include also an appreciation, a nurturing, a pushing forward, a blazoning. All these remain separable and evident to practiced readers of the codes. Nesting codes persist despite, beneath, and in addition to their inevitable warping—their abuse, investments with unwarranted sentiment, forgetting, dilution. By using a relatively neutral word like *nest,* I point at a politics in the process that includes identification *with* as well as distinction *from.* In this politics it is everyday experience to live with irresolvable tensions among and within layers. A range of alliances as well as exclusions is extended when the shingle of the market transmutes to the rake of the stage. The point for critics is not to

simplify that range in recovering it but to live up to its expanse. Even to one who believes that the codes one can read are winks, not twitches, it remains shocking how very much still lies nested in those surreptitious bids and beckonings.

36. Henderson, *The City and the Theatre*. The claim that there was throughout the first half of the nineteenth century a unified theatre public, responding robustly to the same fare, until the Astor Theatre riots of 1849, will not stand scrutiny. By the late 1820s working-class theatre was holding its own even in theatres such as the Bowery that mattered to the middle class. There were already separate consciousness and separate agency in the early years of the century. My Chapter 4 will show this separate agency cohering in the West (Mobile, Pensacola, Cincinnati), the East (Philadelphia, New York, Albany), and London. The unified-theatre thesis is one of the last vestiges of the melting-pot mistake in cultural history. For an opposing argument see Lawrence W. Levine, *Highbrow/Lowbrow: The Emergence of Cultural Hierarchy in America* (Cambridge, MA: Harvard University Press, 1988).

37. See Buckley, "To the Opera House," on this painting, its subjects, and the Park Theatre circle within Knickerbocker DeWitt Clinton's "Republican theory of cultural production."

38. Cited ibid., pp. 140–141.

39. Beecher, *Lectures to Young Men*, pp. 218–219.

40. Wyatt-Brown, *Tappan and the Evangelical War against Slavery*.

41. Michael Paul Rogin, *Subversive Genealogy: The Politics and Art of Herman Melville* (New York: Knopf, 1983), p. 24.

42. Susan G. Davis, *Parades and Power: Street Theatre in Nineteenth-Century Philadelphia* (Philadelphia: Temple University Press, 1986); Linda K. Kerber, "Abolitionists and Amalgamators: The New York City Race Riots of 1834," *New York History* 48 (1967); above all Richards, *"Gentlemen of Property and Standing,"* and Sean Wilentz, *Chants Democratic: New York City and the Rise of the American Working Class, 1788–1850* (New York: Oxford University Press, 1984).

43. Peter Linebaugh, "All the Atlantic Mountains Shook," *Labour/Le Travailleur* 10 (1982).

44. Wyatt-Brown, *Tappan and the Evangelical War against Slavery*, p. 155. The most generative work on the images of mob racism in the period that I know about is Phillip Lapsansky, "Graphic Discord: Abolitionist and Antiabolitionist Images," in *An Untrodden Path*, ed. Jean Fagin Yellin and John C. Van Horne (Ithaca: Cornell University Press, 1994).

45. Sanford, "Personal Reminiscences," pp. 24–25.

46. All these tags of identity—national, ethnic, class, regional—are too gross for intimate meaning. Once in a taxi in Bloomington, Indiana, I tried to strike up conversation with the cabbie. Are you from the Midwest, I asked him. No, he replied, I'm from right around here.

47. My phrasing here is from the opening of Thomas Pynchon's novel *V.* (New

York: Lippincott, 1963), p. 10, about the 1950s. Pynchon reckoned the menace of popular culture was even then still Atlantic, conveyed to ports by a cross-racial community of sailors, and derived from their rogue surplus energy and symbolism: "East Main, a ghetto for Drunken Sailors nobody knew what to Do With, sprang on your nerves with all the abruptness of a normal night's dream turning to nightmare. Dog into wolf, light into twilight, emptiness into waiting presence." This is the underlying creed of *Raising Cain.*

48. Jane P. Tompkins, *Sensational Designs: The Cultural Work of American Fiction, 1790–1860* (New York: Oxford University Press, 1985), p. 53.

49. *Bone Squash Diavolo,* MS in Lord Chamberlain's Papers, British Library, scene 1. See my anthology *Jump Jim Crow.*

50. Wyatt-Brown, *Tappan and the Evangelical War Against Slavery,* pp. 54, 67. See also Lydia Maria Child's letter, 22 Aug. 1835, to Ellis Gray Loring: "A virulent little paper is buzzing about here, called the Anti-Abolitionist. Over it is a large wood cut, representing men and women, black and white, hugging and kissing each other; and on the table are decanters marked A.T.B.—which signifies Arthur Tappan's Burgundy." *Lydia Maria Child: Selected Letters, 1817–1880,* ed. Milton Meltzer and Patrica G. Holland, assoc. ed. Francine Krasno (Amherst: University of Massachusetts Press, 1982), p. 34.

51. The two versions of this song I am working from here are in *Jim Crow's Vagaries* (London, dated by the British Library as 1840), p. 9, and *De Susannah, and Thick Lip, Melodist* (New York, [1863]), p. 74. Eric Lott in *Love and Theft* also notices the self-consciousness in this song, calling it subtle, guilty, and unexpected. To me it seems rather the opposite—straightforward, guilt-free, and usual. One of the fundaments of early minstrelsy is that it shows no guilt about black oppression. Even when it is sympathetic to black suffering, its relationship to that suffering is not that of someone, or some class, feeling responsibility for that suffering. Blackface performers owned no slaves, minted no guineas, often could not vote, could make no Fugitive Slave Laws, set no demeaning wages. They did not even exclude black performers from the theatres where they performed. Theatre owners and others more powerful, the very people they were fighting, were responsible for those practices. I am not speaking of the large touring minstrel shows after the Civil War. I speak only of the early blackface performers, of the impulse at Catherine Market and in the Chatham and the early Bowery.

52. In the earlier, English, version, the house is the Franklin rather than the Olympic, and the comedian is John Sefton rather than Holland. "Lester" is probably a reference to a performer named Leicester, who performed at the Franklin.

53. Quoted in Wyatt-Brown, *Tappan and the Evangelical War Against Slavery,* p. 151.

54. *Courier and Enquirer,* 11 July 1834, cited in Kerber, "Abolitionists and Amalgamators," p. 37.

55. *Inventory:* Holograph MS Thr. 391, Harvard Theatre Collection, pp. 47, 50. Charles Bickerstaff's *The Padlock* (1768) was an English comic opera with an early blackface character, Mungo. In London Bickerstaff played Mungo's role himself. In New York Lewis Hallam played the part famously from May 1769, all through that summer. This play was a very mixed bag, playing the suffering of blacks, and their whipping, for laughs, but at other moments indicating sympathy for slaves. Mungo's most famous song drips with pity:

> Dear Heart! what a terrible life am I led!
> A dog has better, that's shelter'd and fed;
> Night and day 'tis the same
> My pain is dere game;
> Me wish to de Lord me was dead.
> Whate'er's to be done,
> Poor Blacky must run;
> Mungo here, Mungo dere,
> Mungo every where.
> Above or below,
> Sirrah, come, sirrah, go;
> Me wish to de Lord me was dead.

Quoted in S. Foster Damon, "The Negro in Early American Songsters," *Papers of the Bibliographical Society of America,* 28 (1934), p. 134.

Inkle and Yarico (1787) was George Colman Jr.'s opera on the century-old story of Yarico, a North American Indian maiden who fell in love with Inkle, who took her to Barbados and almost sold her into slavery. During Colman's handling of the story, Yarico darkened from Indian to Negro. After Inkle tries to betray his lover, but learns better from his servant's example and the outrage of the Governor of Barbados, the story ends in a double miscegenation, wealthy English man and his servant both marrying their dark lovers. This opera was performed in Boston in 1794 and in New York in 1796. See Lawrence Marsden Price, *Inkle and Yarico Album* (Berkeley: University of California Press, 1937). Price's concluding sentence on the story puts it as a lore cycle: "The slave-dealer and the master took on a more definite form and thus the legend grew as legends will, but what it gained in breadth it lost in depth and after a century of praise the name of Yarico was rarely heard again" (p. 138).

2. The Blackface Lore Cycle

1. Europeans have been putting black on their faces and pretending to be Africans and bogeymen since well before *Othello.* Therefore, the issue of when blackface performance accrued enough conventions to become a form is vexed,

maybe unsolvable. The issues are clarified, however, by S. Foster Damon's "The Negro in Early American Songsters," *Papers of the Bibliographical Society of America,* 28 (1934). Damon divided the appearance of Negroes in American song into three categories. His first two song-types were by English whites about blacks; distinguished not by where they placed their sympathy, which was nearly completely with the represented blacks, but by whether they registered abolitionist agitation and the associated fears of amalgamation. Damon illustrates his first category with Mungo's song from Charles Bickerstaff's *Padlock* and his second with examples from George Colman Jr.'s *Inkle and Yarico.* Damon's third category is songs written by Americans about the American Negro. For want of a secure anchor, I am calling this the beginning of blackface minstrelsy. It emerged with the victory of the Americans in the War of 1812, 11 Sept. 1812, at Plattsburgh. "The Siege of Plattsburgh," also known as "Backside Albany," was written by Micah Hawkins—of Catherine Market—to the tune of "Boyne water," and it premiered in the Green Street Theatre at Albany. It was first published in 1815. In it we see a more disturbing characterization, arguably richer, certainly more ambiguous than in Bickerstaff or Colman. This ambiguity is specifically in the uncertain positional relationship of the black figure:

> Back side Albany stan' Lake Champlain,
> One little pond, half full a' water,
> Plat-te-bug dare too, close pon de main,
> Town small—he grow bigger do hereater.
> On Lake Champlain
> Uncle Sam set he boat,
> And Massa M'Donough he sail 'em
> While Gen'ral M'Comb
> Make Plat-te-bug he home,
> Wid de army, who courage nebber fail 'em. (Damon, p. 143)

Here we have the black commenting positively on whites, telling the story of American bravery in dialect that set Americans off distinctly from the English. There is sympathy here, but also diminution; the character is not talking about himself, but his vernacular pronunciation locates both him and the events of his rudimentary narrative. The song was exceedingly popular, and Damon found it in eleven songsters between 1815 and 1830.

The earliest we know George Washington Dixon performed in blackface was in Albany in 1827, in a circus; Carl Wittke, *Tambo and Bones: A History of the American Minstrel Stage* (1930; Westport, CT: Greenwood Press, 1968). That minstrelsy had its earliest currency across upstate New York is perhaps a clue to why it seems to have persisted there, in church socials and school fairs, long after other regions—

especially the South—became embarrassed to perform the stereotypes. Opry: On the tight connection between country music and minstrelsy see Robert Cantwell, *Bluegrass Breakdown: The Making of the Old Southern Sound* (Urbana: University of Illinois Press, 1984).

2. Letter from Dan Emmett to Frank Dumont, quoted in the *New York Commercial*, "The Story of Negro Minstrelsy," n.d., in the Emmett folder of the Museum of the City of New York. Carl Wittke: "The first minstrel show, in which a troupe of burnt cork performers monopolized the whole performance and thereby constructed an entirely new and distinctively American form of entertainment [was when] the famous 'Virginia Minstrels' made their debut." *Tambo and Bones,* pp. 38–39. Hans Nathan: "The Virginia Minstrels deserve to be called the first minstrel band—one consisting of four blackface musicians playing the violin, banjo, tambourine, and bones." *Dan Emmett and the Rise of Early Negro Minstrelsy* (Norman: University of Oklahoma Press, 1962), p. 146. Nathan dates the first performance of a minstrel show by the Virginia Minstrels as 31 Jan. 1943. Robert Toll: "In February 1843, four blackfaced white men, wearing ill-fitting, ragtag clothing, took the stage in New York City, to perform for the first time an entire evening of the 'oddities, peculiarities, eccentricities, and comicalities of that Sable Genus of Humanity.' " *Blacking Up: The Minstrel Show in Nineteenth-Century America* (New York: Oxford University Press, 1974), p. 30. His quotation is from a poster the Virginia Minstrels used in Dublin in 1844, when their program was far more settled and they were, indeed, filling the theatre's whole night. They did not do so at first.

3. *The Diary of Philip Hone, 1828–1851,* ed. Allan Nevins (New York: Dodd, Mead, 1927), pp. 272–273. A. H. Saxon, *Enter Foot and Horse: A History of Hippodrama in England and France* (New Haven: Yale University Press, 1968).

4. British Library Playbill Collection, catalogue 313, sample bills on 22 Aug. 1836, 18 Sept. 1836, and 24 Oct. 1836. Their performance was described by Charles Rice, an audience member: " 'the real Bedouin Arabs,' as they are largely designated in the bills, exhibited some of the best somersets, and other descriptions of tumbling, ever witnessed even in this metropolis; but, as is always the case in this species of entertainment, there is a dwelling on the various tricks which prolongs the performance of them longer than is pleasant." *The London Theatre in the Eighteen-Thirties,* ed. Arthur Colby Sprague and Bertram Shuttleworth (London: Society for Theatre Research, 1950), p. 5.

5. H. P. Grattan, "The Origin of the Christy's Minstrels," *The Theatre* (London) 5 (March 1882), citing details which E. P. Christy first published 30 Jan. 1848 in the *New York Age*. Nathan, *Dan Emmett.* E. P. Christy's troupe had a nearly ten years' run at Mechanics' Hall in New York City. George Harrington Christy became one of the most influential minstrel performers. Son of an Erie Canal roadhouse hostess, he began dancing jigs in blackface at age 12 in Buffalo. There is a drawing of him

as Topsy in *Christy's and White's Ethiopian Melodies* (Philadelphia, 1854), wearing calico and boots and playing a four-string banjo. A fourth member of the early troupe may have been L. Durand.

6. One instance: on 27 Jan. 1843 the Chatham featured itself as having "Lower Prices than any Theatre in the City!" Specifically, "Pit, 61/4 cts. Second and Third Tier Boxes, 121/2 cts. First Tier, 25 cts." Fairly far down the page came this announcement: "The Ethiopian Dancers and the King of the Banjo Players, Messrs. Frank Diamond, Pelham, and W. Whitlock, in Three ORIGINAL EXTRAVAGANZAS." Diamond was one of the best blackface dancers. But the next Wednesday Pelham and Whitlock would become half of the Virginia Minstrels. At the bottom of the playbill appears this announcement: "A GREAT VARIETY OF EXTRAVAGANZAS! VIZ:— 'Lucy Long,' 'Dan Tucker,' 'Smoke House,' 'Farewell My Dinah Gal,' 'Grape Vine Twist,' 'Celeste,' 'Fanny Elssler,' 'Napolean Buonaparte,' &c. &c." Many of these songs would become staples of Emmett's troupe and, like "Dan Tucker," which he claims to have written at age 13, forever associated with them. For further evidence of the sliding size of the minstrel band see Nathan, *Dan Emmett*.

7. Thomas L. Nichols, *Forty Years of American Life*, I (London, 1864).

8. Whitney R. Cross, *The Burned-over District: The Social and Intellectual History of Enthusiastic Religion in Western New York, 1800–1850* (Ithaca: Cornell University Press, 1950), p. 56.

9. Peter Way, *Common Labour: Workers and the Digging of North American Canals, 1780–1860* (Cambridge: Cambridge University Press, 1993), pp. 1, 10–11.

10. Sean Wilentz's masterly history of New York City labor in this period is nevertheless the history of the artisanry, without catching much of the voice of mudsill mutuality: *Chants Democratic: New York City and the Rise of the American Working Class, 1788–1850* (New York: Oxford University Press, 1984). Alexander Saxton, in *The Rise and Fall of the White Republic: Class Politics and Mass Culture in Nineteenth-Century America* (London: Verso, 1990), David Roediger, in *The Wages of Whiteness: Race and the Making of the American Working Class* (London: Verso, 1991), and Eric Lott, in *Love and Theft*, all persuasively trace this dividing wedge. Peter Quinn's novel *Banished Children of Eve* (New York: Viking, 1994) gives an imaginative narrative of the conflict. I am trying to uncover and decode the submerged evidence of cross-"racial" attractions that worked against this wedge and have survived it.

11. I am grateful to Marcus Rediker for showing me his " 'The Outcasts of the Nations of the Earth': The New York Conspiracy of 1741 in Atlantic Perspective," now published in Peter Linebaugh and Marcus Rediker, *The Many Headed Hydra* (Boston: Beacon, 1998).

12. Hoggee: Lionel D. Wyld, *Low Bridge! Folklore and the Erie Canal* (Syracuse: Syracuse University Press, 1962), p. 19. Herman Melville, *The Confidence Man,* ed. Harrison Hayford (1857; New York: Library of America, 1984), p. 848.

13. Karl Marx, *The Eighteenth Brumaire of Louis Bonaparte,* in *The Marx-Engels Reader,* ed. Robert C. Tucker (New York: Norton, 1972). Melville *Moby-Dick; or, The Whale* (1851; New York, Penguin, 1992), p. 132.

14. When E. P. Thompson outlined "The Moral Economy of the Crowd," he meant a "particular equilibrium" achieved over time between paternalist authority and those workers with deeply rooted traditions. Their self-regulating economy was ending at the beginning of the nineteenth century. However, the moral economy had never warranted the lowest, most nomadic, workers—and never appreciated their expression. Thompson's crowd was upright in a market they could be proud of because they shaped it. I seek the slippery gestures created within the uncongenial market conditions of industrial capital—an amoral economy. The groups I am after must find themselves in a place where they are afraid of being caught. Without license of the moral economy, rough workers were constantly having not only to find out who they were, what a just society for them would be, but also act without legitimacy. Thus, it is no accident that much of the evidence of the blackface lore cycle surfaces in the illegitimate theatres of London and their equivalent American low stages. But the great poet of this orphaned condition is Ishmael, imagining Ahab's interior monologue: "Where is the foundling's father hidden? Our souls are like those orphans whose unwedded mothers die in bearing them: the secret of our paternity lies in their grave, and we must there to learn it." *Moby-Dick,* p. 535.

15. Ralph Ellison, *Invisible Man* (1952; New York: Random House, 1982), p. 333. Sure, rough laborers built the skyscrapers, sailed the ships, and laid the rails. But their traces in that labor will forever be organized and unjustly claimed by the people who front the capital—in the way the Erie Canal became "Clinton's Ditch." I am trying to shift the ground of the argument to emphasize the anti-monumentality of lumpen culture. I want to find the features of this fugitive culture made by invisible men and women.

16. Way, *Common Labour,* p. 3.

17. *Christy's Plantation Melodies,* no. 2 (Philadelphia, 1853), p. 60.

18. The classic study of "black" hair as a sign system is Kobena Mercer, "Black Hair/Style Politics," *New Formations,* 7, no. 3 (1987).

19. Dylan, "Visions of Johanna." Nathan, *Dan Emmett,* p. 411.

20. William Thoms coined the term "folklore" in a letter to the English magazine *The Athenaeum,* 22 Aug. 1846, rpt. in Alan Dundes, *The Study of Folklore* (Englewood Cliffs, NJ: Prentice-Hall, 1965).

21. I am not saying that this doubt occurs at the edge of a group, or that marginal members in groups are more likely to doubt its central principles. I am not proposing an insider/marginal/outsider concept of community. I argue instead that community principles are being maintained and adjusted all the time by *all* the community's members. It is quite likely that new or insecure members of a

community are more heavily involved in conserving its aspects rigidly than long-term members.

22. Margaret Fuller, Lize, Fanny Kemble all responded generously and positively to black and to blackface performance, but how uniform, genuine, or long-lasting this response was is impossible to say. In the 1830s there were women in Rice's blackface farces. Women starred in the minstrel versions of *Uncle Tom's Cabin*. And there were female minstrel troupes after the war, as there were blacks in blackface at the same time.

23. "As an acquired system of generative schemes, the *habitus* makes possible the free production of all the thoughts, perceptions and actions inherent in the particular conditions of its production—and only those. Through the *habitus*, the structure of which it is the product governs practice, not along the paths of a mechanical determinism, but within the constraints and limits initially set on its inventions . . . Because the *habitus* is an infinite capacity for generating products—thoughts, perceptions, expressions and actions—whose limits are set by the historically and socially situated conditions of its production, the conditioned and conditional freedom it provides is as remote from creation of unpredictable novelty as it is from simple mechanical reproduction of the original conditioning." Pierre Bourdieu, *The Logic of Practice,* trans. Richard Nice (Cambridge, MA: Polity Press, 1990), pp. 54–55.

24. *Moby-Dick,* pp. 126, 238, 235, 252. On Melville as a chronicler of Atlantic work see C. L. R. James, *Mariners, Renegades, and Castaways: The Story of Herman Melville and the World We Live In* (1953; Detroit, Bewick/ED, 1978). James wrote this book partly as an appeal to the U.S. Government not to expel him. It failed. He became a castaway.

25. See Paul Gilroy, *Small Acts: Thoughts on the Politics of Black Cultures* (London: Serpent's Tail, 1993).

26. Paul Rabinow, *Reflections on Fieldwork in Morocco* (Berkeley: University of California Press, 1977).

27. Richard M. Dorson, *American Negro Folktales* (Greenwich, CN: Fawcett, 1967).

28. Herman Melville, "Benito Cereno," in *The Piazza Tales* (1856; New York: Library of America, 1984), p. 720. Further citations to this work will appear in the text.

29. Papers of Dan D. Emmett, State Library of Ohio, Columbus. "Pompey Smash" was a stereotypical name for minstrel blacks as well as one of the classic show's most popular songs. It appears, for instance, in *De Susannah, and Thick Lip, Melodist* (New York, [1863]).

30. Leslie Fiedler, "Come Back to the Raft Ag'in, Huck Honey!" in *An End to Innocence: Essays on Culture and Politics* (Boston: Beacon, 1955).

31. Eric Sundquist, *To Wake the Nations: Race in the Making of American Literature* (Cambridge, MA: Harvard University Press, 1993), p. 221.

32. Martin Delany, *Blake: or, The Huts of America* (1859–1862; Boston: Beacon, 1970); further citations will appear in the text. For the split with Douglass see Robert S. Levine, "*Uncle Tom's Cabin* in Frederick Douglass' Paper," in *Uncle Tom's Cabin*, ed. Elizabeth Ammons (New York: Norton, 1994).

33. See Herbert Aptheker, "Maroons within the Present Limits of the United States," in *Maroon Societies: Rebel Slave Communities in the Americas*, ed. Richard Price (Baltimore: Johns Hopkins University Press, 1979).

34. Ronald Segal, *The Black Diaspora* (London: Faber and Faber, 1995). Delano's ship, the *Bachelor's Delight*, echoes the shallow success and casual racism celebrated on the ship the *Bachelor* in Melville's *Moby-Dick*, and the shallowness of the Inns of Court in "The Paradise of Bachelors," published April 1855 in *Harper's*. Ahab's doomed *Pequod*, still outward bound, encountered the *Bachelor* when she was on her homeward way. The *Bachelor's* hatches were bursting ("the steward had plugged his spare coffee-pot and filled it; . . . the harpooners had headed the sockets of their irons and filled them; . . . indeed everything was filled with sperm" (p. 537). Melville's implication is that this sperm-rich happiness, and its necessarily attendant self-focus, is what gives these bachelors their capacity to racism and other faults— for the *Bachelor* in *Moby-Dick* is a racist joke of some repeated resonance. Ahab to *Bachelor's* captain: "Hast lost any men?" *Bachelor's* captain to Ahab: "Not enough to speak of—two islanders, that's all." Martin Delany gives a similar interchange at a gruesome moment in the middle-passage sequence of *Blake*. The Spanish captain goes below to inspect the 1,800 packed Africans he has bought in Dahomey to sell in Cuba. He finds them "In very good condition, none dead worth naming," but Delany goes on in the same sentence to tell us of "two fine children—a boy and girl of three years of age—having died through the night for want of air and water" (p. 223). This is also the bitter jest that Twain repeats in *The Adventures of Huckleberry Finn*, ch. 32. Huck explaining his accident to Aunt Sally: "We blowed out a cylinder-head." Sally: "Good Gracious! anybody hurt?" Huck: "No'm. Killed a nigger." Sally to Huck: "Well, it's lucky; because sometimes people do get hurt." It is significant that when Huck makes this remark he is impersonating Tom Sawyer. Tom Sawyer is the "bachelor" of Melville's scorn to the nth degree.

35. See Philip Fisher, "Democratic Social Space: Whitman, Melville, and the Promise of American Transparency," in *The New American Studies: Essays from Representations*, ed. Fisher (Berkeley: University of California Press, 1991).

36. Jonathan Dollimore and Alan Sinfield, eds., *Political Shakespeare: New Essays in Cultural Materialism* (Manchester: Manchester University Press, 1985).

37. "Sign of the train" is Hazel Carby's term for the complex meaning of the train whistle in the blues when such classic blues singers as Trixie Smith and Clara

Smith, in 1924, record "Freight Train Blues" and claim the literally alienating power of the locomotive for their sex: "Every time I hear it blowin'," they sing, "I feel like ridin' too." Carby remarks: "The sound of the train whistle, a mournful signal of imminent desertion and future loneliness was reclaimed as a sign that women too were on the move." "It Jus Be's Dat Way Sometime: The Sexual Politics of Women's Blues," in *Unequal Sister: A Multi-cultural Reader in U.S. Women's History*, ed. Vicki L. Ruiz and Ellen Carol Dubois (New York: Routledge, 1994), p. 335.

38. Rice clipping in Enthoven Collection, Theatre Museum, Covent Garden. Whitlock clipping in Samuel S. Sanford, "Personal Reminiscences of Himself Together with the History of Minstrelsy from the Origan [sic] 1843 to 1893 with a sketch of all the celebrities of the Past and Present," holograph MS, Special Collections, Harry Ransom Humanities Research Center, University of Texas. The next month, at the Adelphi Theatre, Whitlock was featured doing a "GRAND LOCOMOTIVE IMITATION"; theatre bill in Adelphi folder, 1843, Enthoven Collection. Whitlock probably did not originate this locomotive imitation. There is an advertisement dated 10 Jan. 1843 for an entr'acte at the Chatham Theatre by a performer called Great Western: "Great Western in his laughable Adventures at Negro Ball, Imitations of a Locomotive, and Elegant Dancing"; Chatham Folder, Harvard Theatre Collection.

39. Leo Marx, *The Machine in the Garden: Technology and the Pastoral Ideal in America* (New York: Oxford University Press, 1964).

40. *Old Plantation Songster* (Philadelphia, [1850]), pp. 154–155.

41. My references to *Uncle Tom's Cabin* are to the edition edited by Elizabeth Ammons (New York: Norton, 1994), here pp. 332, 93, 94.

42. *Uncle Tom's Cabin*, p. 52. e. e. cummings, *Tom* (New York: Arrow, 1935), p. 17. William Wells Brown, "View Twentieth, Escape of a Woman—Fearful Passage of the River" (1850), in C. Peter Ripley, ed., *The Black Abolitionist Papers*, vol. 1 (Chapel Hill: University of North Carolina Press, 1985). Brown tells a story of an unnamed slave woman escaping across the ice of the Ohio river. Brown's skit precedes *Uncle Tom's Cabin* by two years. Thus Stowe's famous scene was a stock image of the abolitionists. Indeed, Brown's biographer cites three earlier appearances of this story in the abolitionist press; William Edward Farrison, *William Wells Brown: Author and Reformer* (Chicago: University of Chicago Press, 1969). Russell B. Nye cites two further appearances of the story in "Eliza Crossing the Ice: A Reappraisal of Sources," (1950), in Elizabeth Ammons, ed., *Critical Essays on Harriet Beecher Stowe* (Boston: G. K. Hall, 1980). Nye, in discussing the sources, writes of "the incident's authenticity" (p. 98). These multiple sources indicate, to the folklorist in me, on the contrary, its legendary status, its authorization neither in fact nor in Stowe's imagination but in the lore of the era she elaborates. "Authentic" or not, the story had been well rehearsed before Stowe used it. She brilliantly touched up an urban legend.

43. *The Autobiography of Joseph Jefferson,* ed. Alan S. Downer (1889; Cambridge, MA: Harvard University Press, 1964), pp. 9–10.

44. The contender for a scene more grueling would be the tableau of 600 slaves, one-third of the slaveship's cargo, being thrown overboard by the American and Spanish crew trying to outrun a pursuing English patrol and an impending storm. Paul Gilroy, in *The Black Atlantic* (Cambridge, MA: Harvard University Press, 1994), shows that this scene, too, forms part of an Atlantic train extending from oral report through abolitionist legend, through paintings and art history, to Delany's novel.

45. Charles Mathews Sr. is to be kept separate from his son, Charles Jr., whose partnership with Madame Vestris often had him appearing on the same bill with T. D. Rice on both sides of the Atlantic. The senior Mathews was early on the track of ethnographic sketches. From about 1803 he had "Jabal the Jew" and a (I presume Irish) character named Lingo in his repertoire. He went on to create "hundreds of beings that live their brief moment in his dialogue songs," according to a contemporary memoir in the Mathews file at the Harvard Theatre Collection. After he retired from his polymonologues, Charles Mathews Sr. went into successful partnership with Francis Yates at the Adelphi Theatre until his death in 1835; see James Grant, *The Great Metropolis* (London, 1837).

46. Each of these characters is a further reference to another, shadowing range. Armsted is based on St. Clare in *Uncle Tom's Cabin*. Armsted has promised to buy and free Blake's wife "at the earliest possible opportunity" (p. 65), but he fails to do so, just as St. Clare fails to act on his similar promise to Eva. As a northern judge who has decided in favor of the South concerning fugitive slaves, Ballard is an allusion to Lemuel Shaw, Melville's father-in-law, who as Chief Justice of Massachusetts first enforced the Fugitive Slave Law compromise of 1850 by sending the fugitive Thomas Sams back to his southern owner. And Rube is a reference to Harry Harris's long line of little Jim Crows. For Delany's use of King's Day see Eric Sundquist, *To Wake the Nations.*

47. "My Mammy," on Al Jolson, *Let Me Sing and I'm Happy* (CD RMB 75019).

48. The inspiration for Sampson Raphaelson's original short story had been a performance of Jolson's in Illinois in *Robinson Crusoe, Jr.* Raphaelson had subsequently turned his story into a play for George Jessel. When Warner Brothers decided to do the play as the introduction of the Vitaphone coordination, Jessel was meant to continue in the part. Alfred Cohn was assigned to do the screen continuity for him. The film both follows and deviates from Cohn's treatment. The deviation was especially pronounced in the song choices, in the ways the film's momentum builds up to and springs from Jack Robin's blacking up, and in the film's ending, which has Robin affirm his Jewishness by singing *kol nidre* then also return to the theatre to star in its secular alternative, *April Follies.* Robert L. Carringer reprints Cohn's screenplay in *The Jazz Singer* (Madison: University of Wisconsin Press, 1979).

49. British Library Add 42940, ff. 822–867. The cast list for first production in Mobile appears at the head of the MS. The "She nigga" appellation in it has a faint alternative in the manuscript penciled in Rice's hand, "Queen Shebera." On the orientalism of *Uncle Tom's Cabin* see Diane Roberts, *The Myth of Aunt Jemima: Representations of Race and Region* (London: Routledge, 1994).

50. Laurence Bergreen, *As Thousands Cheer: The Life of Irving Berlin* (London: Hodder and Stoughton, 1990).

51. Sam Sanford, *Sanford's Plantation Melodies* (Philadelphia, 1860), pp. 31–32.

52. Probably the most starkly argued of these is Michael Rogin, *Blackface, White Noise: Jewish Immigrants in the Hollywood Melting Pot* (Berkeley: University of California Press, 1996).

53. "Sidewalk Blues," *Jelly Roll Morton,* vol. 1 (London: JSP, CD 321, 1989).

54. Robert Oberfirst, *Al Jolson: You Ain't Heard Nothin' Yet* (San Diego: A. S. Barnes, 1980). Goldman, *Jolson.*.

55. Toll, *Blacking Up.*

56. RMB 75019.

3. Blame It on Cain

1. The best book on the Cain legends is Ricardo Quinones, *The Changes of Cain: Violence and the Lost Brother in Cain and Abel Literature* (Princeton: Princeton University Press, 1991). But neither Quinones nor the commentators on minstrelsy—except the performers themselves—acknowledge a connection between blackface and the mark of Cain. Francis Lee Utley, the one critic who saw the connection between the minstrel mask and Cain's mark, denounced it. See his preface to Ike Simond's *Old Slack's Reminiscence and Pocket History of the Colored Profession from 1865 to 1891* (1892; Bowling Green, OH: Bowling Green University Popular Press, 1974).

2. Hans Nathan, *Dan Emmett and the Rise of Early Negro Minstrelsy* (Norman: University of Oklahoma Press, 1962), pp. 411–412. On this passage see William F. Stowe and David Grimsted's review of Robert Toll's *Blacking Up:* "White-Black Humor," *Journal of Ethnic Studies,* 3 (1975).

3. See Hennig Cohen, "A Negro 'Folk Game' in South Carolina," *Southern Folklore Quarterly,* 16 (1952); also John W. Blassingame, *The Slave Community: Plantation Life in the Antebellum South* (New York: Oxford University Press, 1979); William D. Piersen, *Black Legacy: America's Hidden Heritage* (Amherst: University of Massachusetts Press, 1993); Roger Abrahams, *Singing the Master: The Emergence of African American Culture in the Plantation South* (New York: Pantheon, 1992).

This material is related to the license given the African-American syncretizations come down to us as "John Canoe." See Richardson Wright, *Revels in Jamaica: 1662–1838* (New York: Dodd, Mead, 1937). Frederick G. Cassidy, in " 'Hipsaw' and 'John

Canoe,' " *American Speech,* 41 (Feb. 1966), proposes African and French etymologies for the term; if true, these would confirm the revelry's syncretization from Africa, through the West Indies, to North Carolina. Harriet Jacobs gives a full description of what she calls the *Johnkannaus* in *Incidents in the Life of a Slave Girl,* ed. Jean Fagan Yellin, (Cambridge, MA: Harvard University Press, 1987).

In addition to the market dancing, Pinkster celebrations, martial revues, and the like in the North, this south Atlantic material is clearly an additional determinant of blackface performance. Its transfer from folk to commercial performance, however, is indirect. It is warped as it passes from folk to commercial use, and this warping is what interests me.

4. Mary H. Kingsley, *West African Studies* (1899; London: Frank Cass, 1964), p. 328.

5. Ralph Ellison's "On Initiation Rites and Power" and "If the Twain Shall Meet," in *Going to the Territory* (New York: Random House, 1986), are good on secular rites and their importance to Americans.

6. John K. Terres, *Audubon Society Encyclopedia of North American Birds* (New York: Knopf, 1980), p. 958. Enslaved Ibos in the Americas imaginatively employed buzzards and vultures to form a roaming, fugitive African-American consciousness; see Sterling Stuckey, *Slave Culture: Nationalist Theory and the Foundations of Black America* (New York: Oxford University Press, 1987).

7. "Skitt" [Harden E. Taliaferro], *Fisher's River (North Carolina) Scenes and Characters* (New York, 1859), pp. 188–189.

8. Anonymous, *Minstrel Gags and End Men's Handbook* (1875; Upper Saddle River, NJ: Literature House/Gregg Press, 1969), p. 144; my emphasis. "Bressed Am Dem Dat 'Spects Nuttin', Kaze Dey Aint A Gwine to Git Nuttin'!" in Nathan, *Dan Emmett,* p. 411.

9. Dan Emmett Box, Ohio Historical Society, Columbus. Charles Burleigh Galbreath, *Daniel Decatur Emmett: Author of "Dixie"* (Columbus, 1904), p. 9: Emmett was "connected with the shows of Spalding and Rogers, Samuel Stickney, Seth Howe and Dan Rice."

10. Harriet Beecher Stowe, *Uncle Tom's Cabin; or, Life among the Lowly,* ed. Elizabeth Ammons (1851–1852; New York: Norton, 1994), p. 216. Herman Melville, *Moby-Dick; or, The Whale* (1851; New York: Penguin, 1992), p. 192. Quinones discusses Cain and *Billy Budd* in *Changes of Cain.*

11. I have described this momentum as the Law of Passé Pursuit. In such conditions, old media and maturing authors do not fade away, "they grow more vital . . . They stop seeking the majority audience, formulate instead a minority aesthetic, and please fewer people more thoroughly." *Deliberate Speed,* pp. 23–25, 43–44.

12. *The Confidence Man,* ed. Elizabeth S. Foster (1857; New York: Hendricks House, 1954), p. 156.

13. Derrick Stewart-Baxter, *Ma Rainey and the Classic Blues Singers* (London: Studio Vista, 1970). Thanks to Mike Hart of Compendium Books, Camden Town, London, for generously giving me his copy of this book. Rosetta Records released an Ida Cox LP in 1981, named after her most famous song: *Wild Women Don't Have the Blues* (Rosetta Records 1304). In the United States one still sees her famous title declared on bumper stickers. The most revealing stories of Ida Cox are those Earl Palmer has told Tony Scherman; a *soupçon* appears in Tony Scherman, "Earl Palmer the Rhythm Bomber, the Funk Machine from New Orleans," in Scherman, *The Rock Musician* (New York: St. Martin's, 1994). Much more is forthcoming in Scherman's oral biography of Palmer.

14. Wesley Brown, *Darktown Strutters* (New York: Cane Hill, 1994), p. 40.

15. The phrase *"first black face turn"* was coined and emphasized by Edward Le Roy Rice in the first full-scale study of minstrelsy, *Monarchs of Minstrelsy, from "Daddy" Rice to Date* (New York, 1911), p. 5. Rice had experience as a blackface performer. Twenty-one years before his book was published, he first blacked up for a small part as a cross-dressed wench in the show of his father, Billy Rice, himself a cross-dressing Prima Donna. Edward Rice was no relation of Thomas Dartmouth "Daddy" Rice, nor of George Rice (brother to T. D. Rice), nor of Dan Rice, another blackface comedian in the nineteenth century. Independently, however, they all related themselves to Cain and, in that mutual affiliation, shared a genealogy if not genes.

16. Quinones, *Changes of Cain*, p. 19. Unlike a lot of now-canonical art, Byron's Cain was an available model to popular playwrights, their publics, and the reading artisanry: Lord Byron, *Cain: A Mystery* (London: Dicks' Standard Plays, no. 203, n.d.).

17. "Cain," in *Byron*, ed. Jerome J. McGann (New York: Oxford University Press, 1986), p. 936, ll. 482–483, 499–501.

18. Rice, *Monarchs of Minstrelsy*, p. 5.

19. These phrases, from the last paragraph of Foucault's *Discipline and Punish* (New York: Vintage, 1979), p. 308, name his ultimate concern.

20. Peter Linebaugh, *The London Hanged: Crime and Civil Society in the Eighteenth Century* (Cambridge: Cambridge University Press, 1992), p. 23.

21. Trinh T. Minh-Ha, *When the Moon Waxes Red: Representation, Gender and Cultural Politics* (New York: Routledge, 1991), p. 74.

22. Richard Price, ed., *Maroon Societies: Rebel Slave Communities in the Americas* (Baltimore: Johns Hopkins University Press, 1979), p. 425.

23. " 'Jump Jim Crow' is a dance native to this country," wrote Fuller, "and one which we plead guilty to seeing with pleasure, not on the stage, where we have not seen it, but as danced by children of an ebon hue in the street." "Entertainments of the Past Winter," *Dial*, 3 (July 1842), p. 52.

24. Emmett, untitled song, handwritten on a single sheet, Dan Emmett papers,

State Library of Ohio, Columbus. Joe: E. P. Christy, *Plantation Melodies*, no. 1 (New York, 1851), p. 66.

25. "Farewell, My Lilly Dear" (1851), in E. P. Christy, *Christy's Plantation Melodies*, no. 2 (New York, [1852]), p. 16.

26. Toll, *Blacking Up*, p. 161.

27. Ludwig Wittgenstein, *Philosophical Investigations*, trans. G. E. M. Anscombe (Oxford: Basil Blackwell, 1953), p. 194e (II: xi).

28. Frances Anne Kemble, *Journal of a Residence on a Georgian Plantation in 1838–1839*, ed. John A. Scott (1863; Athens: University of Georgia Press, 1984), pp. 130–131. Nicholas Cresswell, *The Journal of Nicholas Cresswell, 1774–1777* (London: Jonathan Cape, 1925), p. 19. Pauline E. Hopkins, *Contending Forces: A Romance Illustrative of Negro Life North and South* (1900; New York: Oxford University Press, 1988), p. 164. Robert L. Carringer, *The Jazz Singer* (Madison: University of Wisconsin Press, 1979), p. 11. Gary D. Engle, *This Grotesque Essence: Plays from the American Minstrel Stage* (Baton Rouge: Louisiana State University Press, 1978).

29. Bakhtin, *Rabelais and His World*, trans. Hélène Iswolsky (Bloomington: Indiana University Press, 1984), p. 39.

30. "Callows" is an entomologist's term for the youngest workers compressed in the lowest depths of the anthill. Blacks as childlike or as (playing) stupid is the dimension of the phenomenon that captured most white and black writers from the late nineteenth century until Ralph Ellison—that is, from Twain and Richard Wright, and their boy-men, to the Invisible Man. Charles Chesnutt, Hughes, Toomer, Du Bois, and most other African-American novelists of course no more subscribed to the belief that black men could not be adult than did Wright in private or in his essays, but the problem was to secure fictional conventions that displayed ways to be adult in a world that was determined to see black men as children and black women as mammies. Huck and Jim going down the river ever more into the worlds of Euroromanticism and the confining racism of the Phelps family goodness are examples of this identification with childlikeness that the minstrel show mirrored, though of course it hardly invented it.

31. Piersen, *Black Legacy*, p. 53. James Clifford, "On Ethnographic Allegory," in James Clifford and George E. Marcus, *Writing Culture: The Poetics and Politics of Ethnography* (Berkeley: University of California Press, 1986).

32. *Uncle Tom's Cabin*, ed. Ammons, p. xiii; further citations will appear in the text.

33. Shane White argues in *Somewhat More Independent: The End of Slavery in New York City, 1770–1810* (Athens: University of Georgia Press, 1991) that the slave's rolled eyes were a defiant, negating gesture, and recognized as such by both blacks and whites very early in the nineteenth century. The glossary of Harlem slang appended to Rudolph Fisher's novel *The Walls of Jericho* (1928; New York,

Arno, 1969) defines "Martin" as "Jocose designation of death. Derived from Bert Williams' story, *Wait Till Martin Comes*" (p. 302).

34. George Marcus, " 'What did he reckon would become of the other half if he killed his half?': Doubled, Divided, and Crossed Selves in *Pudd'nhead Wilson;* or, Mark Twain as Cultural Critic in His Own Times and Ours," in *Mark Twain's Pudd'nhead Wilson: Race, Conflict, and Culture*, ed. Susan Gillman and Forrest G. Robinson (Durham: Duke University Press, 1990). For Marcus, fictional form corresponds to shifts in theories of personality at the end of the nineteenth century. During that period those fictions which entertained divided selves—which after their irruption could be properly resolved and repressed—were succeeded by those which acknowledged the normality of crossed selves that remained irresolvable. Marcus's ideas have helped me conceptualize minstrelsy as a popular forum that produced the crossed and nomadic selves that polite society would later approve.

35. We are "readers" of this scene because it did not appear in the play, at least not in the Aiken variant that was most widely performed.

36. Liner notes to *Wild Women Don't Have the Blues* (Rosetta Records 1304).

37. Kenneth Burke, *The Philosophy of Literary Form: Studies in Symbolic Action* (Baton Rouge: Louisiana State University Press, 1967), p. 1.

38. Stephen Greenblatt, "Filthy Rites," in *Learning to Curse: Essays in Early Modern Culture* (New York: Routledge, 1990), pp. 64, 70. This essay is too little known; an earlier incarnation of the piece provoked my theorizing the blackface lore cycle as rites of baptism in filth.

39. *Wages of Whiteness*, p. 104.

40. Robert Lowell, "Children of Light," in *Poems 1938–1949* (London: Faber and Faber, n.d.), p. 30. Elvis Costello, "Blame It on Cain," *My Aim Is True* (Stiff, 1977).

4. Finding Jim Crow

1. C. Vann Woodward, *The Strange Career of Jim Crow* (1955; New York: Oxford University Press, 1966), p. 7.

2. Eric Lott summarizes the general position when he writes that "legend" is "the closest we are going to get to truth in the matter"; see *Love and Theft: Blackface Minstrelsy and the American Working Class* (New York: Oxford University Press, 1993), p. 51.

3. In July 1833, in the District of Columbia, Joseph Jefferson was half-lessor of a popular theatre. He made formal appeal to the District government to lift its curfew on African Americans: "There is at present a law in force which authorizes the constables of the city to arrest the colored people if on the street after nine o'clock without a pass. *A great proportion of our audience consists of persons of this*

caste, and they are consequently deterred from giving us that support that they would otherwise do." Quoted by Edward Ingle, *The Negro in the District of Columbia* (Baltimore, 1893), p. 47, my emphasis. This was the year after Jefferson had presented his 4-year-old son, Joseph Jefferson II, tumbling out of a sack in blackface motley to dance Jim Crow with T. D. Rice in Philadelphia. Ingle's quotation of the theatre lessor's appeal is firmer evidence of this black appreciation that several of Rice's obituarists note when they claim that Rice was popular among black audiences.

4. Richard Brinsley Peake, *The Hundred Pound Note,* in *Cumberland's British Theatre,* vol. 34 (London, n.d.). William Leman Rede, *The Flight to America; or, Ten Hours in New York!* (London, [1837]).

5. See Molly N. Ramshaw, "Jump, Jim Crow! A Biographical Sketch of Thomas D. Rice (1808–1860)," *Theatre Annual 1960,* 17 (1961); James H. Dormon, "The Strange Career of Jim Crow Rice (with apologies to Professor Woodward)," *Journal of Social History* 3, no. 2 (1970). Dormon's *Theatre in the Ante Bellum South: 1815–1861* (Chapel Hill: University of North Carolina Press, 1967) is helpful for background. Frederic R. Sanborn's article in the *New York Times,* "Jump Jim Crow!— The Opening of an Era" (13 Nov. 1932), celebrated the centenary of Rice's first dancing at the Bowery Theatre.

6. *New York Times,* 21 Sept. 1860. Rice is buried in Greenwood Cemetery, Brooklyn.

7. In an obituary, *Frank Leslie's Illustrated Newspaper,* 6 Oct. 1860, says that "the well-known carver" Dodge employed Rice for several years and that Rice "fashioned many figure heads for our merchant vessels."

8. "When Thomas D. Rice was playing 'William Tell' in Cherry Street, New York, he little dreamed of every making a fortune by singing *Jim Crow!" New Orleans Daily Picayune,* 7 May 1841. Obituary, *Frank Leslie's Magazine,* 6 Oct. 1860. On 7 June 1834 at the Bowery, Rice had a benefit performance of *William Tell,* "after which" said the bill, "he proposes jumping Jim Crow across the Atlantic." He also "jumped" and likewise offered *Life in New York,* which may have been an early version of *Bone Squash Diavolo.* See George C. D. Odell, *Annals of The New York Stage,* III (New York: Columbia University Press, 1928), p. 686. He did not perform in England until almost two years later.

9. William Bobo, *Glimpses of New-York City by a South Carolinian (Who Had Nothing Else to Do)* (Charleston, 1852), p. 96.

10. Ibid., p. 119.

11. Bob Dylan, "Minstrel Boy," *Self Portrait* (Columbia, 1970).

12. Noah M. Ludlow, *Dramatic Life as I Found It* (1880; New York: Benjamin Blom, 1966). Odell, *Annals of The New York Stage,* III, cites Joseph Ireland for Rice at the Lafayette on 23 Aug. 1828. And a clipping from "The Sun, May 10, 1908,"

marking the centenary of Rice's birth, includes a drawing of the young actor as Johnny Atkins in 1828, "before he conceived Jim Crow"; Billy Rose Collection, New York Public Library.

"Coal Black Rose" was the lead song in the 1830 edition of George Washington Dixon's songster, *Oddities and Drolleries of Mr. G. Dixon The Celebrated American Buffo Singer; with the likeness of Mr. G. Dixon, in the characters of Billy Grizzel, Major Longbow, &c.* (New York, 1830). S. Foster Damon judged "Coal Black Rose" the first song in the line of "hilarious irresponsibility" to become a great success. The lyrics were by White Snyder, the air was appropriated from an old ballad, and Dixon was singing the song as early as 1827. Dixon sang it first in New York in July 1828, and by the end of the summer someone had expanded the song into an operetta, *Love in a Cloud*. Damon, "The Negro in Early American Songsters," *Papers of the Bibliographical Society of America,* 28 (1934). This interlude was so successful that the next year, at the Chatham, Dixon created a second interlude based on the same song, with an expanded cast, calling it "The Duel or Coal Black Rose"; theatre bill at the Harvard Theatre Collection, Chatham Folder, 28 Oct. 1829.

Damon wonders about T. D. Rice's success: "The cause of his international success is clear: 'Jim Crow' was the first genuine, human American negro to reach the stage. 'Coal Black Rose' was the broadest of burlesque: one laughed *at* the antics of the niggers; but now the audience laughed *with* a character whose wit for the first time was shared and thus appreciated" (p. 149). Subsequent critics of blackface performance have rejected this position. But I think Damon's fundamental point about Rice's sympathy and sharing wit is correct (despite his vocabulary). Both the demeaning laughing *at* and the empathic laughing *with,* or laughing turned toward *themselves,* went forward from about 1828 when Rice started picking up the themes of blackface.

13. The "earliest consistent pattern of American racist caricature," according to Phil Lapsansky, developed in Boston in the years 1815–1820 to attack the free black community's annual celebration of the closing of the Atlantic slave trade. Lapsansky, "Graphic Discord: Abolitionist and Antiabolitionist Images," in *The Abolitionist Sisterhood: Women's Political Culture in Antebellum America,* ed. Jean Fagin Yellin and John C. Van Horne (Ithaca: Cornell University Press, 1994).

14. Lapsansky, ibid., reprints one of the many parodies of African-American celebrations of Abolition Day, 14 July 1808. The Library Company of Philadelphia has several more, including versions of the "Dreadful Riot on Negro Hill!" image. Henry Louis Gates Jr. reproduces this graphic in *The Signifying Monkey: A Theory of African-American Literary Criticism* (New York: Oxford University Press, 1988).

15. "There were not enough good actors available in 1827–28 to keep four theatres going, to the standard of metropolitan taste. The Lafayette and the Chat-

ham offered no such arrays of talent as were seen nightly at the Park and the Bowery; they have sunk to the level of 'minor' theatres." Odell, *Annals of the New York Stage*, III, p. 356. Ludlow, *Dramatic Life*.

16. Ludlow, *Dramatic Life*, pp. 332, 331. The play had been published in London only a year before. When Rice two months later did *A Day after the Fair* in Pensacola, Florida, his lag time way out in the sticks was even more phenomenal. Nicoll says it was licensed on 15 Dec. 1828; it was performed first at the Olympic in London on 5 Jan. 1829; and Rice performed it in Pensacola on 17 Feb. 1829. This is evidence of the sort of position he had in the theatre, searching for new roles and looking to London for cutting-edge material. And Rice was ever capable of making useful alliances. Buckstone was later writing verses of Jim Crow for Rice to perform during his 21 weeks in London, 1836, and acted with him in *Flight to America*, at London's Adelphi Theatre, 1836–1837.

Provenance of *The Lottery Ticket and the Lawyer's Clerk* is at issue. Ludlow and other contemporary commentators in the States thought of it as Buckstone's, but the British Library does not attribute its earliest editions of the play; and it attributes those published from 1836 on to Samuel Beazley. "D.—G.," who glossed and edited the texts for the Cumberland Library, seems to be the fount of this dispute, for he claims Beazley translated *The Lottery Ticket* from the French. But he forgets the play that Henry Fielding wrote in 1775, called simply *The Lottery*. Fielding's plot is clearly a forerunner of *The Lottery Ticket*. So whoever wrote the 1827 *Lottery Ticket*, Beazley or Buckstone, had important English precedents.

17. "D.—G.," preface to *The Lottery Ticket; or, The Lawyer's Clerk: A Farce*, (London, 1836), p. 5.

18. These contextual stories seemed at first extremely rudimentary, as was Rice's *Oh! Hush!* Here is a review of its opening in London, 1836: "*Oh! Hush; or, Life in New York* . . . is the production of Mr. T. D. Rice, or [the] Surrey theatre. In the play-bills it is stated to have been performed 'upwards of two hundred nights in New York.' If it were played 'with applause' the Americans must be very easily pleased, for we never had the misfortune to see anything represented on the stage so completely devoid of plot, character, and dialogue. *Oh! Hush* is divided into four scenes; in the first Mr. Rice and some other persons, acting the parts of negroes sing, in the second there was the same, and in the fourth the same, with all the characters joining in an old figure of a country dance. The only novelty in the last scene was, that Mr. W. Smith, who personated a negress, attracted the applause of the galleries by pulling up his dress so as to display a very considerable portion of his black stockings." Unattributed newsprint clipping, Surrey Folder, Harvard Theatre Collection, handwritten date of 30 Oct. 1836.

19. "The Original Jim Crow," lyrics in Harvard Theatre Collection.

20. Ludlow, *Dramatic Life*, p. 332.

21. Ibid. Clipping, Enthoven Collection, Theatre Museum, Covent Garden. Francis Courtney Wemyss, *Theatrical Biography; or, The Life of an Actor and Manager* (Glasgow, 1848), pp. 178–179.

22. George Carlin, e-conversing on Prodigy, 22 April 1996.

23. Sam Sanford, "Personal Reminiscences of Himself Together with the History of Minstrelsy from the Origan 1843 to 1893 with a sketch of all the celebrities of the Past and Present," holograph MS, Special Collections, Harry Ransom Humanities Research Center, University of Texas.

24. Clifford Geertz, "Thick Description: Toward an Interpretive Theory of Culture," in Geertz, *The Interpretation of Cultures* (New York: Basic Books, 1973).

25. William R. Alger, *Life of Edwin Forrest: The American Tragedian,* 2 vols. (Philadelphia, 1877), I, p. 477, cited in Peter George Buckley, "To the Opera House: Culture and Society in New York City, 1820–1860" (Ph.D. diss., State University of New York at Stony Brook, 1984).

26. Lauren Greenbaum, unpublished interview with Mrs. Ruthie Taylor, Oct. 1990, Tallahassee.

27. Wesley Brown, *Darktown Strutters* (New York: Cane Hill Press, 1994), p. 78. Further citations will appear in the text.

28. Brown repeated this device on both sides of the war. His characters propose a blackface mask divided down the middle, half black and half white. It is a fictional fantasy that was presciently connected to actual blackface practice. In T. D. Rice's burlesque *Otello,* which I have discovered in manuscript, there is a powerful moment that appears only in Rice's own variant on the burlesques: it is not in the Maurice Dowling burlesque which Rice is sometimes said to be copying, and not in "Dar's de Money," or the other mock-ups of Shakespeare. (I am grateful to June Piscitelli for noticing this device in *Otello* and bringing it to my attention.)

In Rice's play Desdemona bears Otello a child who embodies the disturbing anxieties of the cross-racial love that is the topic of blackface. In Rice's play this child appears on stage in Desdemona's arms—although the child may have been impersonated by a walking boy in some productions. For instance, at Purdy's National Theatre (yet another name change for the old Chatham) on 30 Aug. 1852, Rice appeared at the end of the evening as Otello and the child was played by "Mast. J. Murray." Otello's child first appears at 1.4.13: "Enter Desdemona, Emilia, ladies, child & Iago L.H." Two lines later Cassio remarks, "Madam I wish you joy / Blood an zouns & whiskey, what a bouncing boy." The child remains on stage through the arrival of his father. Then Desdemona says to her husband, "Behold this pledge—your image here is seen / Not this side love, the other side I mean / points to childs face / Otello takes the boy & kisses him" (*Otello* MS 1.4.63–64). See my *Jump Jim Crow: Plays, Lyrics, and Street Prose of the First Atlantic Popular Culture* (Cambridge, MA: Harvard University Press, forthcoming). I take this child to be made up with one side of his face black, the other side white. I have other images of later minstrel performers who dress and wig themselves as a woman on one side of their costume and as a man on the other side.

29. Although there are real differences between the uses of performance in folk and industrial societies, there are also so many important continuities that I am loath to decouple folk and capitalist cultural products. The first lurks within the other like its DNA. Ancient uses of a tradition lie dormant beneath their commercial inflection and may be found later, perhaps despite (perhaps because of) the limitations of the commercial form.

30. The connection between the blackface Jim Crow and tricksters is overdetermined; it does not rely solely on this menstrual connection. Another connection is the insistent limp in the Jim Crow persona from the legendary Jim Crow, through T. D. Rice, right up to Little Richard Penniman (who always maintains one of his legs is shorter than the other) and Chuck Berry's variant in his athletic duckwalk. The African take on the trickster figure descends from Legba, the limping spirit of the crossroads who provides access to all the other spirits. The protagonist of Ishmael Reed's novel *Mumbo Jumbo* (1972; New York: Atheneum, 1988) is named PaPa LaBas and is meant to be a west Atlantic extension of Legba (generally pronounced LahBah). Daddy Rice and PaPa LaBas, one might say heretically, are mutations of each other. Both are hip to what Reed calls the "dazzling parodying punning mischievous pre-Joycean style-play of your Cakewalking your Calinda your Minstrelsy give-and-take of the ultra-absurd" (p. 152). With Wesley Brown, Reed stands in *Mumbo Jumbo* as a provocative theorist of the blackface conduit.

31. At least one composer of a Jim Crow street biography gives him American Indian parentage: "A Faithful Account of the Life of Jim Crow, The American Negro Poet," appended to an English songster called *Jim Crow's Vagaries* (London, [1840]) tells us that "Oulamou was the Indian name of Jim [Crow's] father . . . His mother, like other Indian women, tilled the ground, and dressed the food." When Jim's parents died, the boy was "taken in charge by a merchant who changed his Indian name into that of Jim Crow" (pp. 21–22). On clowns see Laura Makarius, "Ritual Clowns and Symbolical Behaviour," *Diogenes*, 69 (spring 1970); idem, "The Blacksmith's Taboos: From the Man of Iron to the Man of Blood," *Diogenes*, 62 (spring 1968).

32. Bessie Jones and Bess Lomax Hawes, *Step It Down: Games, Plays, Songs, and Stories from the African-American Heritage* (New York: Harper and Row, 1972), p. 55.

33. Nichols: Carl Wittke, *Tambo and Bones* (1930; Westport, CN: Greenwood Press, 1968). But Nichols was a circus performer in the late 1820s in the Ohio Valley, in the same areas as Rice, so he may have picked up "Jim Crow" from him; even more likely, Nichols, too, picked it up from watching blacks do it. The black performer Picayune Butler reappears as a minor and northern presence in later minstrelsy, as in the song "Picayune Butler" in *The Negro Melodist* (Cincinnati,

[1850s?]). McGregory, personal communication; I am grateful to Professor Mc-
Gregory for pointing out this folk pattern to me.

34. Jones and Hawes, *Step It Down*, pp. 55–56. It is worth looking up the way
Jones and Hawes render this song, if only to note the nimbleness of its poly-
rhythms, steps on the downbeat, claps on the offbeat.

35. Jones and Hawes report a slightly different variant on these lines. This 1832
version is now in the Harvard Theatre Collection but was originally distributed at
the Chesnut Theatre, Philadelphia. It may have been the version Rice sang with
Joseph Jefferson III as described in Chapter 2.

36. Sterling Stuckey, *Slave Culture: Nationalist Theory and the Foundations of Black
America* (New York: Oxford University Press, 1987), p. 6. "The King Buzzard" is
in Edward C. L. Adams's *Tales of the Congaree*, ed. Robert G. O'Meally (1927, 1928;
Chapel Hill: University of North Carolina Press, 1987); rpt. in Henry Louis Gates
Jr. et al., *The Norton Anthology of African American Literature* (New York, 1997).

37. Hans Nathan, *Dan Emmett and the Rise of Early Negro Minstrelsy* (Norman:
University of Oklahoma Press, 1962), pp. 130–131.

38. "Rhetoric of blame" is Edward Said's term, coined in *Culture and Imperialism*
(New York: Knopf, 1993).

39. Edward Said: "The power to narrate, or to block other narratives from forming and emerging, is very important to culture and imperialism, and constitutes
one of the main connections between them." Ibid., p. xiii.

40. C. Vann Woodward reports in *The Strange Career of Jim Crow* that the term
"Jim Crow" had become an adjective—I presume for racial segregation—by 1838.

41. Theodore Parker, *Sermon of The Dangerous Classes in Society* (Boston, 1847).

42. Alex Albright, *Boogie in Black and White*, Center for Public Television, WUNC,
Chapel Hill, N.C., 19 February 1988. See Albright, "Scenes from a Dream: (Nearly)
Lost Images of Black Entertainers," in *Images of the South*, ed. Karl G. Heider (Ath-
ens: University of Georgia Press, 1993), pp. 55–73.

43. [T. D. Rice,] *Life of Jim Crow, showing how he got his inspiration as a poet . . .*
(Philadelphia, dated both 1835 and 1837), p. 4. Further citations will appear in
the text. Rice performed *Jim Crow in London* at the Walnut Street Theatre in Philadelphia on 25–28 Oct. 1837; Arthur A. Wilson, *A History of the Philadelphia Theatre,
1835–1855* (Philadelphia: University of Pennsylvania Press, 1935).

44. This image of leaping into the arms of the public anticipates the literal act,
a century and a half later, of Rice's punk rock descendants tumbling among their
fans and being restored to the stage. The image codifies, and the act consolidates,
congeniality.

45. *Davy Crockett: American Comic Legend*, ed. Richard M. Dorson (Rockland,
NY: Spiral Press, 1939), p. 10. I do not intend to specify a clean opposition between
Crockett and Crow—rather the opposite. Rice was amalgamating the two even
while he was separating from Crockett. As Crow, he sang about and embodied

Crockett at least as late as 2 Aug. 1833 (according to a poster at the Harvard Theatre Collection). Rice was then performing *Rent Day* in Philadelphia at the Walnut Street Theatre; he stepped up front during the entr'acte to sing "The Last of Davy Crockett," "De Nigger Ball," "Mr. Crockett and the Coon," "De Callaboose," and "De Louisiana Alligator." As always, Rice tried having things both ways. His capacity to inhabit the border areas between cultural expressions, embody and stretch them out into a combinatory middle ground, is what I believe made him so problematic, and probably so attractive to his cohort.

46. Mrs. Trollope had published her *Domestic Manners of Americans* and *The Refugee in America* in 1832; Fanny Kemble had issued her first *Journal* in Philadelphia in 1835; Harriet Martineau would publish her *Society in America* in 1837, in time, perhaps, to anger readers of Rice's second edition of *The Life of Jim Crow*. David Claypoole Johnston had issued his rejoinder to Kemble and Trollope in a cartoon book, *Outlines Illustrative of the Journal of F_____A_____K_____, Drawn & Etched by Mr. _____* (Boston, 1835). The copy I read was in the Library Company of Philadelphia. Rice had joined this fray in the spring of 1834 at the Bowery Theatre. George Odell reports how Rice became involved: "The Bowery piece was brought out on April 24th [1834], under the title of *Life in New York, or, the Major's Come* . . . The local types filled pit and gallery with unrestrained joy; doubtless peanuts cracked and were crunched and whistles shrilled in ecstasy. For the first night was advertised a feature of 'Mrs. Trollope and family group by a well-bred lady.' I dare say that seemed funny to peanut-eaters whose domestic manners had recently been castigated. On May 20th, new scenes had been written in for Jim Crow Rice; thereafter the farce had even a stronger hold on life." *Annals of the New York Stage*, III, p. 685.

47. Makarius, "Ritual Clowns and Symbolical Behaviour," p. 65; my emphasis.

48. See "A list of the royal family, nobility & gentry who have honoured the Ethiopian Serenaders, Germon, Stanwood, Harrington, Pell, & White with their patronage at the St. James Theatre, London, together with the opinions of the London press," n.d., Harvard Theatre Collection. Beginning with the Queen and Prince Albert, this pages-long list is more garish than the parade at Ascot.

49. *Pensacola Gazette* theatre advertisement, 17 Feb. 1829.

50. C. A. Somerset, *A Day After the Fair* (London, n.d.), pp. 25–26. The printed play's introduction calls Susan Squall's accompanying children, all of them fellow squallers, "ragged minstrels." These minstrels are quite clearly the European variety, singing loudly a "bawling . . . Hungarian Waltz" about their hunger.

51. See Dian Lee Shelley, "Tivoli Theatre of Pensacola," *Florida Historical Quarterly*, 50, no. 4 (1972). According to Shelley the Tivoli was a hotel, brothel, and sometime theatre. Jack L. Bilbo Jr., "Economy and Culture: The Boom-And-Bust Theatres of Pensacola, Florida, 1821–1917" (Ph.D. diss., Texas Tech University, 1982), has additional useful information about the Tivoli. The 1829 season was

the second season Mrs. Hartwig had performed there. Shelley and Bilbo both conclude from a typographical error in the *Pensacola Gazette* that Rice was married this early. He was not.

52. In the summer of 1996 National Public Radio and the *New York Times* reported that many young people learn most of their political information from the jokes of Jay Leno, David Letterman, and other late-night comics. *The Life of Jim Crow* suggests that it was always thus, or that popular informances have provided youth culture with news at least since the 1830s.

53. Zora Neale Hurston, *Mules and Men* ([1935]; New York: Harper/Perennial, 1990), pp. 82–83.

54. Ritual "as a busy intersection," Renato Rosaldo writes, contrasts "with the classic view, which posits culture as a self-contained whole made up of coherent patterns." Instead, culture may be "a more porous array of intersections where distinct processes crisscross from within and beyond its borders. Such processes often derive from differences of age, gender, class, race, and sexual orientation." *Culture and Truth: The Remaking of Social Analysis* (Boston: Beacon, 1989), pp. 20–21.

55. Molly Ramshaw claims Rice paid a prisoner in Cincinnati to send him twenty or thirty verses a night for his song; Ramshaw, "Jump, Jim Crow!" p. 40. To try to follow all the multiple traces in "liderary hemporium," would clog this chapter: lid/clampdown, liderarity vs. orality, hemp/marijuana, hemp/cockney vowel, emporium/market, and more. Whether the voice is African American is a thorny issue; some of the best work on it is by William Mahar. See his "Black English in Early Blackface Minstrelsy: A New Interpretation of the Sources of Minstrel Show Dialect," *American Quarterly,* 37 (summer 1985). What's important to me is not whether Rice rendered authentic blackness, a topic impossibly vexed, but whether he projected a more complex blackness than his predecessors and contemporaries. He did; early blackface did; that was why its publics clapped it into existence.

56. This dream of reversing entropy was a fantasy of cost-free rationality that Leon Brillouin would demonstrate to be impossible. Richard Poirier has called attention to the demon and Brillouin's critique of it as a model for cultural history and its limitations: "The Importance of Thomas Pynchon," in *Mindful Pleasures,* ed. George Levine and David Leverenz (Boston: Little, Brown, 1976).

57. Arthur LaBrew, *Francis Johnson, 1792–1844* (Detroit: privately published, 1977); Eileen Southern, *The Music of Black Americans* (New York: Norton, 1983). It may be that opportunities opened for Johnson to tour abroad in 1837 because of Rice's popularity the year before. Indeed, in London Johnson billed his band as "The American Minstrels." During their run at the Argyll Rooms on Regent Street the band played Rossini and Mozart as well as his own works, including "Crows in a Cornfield." Charles K. Jones and Lorenzo K. Greenwich, 2nd, *A Choice Collection of the Works of Francis Johnson,* 2 vols. (New York: Point Two Publications,

1982), I, 43. The "crossover" claim is Phil Lapsansky's, letter to the author, 25 June 1996.

58. *Bone Squash Diavolo*, ADD MSS 42953, Lord Chamberlain's Papers, British Library. The opening date at the Surrey is attested to in a playbill in the British Library collection. And here is the Surrey's announcement in the *Times*: "Royal Surrey Theatre American Novelty, a new Black Opera. This evening will be presented the tragedy of *Douglas*. Principal characters by Messrs. Cobham, Cullen and C. H. Pitt; Miss Macarthy and Miss Watson. After which (1st time) a new Black Opera called *Ben Squash*. In which, Mr. T. D. Rice the American comedian will make his first appearance. To conclude with Valentine and Orson." The *Times* does not review this production.

At this point in its history the Surrey was not announcing its acts regularly in the *Times*. But when Rice started to appear it began to do so several days a week, and to spell his productions correctly. Until Rice appeared on its stage the Adelphi also did not announce its bill. But when he started, with *Flight to America*, they announced daily in the *Times*. And the reviewers covered the Adelphi, too—not only Rice but all the farces the Adelphi put on after Rice. It really was an achievement for him and cultural enfranchisement for his public when Rice began to give his opinions "Along wid all de rest."

59. Karl Marx, *The Eighteenth Brumaire of Louis Bonaparte* (1852), in Robert C. Tucker, ed., *The Marx-Engels Reader* (New York: Norton, 1972), p. 516 (ch. 7 of *The Eighteenth Brumaire*). Strictly speaking, Marx referred to the French peasantry in this remark, not the lumpenproletariat. As Edward Said suggested when he chose these words for his epigraph to *Orientalism*, however, Marx's attitude toward the low groups that developed out of the atomization of a peasantry gone to cities was that they needed representation by their betters. The spirit of Marx's attention to the politically ineffective peasantry and lumpenproletariat comes out more fully in the next sentence: "Their representative must at the same time appear as their master, as an authority over them, as an unlimited governmental power that protects them against other classes and sends them the rain and the sunshine from above."

60. Five plays were written for Rice while he was in London, 1836–1837: *Black God of Love, Flight to America, Cowardy Cowardy Custard, The Peacock and the Crow,* and *The Court Jester*. Also that season, *Mr. Midshipman Easy* and *Peregrinations of Pickwick* were adapted for his impersonations. In 1842 two more plays were written for him: *Jim Crow in His New Place* and *The Foreign Prince*. And, somewhat later, Rice so freely adapted Maurice Dowling's *Otello* that he legitimately performed it as his own play in the United States. I will edit all the extant manuscripts of these plays in my forthcoming *Jump Jim Crow*.

I distinguish between the plays that Rice performed and the way they have come down to us in versions adapted by Charles White, a much later minstrel performer.

It is these "White" versions that other commentators on Rice have quoted and judged. For all that Rice has been assumed to be a known quantity, reference to any of his own scripts is almost nonexistent, for these have been presumed lost, until now.

61. *The Virginia Mummy*, Add MS 42940, ff. 822–867, Lord Chamberlain's Papers, British Library. Lurking behind my understanding of the dividing line is Edward Said's explanation of his method in *Culture and Imperialism:* " 'contrapuntal reading' . . . means reading a text with an understanding of what is involved when an author shows, for instance, that a colonial sugar plantation is seen as important to the process of maintaining a particular style of life in England" (p. 66)—or in the States.

62. "In order to understand the productivity of colonial power it is crucial to construct its regime of 'truth,' not to subject its representations to normalising judgement. Only then does it become possible to understand the *productive* ambivalence of the object of colonial discourse—that 'otherness' which is at once an object of desire and derision, an articulation of difference contained within the fantasy of origin and identity." Homi Bhabha, *The Location of Culture* (London: Routledge, 1994), p. 67. Like a lot of besieged popular art, blackface farce was on to this "productive ambivalence" long before Bhabha named it.

63. [T. D. Rice], arranged by C[harles] White, *Bone Squash* (New York, n.d.), p. 24.

64. I distinguish *Bone* and *Mummy* from *Oh! Hush!* because the last was built around G. W. Dixon's song "Coal Black Rose" and was inevitably tainted still by its smirk.

65. Edward Said's "contrapuntal reading" is a strategy for discovering oppositional traces within high culture. As such, it comes close to what I am describing, and I admire its effects. But in limiting its range during the early colonial years to accepted canonical texts, and denying the self-activating effectiveness of the underclass, Said ignores the vital presence of oppositional voices within the imperial center. Rice's theatre was playing out that recalcitrance smack in the middle of London and New York, Charleston and New Orleans. It's time we acknowledged it.

66. Marx, *Eighteenth Brumaire*, p. 479. For more on this theme in its recent variants, see my *Deliberate Speed* (Washington: Smithsonian Institution Press, 1990).

67. See Peter Stallybrass, "Marx and Heterogeneity: Thinking the Lumpenproletariat," *Representations,* 31 (1990).

68. Uncredited newspaper clipping, 15 July 1837, Royal Surrey folder, Enthoven Collection.

69. Marvin Carlson, "The Old Vic: A Semiotic Analysis," in *Theatre Semiotics: Signs of Life* (Bloomington: Indiana University Press, 1990); Ann Saunders, *The Art*

and *Architecture of London: An Illustrated Guide* (London: Phaidon, 1988); Joseph Donohue, *Theatre in the Age of Kean* (Oxford: Basil Blackwell, 1975).

70. Jim Davis points out the Surrey's 1827 poster in an unpublished paper, "Melodrama, Community, and Ideology: London's Minor Theatres in the Nineteenth Century"; the bill is in the Enthoven Collection. The omnibus to Islington is announced in a theatre bill in the Surrey folder at the Enthoven Collection for 1836. The announcements proving Rice's appearance at both theatres on the same night are in the Enthoven Collection and in the British Library Playbill Collection, casebook 313. The "Grand Union" of the two companies is attested in the Enthoven Collection, Surrey folder for 1837.

71. Thomas Dartmouth Rice, arranged by Charles White, *The Virginia Mummy* (New York, n.d.), p. 20. Examples of pathetic blackface characters in English melodrama are Zinga and Zanga in *My Poll and My Partner Joe*, by John Thomas Haines (Dicks' #500), first performed at the Surrey on 7 Sept. 1835, and in constant rotation during the year before Rice started jumping Jim Crow at the Surrey, and again while he was touring the continent. Zinga and Zanga are married African slaves in the middle passage, when the slaver discovers he needs to lighten his load to flee the English Navy. He tears Zanga from Zinga's arms and throws her in the ocean, where she is saved by T. P. Cooke, playing the hero, a white English sailor.

72. Newspaper clipping, Enthoven Collection, Adelphi folder 1836.

73. *The Collected Essays of Ralph Ellison*, ed. John F. Callahan (New York: Modern Library, 1995), p. 350.

74. On dance: Peter H. Wood,, " 'Gimme de Kneebone Bent': African Body Language and the Evolution of American Dance Forms," in *The Black Tradition in American Modern Dance,* ed. Gerald E. Myers (American Dance Festival, 1988); Jacqui Malone, *Steppin' on the Blues: The Visible Rhythms of African American Dance* (Urbana:. University of Illinois Press, 1996); Brenda Dixon Gottschild, *Digging the Africanist Presence in American Performance: Dance and Other Contexts* (Westport, CN: Greenwood, 1996); Katrina Hazzard-Gordon, *Jookin': The Rise of Social Dance Formations in African-American Culture* (Philadelphia: Temple University Press, 1990). On toasts: Roger Abrahams, *Deep Down in the Jungle: Negro Narrative Folklore from the Streets of Philadelphia,* 2nd ed. (Hawthorne, NY: Aldine, 1970); Gates, *The Signifying Monkey.* On the relationship of black and blackface theatre to the American musical: Thomas L. Riis, *Just before Jazz: Black Musical Theater in New York, 1890–1915* (Washington: Smithsonian Institution Press, 1989); idem, *More than Just Minstrel Shows: The Rise of Black Musical Theatre at the Turn of the Century* (New York: Institute for Studies in American Music, 1992).

75. *Kansas City 1926 to 1930*, BBC CD691.

76. The dance critic and historian Sally Sommer talked me through several of the ideas in the following paragraphs.

77. Note in Figure 4.3 the white pitch man, accompanied by two confeder-

ates—the black performer whose mask has by now focused down to enlarged white lips (which McCartney and Jackson copy exactly), and the man in Indian headdress on the ground.

Three accounts that can contribute to recovery of this material: Alex Albright, "Scenes from a Dream,"; idem, "Noon Parade and Midnight Ramble," in *Good Country People: An Irregular Journal of the Cultures of Eastern North Carolina* (Rocky Mount: North Carolina Wesleyan College Press, 1995); Milton D. Quigless Sr., "Two Weeks on a Minstrel Show," also in *Good Country People,*.

78. Malone, *Steppin' on the Blues*, pp. 55, 126.

79. Rupert Wainwright directed "U Can't Touch This." Its online editor was Rod Klein. Hammer did his own choreography.

80. "The Making of 'Please Hammer Don't Hurt 'Em' " was directed by Susan Friedman and is included on *Hammer Time*.

Acknowledgments

I had financial support making this book. The National Endowment for the Humanities supported a year of research in 1992–93. The Florida State University Committee on Faculty Research Support twice granted me summers to write; Provost Larry Abele, then Dean of Arts and Sciences, supplemented the NEH grant with additional travel and copy funds. The English Department at Florida State made possible several archival trips.

Big thanks to Alex Albright, Eleanor Jones Baker, Genyne Boston, Simon Bronner, Bart Bull, Robert Cantwell, James Clifford, Dale Cockrell, Hennig Cohen, Frederick Crews, Rosemary Cullen, Dominique de Lerma, Bruce Dick, John Dougan, Marjorie Garber, Paul Gilroy, Augusta S. Goennel, Lauren Greenbaum, James Hatch, Hunt Hawkins, Bill Humphries, Joseph Keller, Phil Lapsansky, Dan Lhamon, Peter Linebaugh, Eric Lott, Barbara Luck, William Mahar, Greil Marcus, Chuck Martin, Jerrilyn McGregory, Brooks McNamara, Melissa Miller, Jane Moody, June Piscitelli, Marcus Rediker, David Riesman, Peter Ripley, Diane Roberts, Dave Roediger, Michael Rogin, Tricia Rose, Sarah Royalty, Tony Scherman, Rob Silberman, Camille Smith, Sally Sommer, Ann Spangler, Sally Stein, Robert Toll, Walter Tschinkel, Vron Ware, Lindsay Waters, Stanley Wells, Craig Wilder, Don B. Wilmeth, Peter H. Wood, and Huey Young.

The members of this widespread community showed me books and manuscripts, lyrics and images. They tried to stop my racing down blind alleys. They grunted astonishment and snorted disapproval. They passed me tips and connected me with others. They sheltered me while I was on the road. If my conclusions differ from the claims I made when I knocked on their doors, asking for help, that's likely because our conversation put more pepper in the gumbo.

Fita Ferguson made time to listen skeptically to all the arguments. She counseled on matters of fact, tact, and clarity. She read every page of every draft I hoped would be final. Her own Atlantic diaspora kept real the history I was tracing in this book.

Index